2nd Workshop on Human Evaluation of NLP Systems (HumEval 2022)

Dublin, Ireland
27 May 2022

ISBN: 978-1-7138-6739-5

Printed from e-media with permission by:

Curran Associates, Inc.
57 Morehouse Lane
Red Hook, NY 12571

Association for Computational Linguistics
209 N. Eighth Street
Stroudsburg, Pennsylvania 18360

Phone: 1-570-476-8006
Fax: 1-570-476-0860

acl@aclweb.org

Additional copies of this publication are available from:

Curran Associates, Inc.
57 Morehouse Lane
Red Hook, NY 12571 USA
Phone: 845-758-0400
Fax: 845-758-2633
Email: curran@proceedings.com
Web: www.proceedings.com

HumEval 2022

The 2nd Workshop on Human Evaluation of NLP Systems

Proceedings of the Workshop

May 27, 2022

Introduction

Welcome to HumEval 2022!

We are happy to present the second edition of the workshop on Human Evaluation of NLP Systems (HumEval) that is taking place as a hybrid event at the 60th Annual Meeting of the Association for Computational Linguistics (ACL 2022).

Human evaluation is vital in NLP, and it is often considered as the most reliable form of evaluation. It ranges from the large-scale crowd-sourced evaluations to the much smaller experiments routinely encountered in conference papers. With this workshop we wish to create a space for researchers working with human evaluations to exchange ideas and begin to address the issues that human evaluation in NLP currently faces, including aspects of experimental design, reporting standards, meta-evaluation and reproducibility.

We are truly grateful to the authors of the submitted papers that showed interest in human evaluation research. Based on program committee recommendations, the HumEval workshop accepted 10 submissions: 9 through a regular submission process and 1 through ACL Rolling Review commitment out of 12 submitted and 3 committed papers respectively. The accepted papers cover a broad range of NLP areas where human evaluation is used: machine translation, natural language generation, word sense disambiguation, coreference resolution, and tokenisation. There are also papers dealing with automatic metric validation and human evaluation reporting in NLP.

This workshop would not have been possible without the hard work of the program committee. We would like to express our gratitude to them for writing detailed and thoughtful reviews in a very constrained span of time. We are in particular indebted to our emergency reviewers, who agreed to volunteer their time for last-minute reviews. We also thank our invited speakers, Markus Freitag, and Samira Shaikh, for their contribution to our program with thought-provoking keynotes. As the workshop is co-located with ACL, we appreciated help from the ACL Workshop Chairs, Elena Cabrio, Sujian Li, and Mausam, from the ACL Publication Chairs, Danilo Croce, and the whole team behind `aclpub2`, and we are grateful to all other members of the organising committee involved in the conference management.

We are looking forward to a productive workshop, and we hope that it will create a forum for human evaluation research.

You can find more details about the workshop on its website: `https://humeval.github.io/`.

Anya, Ehud, Maja, Anastasia

Organizing Committee

Program Chairs

Anya Belz, ADAPT Centre, Dublin City University, Ireland
Maja Popović, ADAPT Centre, Dublin City University, Ireland
Ehud Reiter, University of Aberdeen, United Kingdom
Anastasia Shimorina, Orange, Lannion, France

Program Committee

Program Committee

Eleftherios Avramidis, DFKI, Germany
Ondřej Dušek, Charles University, Czechia
Albert Gatt, Utrecht University, Netherlands
Behnam Hedayatnia, Amazon, United States
David Howcroft, Heriot Watt University, United Kingdom
Filip Klubička, ADAPT, Technological University of Dublin, Ireland
Tom Kocmi, Microsoft, Germany
Samuel Läubli, University of Zürich, Switzerland
Chris van der Lee, Tilburg University, Netherlands
Margot Mieskes, UAS Darmstadt, Germany
Emiel van Miltenburg, Tilburg University, Netherlands
Mathias Müller, University of Zürich, Switzerland
Sergiu Nisioi, University of Bucharest, Romania
Juri Opitz, University of Heidelberg, Germany
Maike Paetzel-Prüsmann, University Potsdam, Germany
Maxime Peyrard, EPFL, Switzerland
Martin Popel, UFAL, Charles University, Czechia
Joel Tetreault, Dataminr, United States

Invited Speakers

Markus Freitag, Google, United States
Samira Shaikh, University of North Carolina at Charlotte / Ally, United States

Keynote Talk: Cognitive Biases in Human Evaluation of NLG

Samira Shaikh
University of North Carolina at Charlotte / Ally, United States

Abstract: Humans quite frequently interact with conversational agents. The rapid advancement in generative language modeling through neural networks has helped advance the creation of intelligent conversational agents. Researchers typically evaluate the output of their models through crowdsourced judgments, but there are no established best practices for conducting such studies. We look closely at the practices of evaluation of NLG output, and discuss implications of human cognitive biases on experiment design and the resulting data.

Bio: Samira Shaikh is an Assistant Professor in the Computer Science Department in the College of Computing and Informatics at the University of North Carolina - Charlotte (UNCC). She has a joint appointment with the Department of Psychology as an Assistant Professor in Cognitive Science. Samira directs the SoLID (Social Language and Intelligent Dialogue) Agents Lab at UNCC, with a focus on Computational Sociolinguistics and Natural Language Generation.

Keynote Talk: Experts, errors, and context: A large-scale study of human evaluation for machine translation

Markus Freitag
Google, United States

Abstract: Human evaluation of modern high-quality machine translation systems is a difficult problem, and there is increasing evidence that inadequate evaluation procedures can lead to erroneous conclusions. While there has been considerable research on human evaluation, the field still lacks a commonly accepted standard procedure. As a step toward this goal, we propose an evaluation methodology grounded in explicit error analysis, based on the Multidimensional Quality Metrics (MQM) framework. We carry out the largest MQM research study to date, scoring the outputs of top systems from the WMT 2020 shared task in two language pairs using annotations provided by professional translators with access to full document context. We analyze the resulting data extensively, finding among other results a substantially different ranking of evaluated systems from the one established by the WMT crowd workers, exhibiting a clear preference for human over machine output. Surprisingly, we also find that automatic metrics based on pre-trained embeddings can outperform human crowd workers. We further discuss the impact of this study on both the WMT metric task, and the general MT task. We will close the talk by showcasing research that benefits from the new evaluation methodology: Minimum Bayes Risk Decoding with neural metrics significantly outperforms beam search decoding in expert-based human evaluations while the previous human evaluation standards using crowd-workers set both decoding strategies on par with each other.

Bio: Dr. Markus Freitag is a Staff Research Scientist at Google Research in Mountain View, CA. His current research interests are in machine translation, focusing on human and automatic evaluation, decoding strategies, model training, and data processing. Prior to joining Google, he worked as a Research Staff Member at IBM in Yorktown Heights, NY. Markus received a PhD in Computer Science in 2015 from the RWTH Aachen University under the supervision of Prof. Dr. Hermann Ney.

Table of Contents

Program

Friday, May 27, 2022

09:00 - 10:00 *Invited talk by Markus Freitag*

10:00 - 10:30 *Session 1*

A Methodology for the Comparison of Human Judgments With Metrics for Coreference Resolution
Mariya Borovikova, Loïc Grobol, Anaïs Lefeuvre Halftermeyer and Sylvie Billot

Perceptual Quality Dimensions of Machine-Generated Text with a Focus on Machine Translation
Vivien Macketanz, Babak Naderi, Steven Schmidt and Sebastian Möller

Towards Human Evaluation of Mutual Understanding in Human-Computer Spontaneous Conversation: An Empirical Study of Word Sense Disambiguation for Naturalistic Social Dialogs in American English
Alex Lưu

10:30 - 11:00 *Coffee Break*

11:00 - 12:20 *Session 2*

A Study on Manual and Automatic Evaluation for Text Style Transfer: The Case of Detoxification
Varvara Logacheva, Daryna Dementieva, Irina Krotova, Alena Fenogenova, Irina Nikishina, Tatiana Shavrina and Alexander Panchenko

Beyond calories: evaluating how tailored communication reduces emotional load in diet-coaching
Simone Balloccu and Ehud Reiter

Human Judgement as a Compass to Navigate Automatic Metrics for Formality Transfer
Huiyuan Lai, Jiali Mao, Antonio Toral and Malvina Nissim

The Human Evaluation Datasheet: A Template for Recording Details of Human Evaluation Experiments in NLP
Anastasia Shimorina and Anya Belz

12:20 - 14:00 *Lunch*

14:00 - 15:00 *Session 3*

Human evaluation of web-crawled parallel corpora for machine translation
Gema Ramírez-Sánchez, Marta Bañón, Jaume Zaragoza-Bernabeu and Sergio Ortiz Rojas

Friday, May 27, 2022 (continued)

	Toward More Effective Human Evaluation for Machine Translation Belén C Saldías Fuentes, George Foster, Markus Freitag and Qijun Tan
	Vacillating Human Correlation of SacreBLEU in Unprotected Languages Ahrii Kim and Jinhyeon Kim
15:00 - 15:30	*Coffee Break*
15:30 - 16:30	*Invited talk by Samira Shaikh*
16:30 - 17:00	*General discussion and wrap-up*

Vacillating Human Correlation of `SacreBLEU` in Unprotected Languages

Ahrii Kim[1] and **Jinhyeon Kim**[2]
Kakao Enterprise
Gyeonggi-do, Republic of Korea
ria.i, rob.k@kakaoenterprise.com

Abstract

SacreBLEU, by incorporating a text normalizing step in the pipeline, has become a rising automatic evaluation metric in recent MT studies. With agglutinative languages such as Korean, however, the lexical-level metric cannot provide a conceivable result without a customized pre-tokenization. This paper endeavors to examine the influence of diversified tokenization schemes –word, morpheme, subword, character, and consonants & vowels (CV)– on the metric after its protective layer is peeled off.

By performing meta-evaluation with manually-constructed into-Korean resources, our empirical study demonstrates that the human correlation of the surface-based metric and other homogeneous ones (as an extension) vacillates greatly by the token type. Moreover, the human correlation of the metric often deteriorates due to some tokenization, with CV one of its culprits. Guiding through the proper usage of tokenizers for the given metric, we discover i) the feasibility of the character tokens and ii) the deficit of CV in the Korean MT evaluation.[1]

1 Introduction

For almost two decades, BLEU (Papineni et al., 2002) has been a key driver of the development of Machine Translation (MT) and MT Evaluation despite its blind spots. Marie et al. (2021) statistically support such trend, reporting that in the past decade, about 98.8% of research papers of ACL under the title of "MT" regarded it as their prime evaluation metric. However much stern warnings we have got against its use (Tan et al. 2015; Callison-Burch et al. 2006), the fact that one of the most popular metrics besides it since 2018 is its stabilized implementation SacreBLEU (Post, 2018) (Marie et al., 2021) lets us ask ourselves if this rising metric is safe for all .

The biggest strength of SacreBLEU is that it reduces the influence of pre-processing scheme on the score computation that could have fluctuated otherwise upon any minor changes such as a type of tokenizers, a split of compound nouns, use of unknown tokens for rare words, or casing (Post, 2018). By embracing the text normalizing step in the architecture, this automatic metric can provide more trustworthy evaluation scores.

While it is gaining weight in the literature, its trust issue remains prominent in terms of agglutinate languages such as Korean. Languages of such typology by design require language-dependant tokenization to convey the morphological implications hardly expressible by whitespaces. Presumably for that reason, SacreBLEU specifics a customized tokenizer for some languages such as Japanese. When assessing Korean texts, therefore, the Workshop on Asian Translation directs that the texts be tokenized by MeCab-ko[2] before running any automatic metrics (Nakazawa et al., 2017), but their correlation to human judgment has not been officially confirmed.

In the context where Korean is not capable of taking advantage of SacreBLEU's protective layer, we shed light on the influence of varied pre-tokenization types on the human correlation of the given metric that features three surface-based metrics: BLEU, TER (Snover et al., 2006), and ChrF (Popović, 2015). With that information, we share empirical lessons for SacreBLEU when applying it in the Korean language in MT evaluation, some of which are summarized as such:

On the segment level:

1. Almost any pre-tokenization enhances the human correlation of BLEU or TER, but not ChrF.

[1]Link to our code is available at https://github.com/kakaoenterprise/korean-sacrebleu

[2]https://bitbucket.org/eunjeon/mecab-ko

Proceedings of the 2nd Workshop on Human Evaluation of NLP Systems (HumEval), pages 1 - 15
May 27, 2022 ©2022 Association for Computational Linguistics

2. The character-level decomposition guarantees a feasible human correlation and fast deployment.

3. The influence of the CV level is detrimental. It degrades the human correlation of ChrF.

On the corpus level:

1. The morpheme level, in general, achieves a higher correlation, among which Kiwi and Khaiii are noteworthy.

2. Contrary to the segment level, the character-level tokens harm the human correlation of the metrics.

3. The raw score of the metrics can be inflated up to twice when different tokenizers are involved. Thus, comparing scores by simply copying from other studies is invalid.

Cost-Efficiency:

1. TER can be slower than the other two metrics by up to seven times. In the worst scenario, the metric was combined with CV and it took 360 times more than BLEU for computation.

2. No matter how beneficial the CV can be, cost-ineffectiveness is its blind spot.

2 Related Works

Recently, the research topic of word segmentation has got the limelight in many NLP tasks (Zhang et al. 2015; Park et al. 2018; Kim et al. 2020; Yongseok and Lee 2020; Park et al. 2020), especially with the outstanding achievement of subword-level pipelines such as SentencePiece (SPM) (Kudo and Richardson, 2018) or Byte-Pair Encoding (BPE) (Sennrich et al., 2016). In MT in specific, interest is growing in handling unseen vocabularies (OOVs) through an optimal token type, whereas the influence of tokenization in MT evaluation is rarely explored. Thus, this section is devoted to the studies identifying the relation between tokenization and translation quality, but with a particular focus on its language dependency.

Huck et al. (2017) discovered that their model displayed the highest performance when BPE was coupled with a suffix split in German. In a similar manner, Lee et al. (2017) suggested that their fully character-level NMT model outperformed BPE models, especially in the Finnish-English pair. Domingo et al. (2018) demonstrated that no single best tokenizer could lead to a more refined translation quality for all languages when five languages were under study. Furthermore, they remarked that such phenomenon was striking in morphologically rich languages such as Japanese.

Similarly, concerning Korean, Park et al. (2019) found that SPM Unigram allowed their NMT model to attain a higher BLEU score than simple BPE. While they mentioned that a smaller token unit was not always an answer in the case of Korean, recent studies paid more and more attention to the sub-subword token unit called *Jamo*, referring to consonants and vowels.[3] Moon and Okazaki (2020) introduced Jamo-Pair Encoding, combining Jamo with BPE. Eo et al. (2021) suggested a new division of Jamo by sub-grouping it position-wise. They demonstrated that the model with such a word decomposition outperformed Park et al. (2019).

We differ from the studies above in exploring the impact of tokenization on the MT evaluation. Our keen interest is i) to observe how vulnerable this metric is to the agglutinative languages and ii) to find a way to ensure that the metric is in line with human perception in this regard.

3 Background

This section describes the linguistic characteristics of Korean as an agglutinative language. Unlike most European languages, it features deeper layers and diversified decomposition.

3.1 Token Level

We define five meta-levels of segmentation for our experiment: word, morpheme, subword, character, and CV. The fork of a road to the classification is in the dependence of three elements: particles (or *Josa*), endings, and affixes.

- **Word**: A whitespace is a separator between this level of tokens. A token does not consider any of the three components independent.

- **Morpheme**: This token level considers particles, endings, and affixes as dependent elements. The degree of segmentation, however, varies from tokenizer to tokenizer by their tag set or algorithm.

[3] For those who are not familiar with Korean, the in-depth information about its word decomposition is provided in Appendix A.

Source		model		Leon		Dame			before		no one has strutted										like				the catwalk				strutted down			
Word		모델		레옹		데임은			아직		그	누구도			시도한			적	없는		방식으로				캣워크를				활보했다			
Morpheme				레	옹	데	임	은				누구		도	시도		한		없	는	방식		으로		캣워크			를	활보		했다	
						데	이 ㅁ					누	구도				하 ㄴ								캣	워크			활	보	했	다
																									캐 엇						하 었	다
																															하 았	다
Subword							임		아	직		누구		도			한						으	로	캣						했	다
Character		모	델				임					누	구	도	시	도	한				방	식				워	크					
CV	Choseong	ㅁ	ㄷ	ㄹ	ㅇ	ㄷ	ㅇ	ㅇ	ㅇ	ㅈ	ㄱ	ㄴ	ㄱ	ㄷ	ㅅ	ㄷ	ㅎ	ㅈ	ㅇ	ㄴ	ㅂ	ㅅ	ㅇ	ㄹ	ㅋ	ㅇ	ㅋ	ㄹ	ㅎ	ㅂ	ㅎ	ㄷ
	Jungseong	ㅗ	ㅔ	ㅔ	ㅗ	ㅔ	ㅣ	ㅡ	ㅏ	ㅣ	ㅡ	ㅜ	ㅜ	ㅗ	ㅣ	ㅗ	ㅏ	ㅓ	ㅓ	ㅡ	ㅏ	ㅣ	ㅡ	ㅗ	ㅐ	ㅝ	ㅡ	ㅡ	ㅘ	ㅗ	ㅐ	ㅏ
	Jongseong		ㄹ		ㅐ		ㅁ	ㄴ		ㄱ							ㄴ	ㄱ	ㅂㅅ	ㄴ	ㅇ	ㄱ			ㅅ			ㄹ	ㄹ		ㅆ	

Table 1: All possible tokenization schemes with the tokenizers applied in this study. The English source sentence is "*Model Leon Dame strutted down the catwalk like no one has strutted before.*", and their corresponding Korean words are given by the token space.

- **Subword**: It is an arbitrary sequence of strings. It is to note that the surface form of this token resembles morphemes unless the dictionary is intentionally built at the sub-subword level. We, nevertheless, categorize it in isolation, given the absence of morphological meaning in its token.

- **Character**: This token level denotes a string. No tokenizer is needed for the decomposition.

- **CV**: It refers to the smallest token unit, Jamo, meaning consonants and vowels (CV). A certain tokenizer is required to segment a string (equal to a character) into the CV.

3.2 Tokenizer

The meta-level tokens come into shape with the help of tokenizers in most cases. We implement seven tokenizers on the morpheme level – Kkma, Hannanum, Komoran, Okt and MeCab from KoNLPy (Park and Cho, 2014), Kiwi (Korean Intelligent Word Identifier)[4], data-driven Khaiii (Kakao Hangul Analyzer III)[5], a subword tokenizer SPM (Kudo and Richardson, 2018), and a CV-level tokenizer, Jamo[6]. Their systematic details are given in Appendix B.

3.2.1 Tag Set

Most Korean morphological analyzers have their roots in the 21st Century Sejong Project launched in 1998 intending to build a national framework for large-scale Korean corpora (21st Sejong Project, 1999). The tokenizers feature a different number of tag sets derived from the Sejong tag sets, as described in Table 7 in Appendix C.

The prototypical tag set is preserved in Komoran or similarly in MeCab and Khaiii. The tokenizer with the most fine-grained tag set is Kkma (56 tags). It provides a detailed analysis of endings. The most coarse form is observed in Okt (19 tags), a tokenizer for Twitter. Woo and Jung (2019) report its outstanding performance in terms of typos, emojis, and punctuation. Hannanum also features a small-sized tag set (22 tags). The particle-related tags are exceptionally reduced in this tokenizer. As mentioned previously, the central divergence of the tag sets is in particles, endings, and affixes.

3.2.2 Tokenization Scenario

The exemplary sentence depicted in Table 1 gives a glimpse of all possible cases of tokens in our experiment. It illustrates that the the most diversified segmentation occurs with verbs (*strutted down*). Intriguingly, some morphological tokenizers partially employ CV, such as shown in 한 versus 하, -ㄴ (the part of *no one has strutted*). Such are the cases of Hannanum, Kkma, Komoran, Khaiii, and Kiwi.

4 Experiment

4.1 Experiment Setup

As Korean evaluation data is scarce, we have organized human evaluation of four commercial NMT systems for the English-to-Korean translation with Direct Assessment (DA), the conventional human evaluation metric employed in Conference on Machine Translation (Barrault et al., 2020). Subsequently, automatic evaluation is performed with BLEU, TER, and ChrF built in `SacreBLEU`. With the resources at hand, the correlation between the two evaluation results is computed on the segment and corpus level.

4.1.1 Dataset

- **Source Test Set**: The original English texts are borrowed from WMT 2020 English III-type test set, composed of 2,048 sentences (61 documents) with a segment split maintained.

[4] https://github.com/bab2min/Kiwi

[5] https://github.com/kakao/khaiii

[6] https://github.com/JDongian/python-jamo

		Word	Morpheme							Subword	Char	CV
			Hannanum	Kkma	Kiwi	Khaiii	Komoran	MeCab	Okt			
Ratio	Ref	1	2.04	2.27	2.24	2.24	2.22	2.06	1.78⋆	2.30	3.22	7.51‡
	Hyp	1	2.02	2.15	2.14	2.14	2.12	1.97	1.70⋆	2.20	3.16	7.23‡
Time (ms)		-	4,326.91	27,112.96‡	1,959.96	1,494.13	1,084.10	152.59	3,029.68	51.57	5.00⋆	89.07

Table 2: Given our reference and hypothesis translations, a token ratio per word is measured by category. ‡ and ⋆ denote the biggest and smallest values, respectively. In addition, the time to decompose 1,000 sample sentences is calculated in milliseconds.

- **Reference Translation**: We hire a group of professional translators to create Korean reference translations. They are advised not to post-edit MT. To guarantee the highest translation quality, one of our in-house translator double-checks the final version. The revision, nevertheless, is implemented only if the sentence is semantically erroneous.
- **System Translation**: We employ four online MT models including our own –*Kakao i*[7]–. They are anonymized as Sys_A, Sys_B, Sys_P and Sys_Q for legal reason. The system translations are obtained on July 21, 2021.
- **Token Ratio & Time**: Given a word ($ratio = 1.0$), an average token ratio per token type is displayed in Table 2. The size of character and CV tokens are about 1.5 and 4 times larger than that of the average morpheme tokens. In addition, time taken to process 1,000 sentences is logged per token unit. The character level is about 5,000 times faster than Kkma.

In terms of normalizing data, errors in the source test sets and their subsequent impact on the system translations as discussed in Kim et al. (2021) remain undealt with. Only some minor technical issues, i.e. a single quote (') versus a backtick (`), are normalized.

4.1.2 Human Evaluation

DA is a metric where an evaluator scores each sentence on a continuous scale of [0, 100] in the category of Adequacy and Fluency. We hire 25 professional translators and assign each person a set of more or less 300 translated sentences. The contextual information of the documents is maintained to help them consider when making a judgment. They are allowed to reverse their previous decisions within a document boundary.

Regarding their qualification, they are either holders of a master's degree in interpretation and translation in the English-Korean language pair or freelance translators with a minimum of two years of experience. In light of the fact that all participants are new to MT evaluation, we provide a detailed guideline for the experiment.

One judgment per system translation is gathered, amounting to 16,116 (8,058 of Adequacy and Fluency) evaluation data. The judgment on Fluency is only utilized as supplementary information.

4.1.3 Quality Control

Out of the 8,058 Adequacy judgments, the first 10 judgments of each evaluator are removed from the calculation. The scores are then normalized with judge-wise Z-scores. Then, Inter-Quartile Range (IQR) is computed as in Equation 1, where Q_1 and Q_3 signify the first and third quartile values and x denotes outliers that fall into the two categories. Having removed 4.1% of the data, we base our observation on 7,727 judgments.

$$x < Q_1 - 1.5 \cdot (Q_3 - Q_1)$$

or

$$x > Q_3 + 1.5 \cdot (Q_3 - Q_1) \tag{1}$$

4.1.4 Computation

The hypothesis and reference translations are tokenized by the aforementioned 11 token units without applying any additional normalization. Consequently, the scores of the automatic metrics are computed, and their Pearson's correlation coefficient r are measured against the human Adequacy judgment by:

$$r = \frac{\sum_{i=1}^{n}(H_i - \overline{H}) \cdot (M_i - \overline{M})}{\sqrt{\sum_{i=1}^{n}(H_i - \overline{H})^2}\sqrt{\sum_{i=1}^{n}(M_i - \overline{M})^2}} \tag{2}$$

where H and M refer to the machine and human DA scores, respectively, and $\overline{H}$ and $\overline{M}$, their mean values. The Pearson's r measures the linear relationship between the two variables. During the process, some of the issues have concerned us:

[7] https://www.translate.kakao.com

		Default	**Word**	**Morpheme**							**Subword**	**Char**	**CV**
				Hannanum	Kkma	Kiwi	Khaiii	Komoran	MeCab	Okt			
BLEU	*ngrams*	4	1	2	2	2	2	2	2	2	2	2	5
ChrF	*char_order*	6	3	3	3	3	3	3	3	3	3	3	5
	word_order	0	0	0	0	1	1	1	1	1	1	2	0

Table 3: The adjusted parameters of BLEU and ChrF per token type.

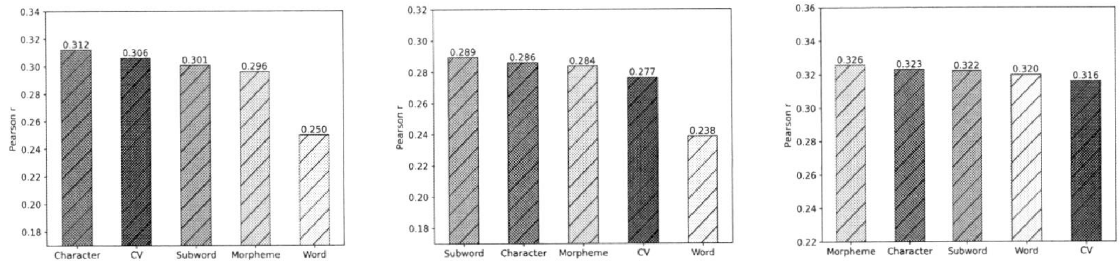

(a) BLEU (b) TER (c) ChrF

Figure 1: The Pearson correlation on the segment level: concerning the meta-token level. The morpheme corresponds to the average value of all morpheme tokens.

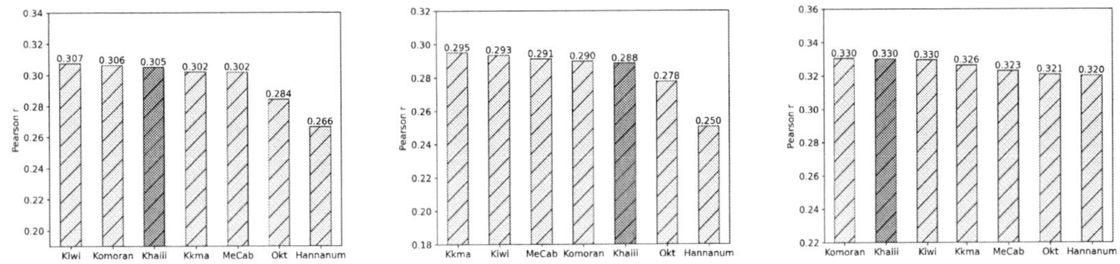

(a) BLEU (b) TER (c) ChrF

Figure 2: The Pearson correlation on the segment level: concerning the morpheme level. Khaiii is in red to inform its different basis.

- **Do we adjust n-gram parameters?**
The BLEU score is a geometric mean of four-grams. As the token unit is divergent, on the one hand, we attempt to avoid a circumstance where any tokenizer benefits from the n-gram parameter. On the other, the default word n-gram of ChrF is zero, which leads to the same conclusion for some tokens. To make the consequence of the token unit clear and compatible, we have organized a preliminary study to obtain the best-correlated n-gram parameters per token typology. The result is provided in Table 3 along with the default values.

- **TER scores over 1.0**
Theoretically speaking, a TER score of 1.0 represents a total mismatch between a hypothesis and reference. Yet, when a reference is too short for its hypothesis, the computation is programmed to exceed 1.0, which becomes an outlier to the Pearson correlation. We, thus, normalize such cases by cutting down to 1.0.

- **Is the sample size enough?**
Koehn (2004) reported that they reached a near 100% confidence with 3,000 samples when assessing MT systems with BLEU. In light of their work, we believe that our sample size is affordable to draw a valid conclusion.

4.2 Experiment Result

The Pearson correlation of `SacreBLEU` to human DA scores when with different token types is reported on the segment and corpus level. On each level, the results are organized by the meta level, with the morpheme represented by the average score of seven types. Afterward, the morpheme tokens are compared among themselves. Khaiii is

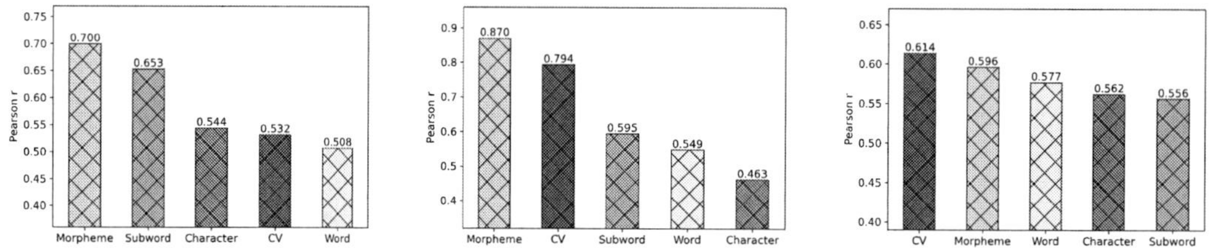

(a) BLEU (b) TER (c) ChrF

Figure 3: The Pearson correlation on the corpus level: concerning the meta-token level.

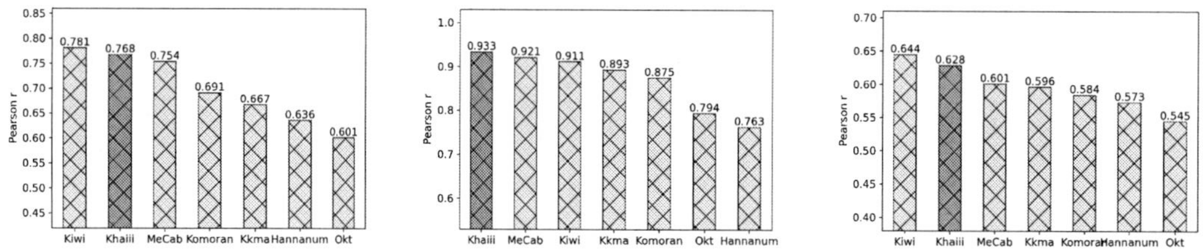

(a) BLEU (b) TER (c) ChrF

Figure 4: The Pearson correlation on the corpus level: concerning the morpheme level.

highlighted with a different color to present its algorithmic divergence.

4.2.1 Segment Level

Figure 1 and Figure 2 reports the Pearson correlation of the meta- and morpheme level, respectively. The scores range from 0.23 to 0.33.

BLEU achieves better human correlation when the token is more fine-grained. When a sentence is not decomposed, the score is likely to lose validity. The best fit for this metric is a character ($r = 0.312$). Among the morphemes, we witness an insignificant correlation of MeCab.

The result of **TER** coincides with BLEU in that any tokenizer can enhance the correlation of the metric. The result shows that SPM goes best with this metric. It is also noticeable that CV results in a poor correlation. Moreover, Khaiii is insignificant to this metric.

ChrF has obtained relatively consistent correlations in all token types despite its re-adjusted parameters. The morpheme level is best suited for this metric, among which Khaiii stands out for a good reason and CV for a wrong reason. CV often deteriorates the correlation of ChrF.

We conclude that any pre-tokenization is essential for BLEU and TER, while ChrF should be approached with caution on the segment level. On the bright side, the performance of Kiwi is noteworthy among the morpheme tokenizers. Furthermore, as a whole, we stress the effectiveness of the character-level segmentation, which guarantees a fast deployment and the human correlation that is often better than MeCab. On the other side, the CV level is undependable in the Korean MT evaluation, unlike in other NLP tasks. Furthermore, Hannanum and Okt are not an option for this task.

4.2.2 Corpus Level

Figure 3 to Figure 4 depict the result of the meta- and morpheme levels, respectively. The score ranges from 0.46 to 0.93, which is much higher and broader than the segment level.

On the meta level, the morpheme tokens are likely to attain a higher correlation to human judgment in all cases. Moreover, the performance of Kiwi and Khaiii is striking. However, the correlation of TER and ChrF degrades with character tokens or SPM in the case of ChrF. Such a tendency is in clear contrast to the finding observed at the segment level.

Additionally, the raw scores of each metric are compared to human DA scores, as shown in Table 4. As expected from the characteristics of the lexical matching system, the smaller units result in higher raw scores, which, however, can soar up to twice in the case of BLEU (from 28.1 to 48.5 in Sys_A). Likewise, the most severe version of TER

	Ave. DA ↑	Ave. z	Word	Okt	MeCab	Komoran	Kkma	Kiwi	Khaiii	Hannanum	SPM	Character	CV
Sys_A	68.783	0.203	28.099	33.398	38.341	40.275	40.986	41.022	40.005	36.939	41.015	48.712	48.467
Sys_B	67.160	0.112	28.932	34.351	39.185	41.007	41.920	41.997	40.881	37.793	41.948	49.553	49.188
Sys_P	64.688	0.027	23.941	30.415	35.605	36.621	37.236	38.458	37.034	32.902	37.213	45.924	45.098
Sys_Q	57.734	-0.220	25.941	31.382	35.602	37.304	38.063	38.138	36.939	34.058	38.155	47.096	46.602

(a) BLEU

	Ave. DA ↑	Ave. z	Word	Okt	MeCab	Komoran	Kkma	Kiwi	Khaiii	Hannanum	SPM	Character	CV
Sys_A	68.783	0.203	82.811	68.223	64.142	63.041	62.253	62.352	63.412	67.833	62.391	57.718	52.932
Sys_B	67.160	0.112	82.334	67.332	63.519	62.585	61.545	61.649	62.867	67.249	61.083	56.364	51.962
Sys_P	64.688	0.027	89.652	69.882	64.898	64.859	63.479	62.983	64.346	71.199	65.914	62.163	54.063
Sys_Q	57.734	-0.220	86.699	70.356	66.611	65.641	64.751	64.758	66.126	71.199	64.767	59.771	54.697

(b) TER

	Ave. DA ↑	Ave. z	Word	Okt	MeCab	Komoran	Kkma	Kiwi	Khaiii	Hannanum	SPM	Character	CV
Sys_A	68.783	0.203	44.897	46.508	47.544	48.904	46.326	49.299	48.763	46.019	47.932	47.887	53.140
Sys_B	67.160	0.112	45.725	47.345	48.370	49.635	47.131	50.096	49.560	46.826	48.807	48.707	53.807
Sys_P	64.688	0.027	42.742	44.171	45.342	46.182	43.796	47.017	46.354	43.401	45.357	45.699	51.198
Sys_Q	57.734	-0.220	43.505	45.134	46.031	47.166	44.639	47.557	47.011	44.378	44.378	46.533	51.775

(c) ChrF

Table 4: The raw scores of the metrics of the four MT systems by token type along with the human DA scores and their z-scores. The highest scores are in blue & red.

scores is before the tokenization (82.33 - 89.69). The ChrF scores, on the other hand, fluctuate moderately from 44.9 to 53.1 (in Sys_A). We, therefore, advise not to copy raw `SacreBLEU` scores from any studies when this language is concerned.

While so, we discover a substantial problem that the system rankings calculated by the automatic metrics do not comply with the human judgment at all. As the highest scores in blue and red demonstrate such a trend, the human average scores place the systems in the order of $[Sys_A = 1, Sys_B = 2, Sys_P = 3, Sys_Q = 4]$, but almost all automatic scores position them as $[Sys_A = 2, Sys_B = 1, Sys_P = 3, Sys_Q = 4]$. In the worst case, the third and fourth ranks are swapped according to BLEU when tokenized by MeCab, Kiwi, or Khaiii. Such an erroneous conclusion by the metrics can be drawn due to either the small number of systems or possible outlier systems in the experiment setup (Mathur et al., 2020). We leave the verification of this issue to our future work.

5 Extra Meta-Evaluation

As an extended work, we investigate the influence of pre-tokenization on other homogeneous automatic metrics: `NLTK-BLEU`[8], `GLEU`[9] (Wu et al., 2016), `NIST`[10], `RIBES` (Isozaki et al., 2010), `CharacTER` (Wang et al., 2016), and `EED` (Stanchev et al., 2019). We compute the Person correlation r of a total of nine metrics per tokenization on the segment and corpus level under the same environment. The results are provided in Figure 5 through Figure 8 in Appendix D.

5.1 Segment Level

Albeit minor differences from `SacreBLEU`, NLTK-BLEU is most benefited from the CV level, not the character level. GLEU features a more robust correlation to any given token type than BLEU. Consistent with such a tendency, the CV level increases the correlation of RIBES. Interestingly enough, however, NIST turns out to be vulnerable to any token types except SPM, and the scope of the scores is markedly low (0.1 - 0.19).

In terms of edit-distance-based metrics, the result does not vacillate much and, at the same time, presents high human correlations. CharacTER favors the morpheme level, such as Komoran. EED, on the other hand, does not favor any token types. The more decomposed a token is, the lower the human correlation becomes in this metric.

To summarize, there is a good chance that the CV level enhances the correlation of many n-gram-based metrics such as BLEU. The metrics that a word should be left as it is are NIST and EED.

5.2 Corpus Level

On the corpus level, the morphological tokens are predominantly helpful in obtaining a higher human correlation, as in the case of BLEU, GLEU, and NIST. Among the morphemes, the role of Kiwi is

[8]https://www.nltk.org/_modules/nltk/translate/bleu_score.html

[9]https://www.nltk.org/_modules/nltk/translate/gleu_score.html

[10]https://www.nist.gov/itl/iad/mig/metrics-machine-translation-evaluation/

	Word	Kkma	Hannanum	Okt	Komoran	MeCab	Khaiii	**Kiwi** ↑	Subword	Character	CV
EED	0.095	0.094	0.093	0.089⋆	0.092	0.093	0.098	0.096	0.094	0.096	0.201
BLEU	0.110	0.110	0.108	0.107	0.111	0.109	0.134	0.106⋆	0.106⋆	0.108	0.128
ChrF	0.111	0.113	0.108⋆	0.115	0.121	0.115	0.121	0.115	0.115	0.129	0.147
CharacTER	0.284⋆	0.827	0.633	0.434	0.77	0.679	0.763	0.816	0.792	2.391	366.65
GLEU	1.018	1.059	1.075	1.036	1.029	1.060	1.038	1.002	0.961⋆	0.979	1.068
NIST	1.016	1.061	1.044	1.042	1.082	1.033	1.011⋆	1.032	1.032	1.085	1.119
NLTK-BLEU	1.072	1.016	0.982	1.011	0.994	1.036	1.140	1.037	0.981⋆	1.020	1.028
RIBES	1.011⋆	3.888	2.867	1.791	3.360	2.735	3.441	3.578	3.476	13.094	628.96
TER	0.332⋆	9.849	5.236	2.413	8.232	5.061	7.768	7.653	8.106	24.933	362.18

Table 5: The time of each metric to compute a score for 100 sentences when combined with different token units. The value is sorted by Kiwi (unit: seconds). The best scores are with a star(⋆) and the abnormal cases are stressed in blue.

significant. This token type is, however, detrimental to RIBES, which scores the highest correlation in this experiment. The character level, on the other hand, is beneficial to this metric. In the case of CharacTER and NIST, the correlation is degraded with word decomposition by the CV or character level.

5.3 Computation Time

Table 5 describes the time to compute metric scores of 100 sentences per token type. From the perspective of token type, the more fine-grained token type takes more time. For instance, treating CV takes 100 times more than words in TER. No matter how good the CV level can be, inefficiency is its blind spot.

From the viewpoint of automatic metrics, RIBES, TER, and CharacTER are one of the most time-consuming ones. The pairing with CV and RIBES, for instance, would end in taking up about 630 seconds (10 minutes) to deal with 100 sentences. On the contrary, EED boasts the utmost efficiency.

6 Limitations & Future Works

We acknowledge some limitations this work has to embrace. First of all, the number of systems in question is small, which, in part, has led to an arguable conclusion on the corpus level. Furthermore, all of the systems are online APIs. Second, while questioning the influence of token type on the agglutinative languages, we base our study solely on Korean.

It is of our future interest to probe into the consequence of token types in other comparable languages other than Korean. We also intend to scale up the experiment by employing state-of-the-art NMT models.

7 Conclusion

This paper analyzes the influence of diversified token units on the human correlation of `SacreBLEU` on both segment and corpus levels when it comes to agglutinative languages such as Korean by performing meta-evaluation with Pearson correlation. We demonstrate that the pre-tokenization with a fit-for-all token type is not always an optimal choice in Korean MT evaluation. We summarize some of the valuable lessons:

- BLEU and TER should always be accompanied by a segmentation process beforehand.
- Tokenizer should be carefully selected in ChrF.
- The human correlation of some metrics, which are mostly related to edit distance, is easily degraded by token type.
- The CV level is beneficial to some metrics. However, its exponential computation time makes it unprofitable in the MT evaluation.
- Instead, we discover the possibility of a character-level segmentation as a quick and easy substitute on the segment level.
- However, the morpheme level is recommended on the corpus level such as Kiwi or Khaiii, among others.
- The raw score on the corpus level can be inflated up to twice. We strongly advise against copying scores from other studies.

Acknowledgements

Special thanks to the members of Business Automation for their thoughtful comments and sound discussions.

References

The 21st Sejong Project. 1999. Construction of korean basic data (academic service report).

Alfred V. Aho and Margaret J. Corasick. 1975. Efficient string matching: an aid to bibliographic search. *Communications of the ACM*, 18(6):333–340.

Loïc Barrault, Magdalena Biesialska, Ondřej Bojar, Marta R. Costa-jussà, Christian Federmann, Yvette Graham, Roman Grundkiewicz, Barry Haddow, Matthias Huck, Eric Joanis, Tom Kocmi, Philipp Koehn, Chi-kiu Lo, Nikola Ljubešić, Christof Monz, Makoto Morishita, Masaaki Nagata, Toshiaki Nakazawa, Santanu Pal, Matt Post, and Marcos Zampieri. 2020. Findings of the 2020 conference on machine translation (WMT20). In *Proceedings of the Fifth Conference on Machine Translation*, pages 1–55, Online. Association for Computational Linguistics.

Chris Callison-Burch, Miles Osborne, and Philipp Koehn. 2006. Re-evaluating the role of Bleu in machine translation research. In *11th Conference of the European Chapter of the Association for Computational Linguistics*, pages 249–256, Trento, Italy. Association for Computational Linguistics.

Miguel Domingo, Mercedes García-Martínez, Alexandre Helle, Francisco Casacuberta, and Manuel Herranz. 2018. How much does tokenization affect neural machine translation? *CoRR*, abs/1812.08621.

Sugyeong Eo, Chanjun Park, Hyeonseok Moon, and Heuiseok Lim. 2021. Research on subword tokenization of korean neural machine translation and proposal for tokenization method to separate jongsung from syllables. *Journal of the Korea Convergence Society*, 12(3):1–7.

Edward Fredkin and Bolt Beranek. 1960. Trie memory. *Communications of the ACM*, pages 490–499.

Matthias Huck, Simon Riess, and Alexander Fraser. 2017. Target-side word segmentation strategies for neural machine translation. In *Proceedings of the Second Conference on Machine Translation*, pages 56–67, Copenhagen, Denmark. Association for Computational Linguistics.

Hideki Isozaki, Tsutomu Hirao, Kevin Duh, Katsuhito Sudoh, and Hajime Tsukada. 2010. Automatic evaluation of translation quality for distant language pairs. In *Proceedings of the 2010 Conference on Empirical Methods in Natural Language Processing*, EMNLP '10, page 944–952, USA. Association for Computational Linguistics.

Ahrii Kim, Yunju Bak, Jimin Sun, Sungwon Lyu, and Changmin Lee. 2021. The suboptimal wmt test sets and their impact on human parity. *Preprints*.

Hwichan Kim, Tosho Hirasawa, and Mamoru Komachi. 2020. Zero-shot North Korean to English neural machine translation by character tokenization and phoneme decomposition. In *Proceedings of the 58th Annual Meeting of the Association for Computational Linguistics: Student Research Workshop*, pages 72–78, Online. Association for Computational Linguistics.

Philipp Koehn. 2004. Statistical significance tests for machine translation evaluation. In *Proceedings of EMNLP 2004*, pages 388–395. Association for Computational Linguistics.

Taku Kudo and John Richardson. 2018. SentencePiece: A simple and language independent subword tokenizer and detokenizer for neural text processing. In *Proceedings of the 2018 Conference on Empirical Methods in Natural Language Processing: System Demonstrations*, pages 66–71, Brussels, Belgium. Association for Computational Linguistics.

Jason Lee, Kyunghyun Cho, and Thomas Hofmann. 2017. Fully character-level neural machine translation without explicit segmentation. *Transactions of the Association for Computational Linguistics*, 5:365–378.

Benjamin Marie, Atsushi Fujita, and Raphael Rubino. 2021. Scientific credibility of machine translation research: A meta-evaluation of 769 papers. In *Proceedings of the 59th Annual Meeting of the Association for Computational Linguistics and the 11th International Joint Conference on Natural Language Processing (Volume 1: Long Papers)*, pages 7297–7306, Online. Association for Computational Linguistics.

Nitika Mathur, Timothy Baldwin, and Trevor Cohn. 2020. Tangled up in BLEU: Reevaluating the evaluation of automatic machine translation evaluation metrics. In *Proceedings of the 58th Annual Meeting of the Association for Computational Linguistics*, pages 4984–4997, Online. Association for Computational Linguistics.

Sangwhan Moon and Naoaki Okazaki. 2020. Jamo pair encoding: Subcharacter representation-based extreme Korean vocabulary compression for efficient subword tokenization. In *Proceedings of the 12th Language Resources and Evaluation Conference*, pages 3490–3497, Marseille, France. European Language Resources Association.

Toshiaki Nakazawa, Shohei Higashiyama, Chenchen Ding, Hideya Mino, Isao Goto, Hideto Kazawa, Yusuke Oda, Graham Neubig, and Sadao Kurohashi. 2017. Overview of the 4th workshop on Asian translation. In *Proceedings of the 4th Workshop on Asian Translation (WAT2017)*, pages 1–54, Taipei, Taiwan. Asian Federation of Natural Language Processing.

Gisim Nam, Yeonggeun Ko, Hyunkyung Yu, and Hyeongyong Choi. 2019. *Korean standard grammar (표준 국어문법론)*. Hankook Munhwasa, Korea.

Kishore Papineni, Salim Roukos, Todd Ward, and Wei-Jing Zhu. 2002. Bleu: A method for automatic evaluation of machine translation. In *Proceedings of the*

40th Annual Meeting on Association for Computational Linguistics, ACL '02, page 311–318, USA. Association for Computational Linguistics.

Chanjun Park, Gyeongmin Kim, and Heuiseok Lim. 2019. Parallel corpus filtering and korean-optimized subword tokenization for machine translation. *Annual Conference on Human and Language Technology*, pages 221–224.

Eunjeong L. Park and Sungzoon Cho. 2014. Konlpy: Korean natural language processing in python. In *Proceedings of the 26th Annual Conference on Human Cognitive Language Technology*, Chuncheon, Korea.

Kyubyong Park, Joohong Lee, Seongbo Jang, and Dawoon Jung. 2020. An empirical study of tokenization strategies for various korean NLP tasks. *CoRR*, abs/2010.02534.

Sungjoon Park, Jeongmin Byun, Sion Baek, Yongseok Cho, and Alice Oh. 2018. Subword-level word vector representations for Korean. In *Proceedings of the 56th Annual Meeting of the Association for Computational Linguistics (Volume 1: Long Papers)*, pages 2429–2438, Melbourne, Australia. Association for Computational Linguistics.

Maja Popović. 2015. chrF: character n-gram F-score for automatic MT evaluation. In *Proceedings of the Tenth Workshop on Statistical Machine Translation*, pages 392–395, Lisbon, Portugal. Association for Computational Linguistics.

Matt Post. 2018. A call for clarity in reporting BLEU scores. In *Proceedings of the Third Conference on Machine Translation: Research Papers*, pages 186–191, Brussels, Belgium. Association for Computational Linguistics.

Rico Sennrich, Barry Haddow, and Alexandra Birch. 2016. Neural machine translation of rare words with subword units. In *Proceedings of the 54th Annual Meeting of the Association for Computational Linguistics (Volume 1: Long Papers)*, pages 1715–1725, Berlin, Germany. Association for Computational Linguistics.

Matthew Snover, Bonnie Dorr, Rich Schwartz, Linnea Micciulla, and John Makhoul. 2006. A study of translation edit rate with targeted human annotation. In *Proceedings of the 7th Conference of the Association for Machine Translation in the Americas: Technical Papers*, pages 223–231, Cambridge, Massachusetts, USA. Association for Machine Translation in the Americas.

Peter Stanchev, Weiyue Wang, and Hermann Ney. 2019. EED: Extended edit distance measure for machine translation. In *Proceedings of the Fourth Conference on Machine Translation (Volume 2: Shared Task Papers, Day 1)*, pages 514–520, Florence, Italy. Association for Computational Linguistics.

Liling Tan, Jon Dehdari, and Josef van Genabith. 2015. An awkward disparity between BLEU / RIBES scores and human judgements in machine translation. In *Proceedings of the 2nd Workshop on Asian Translation (WAT2015)*, pages 74–81, Kyoto, Japan. Workshop on Asian Translation.

Weiyue Wang, Jan-Thorsten Peter, Hendrik Rosendahl, and Hermann Ney. 2016. CharacTer: Translation edit rate on character level. In *Proceedings of the First Conference on Machine Translation: Volume 2, Shared Task Papers*, pages 505–510, Berlin, Germany. Association for Computational Linguistics.

Kyungjin Woo and Suhyeon Jung. 2019. Comparison of korean morphology analyzers according to the types of sentence. *Proceedings of the Korean Information Science Society Conference*, pages 1388–1390.

Yonghui Wu, Mike Schuster, Zhifeng Chen, Quoc V. Le, Mohammad Norouzi, Wolfgang Macherey, Maxim Krikun, Yuan Cao, Qin Gao, Klaus Macherey, Jeff Klingner, Apurva Shah, Melvin Johnson, Xiaobing Liu, Lukasz Kaiser, Stephan Gouws, Yoshikiyo Kato, Taku Kudo, Hideto Kazawa, Keith Stevens, George Kurian, Nishant Patil, Wei Wang, Cliff Young, Jason Smith, Jason Riesa, Alex Rudnick, Oriol Vinyals, Greg Corrado, Macduff Hughes, and Jeffrey Dean. 2016. Google's neural machine translation system: Bridging the gap between human and machine translation. *CoRR*, abs/1609.08144.

Choi Yongseok and Kongjoo Lee. 2020. Performance analysis of korean morphological analyzer based on transformer and bert. *Journal of KIISE*, 47(8):730–741.

Xiang Zhang, Junbo Zhao, and Yann LeCun. 2015. Character-level convolutional networks for text classification. In *Advances in Neural Information Processing Systems*, volume 28. Curran Associates, Inc.

A Word Decomposition

> A single distinct meaningful element of speech or writing, [...] and *typically shown with a whitespace on either side* when written or printed.
> -Oxford Dictionary

The general definition of a word, as shown above, conjectures that it is segmented with whitespaces. While such is the case of most European languages, it is arguable in Korean whose words do not always accompany spaces between themselves, depending on schools. Here we illustrate three approaches in defining a word: *comprehensive*, *compromising*, and *analytic*. Their views on the independence of post-positional particle, ending, or affix as a word diverge (Nam et al., 2019), as displayed respectively in Table 6 of Level *Word*.

Following the comprehensive standpoint, what is typically understood as a word in Western languages is equivalent to *Eojeol* in Korean. Those with the compromising perspective perceives that endings and affixes are not a word while the analytic school recognizes the independence of endings. That much active discussion is possible with the morpheme boundary as well, due to the fact that a character is divisible.

In other words, **a character has a sub-layer**. The word *read*, for instance, is composed of four characters: r-e-a-d. The equivalent Korean word 읽 in Table 6 is also a character, but at the same time it is a combination of two consonants (ㅇ , ㄺ) and one vowel (ㅣ). We call this sub-layer *Jamo* (ㅇ - ㅣ- ㄺ) in Korean or CV in this paper, the abbreviated form from the initial letters of consonant (자음/ja-eum/) and vowel (모음/mo-eum/).

CV is position-wise; it is situated in a fixed position of *Choseong* (initial, ㅇ), *Jungseong* (middle, ㅣ), and *Jongseong* (final, ㄺ), respectively. Some affixes or morphemes take the form of Jongseong, making a diversified token scenario between the morpheme and CV level.

B Architecture of the Morpheme Analyzers

This section delves into the detailed architecture of the morpheme analyzers mentioned in this paper. The aforementioned analyzers are grouped into dictionary-based and data-based by their core algorithm.

B.1 Dictionary-based

Most of the tokenizers applied in this paper belongs to this category. The first step of the tokenization is that when encountered a word, all possible morphological scenarios are represented with some probabilities by referring to a dictionary that contains vocabularies and their morphological information. The next step is to find the optimal morpheme combination that maximizes the observed probability, with the assumption being that the output morpheme m_k of position k is determined by its previous output m_{k-1} and its kth character c_k. Then, as a final procedure m_k is tagged.

For the agglutinative languages whose characters are always divisible, the decomposition depth should be determined whether to separate the character into the CV level. In that sense, we will denominate each case as *non-CV* and *CV level* for convenience's sake.

The non-CV-level decomposition is performed in Kkma, Okt, and Hannanum in our case. Candidate tokens are generated by restoring from the dictionary, and their probabilities are calculated by Dynamic Programming. The CV level segmentation, on the other hand, is the case of Komoran and Kiwi. The probability is calculated by Aho-Corasick string-matching algorithm (Aho and Corasick, 1975) applied on the dictionary which is structured as a look-up table called Tries (Fredkin and Beranek, 1960) of CV.

B.2 Data-driven

Khaiii is the sole analyzer that fits in to this category in this paper. While the previous dictionary-based tokenizers consider the word decomposition as an analysis problem, Khaiii approaches it as a classification problem of determining a morpheme tag for a given input character. One of the main challenges is the disharmonious token length of input and output observed in some cases such as shortened words whose restoration involves the CV-level segmentation. As an instance, the verb 했다 (did) can be segmented into 하/VX + 였/EP + 다/VV. It is clear that just by combining 하 and 였 the original morpheme 했 is not able to be achieved at a character level (하였 vs. 했).

While Recurrent Neural Networks (RNN) is a popular baseline in this regard, Khaiii adopts Convolutional Neural Networks (CNN) to maintain the information of input character and its corresponding output tag. In addition, CNN can speed up the

Level	Denomination	Particle	Ending	Affix	Example
Word	Eojeol	X	X	X	혜미가, 동화를, 읽었다
	Word	O	X	X	혜미, -가, 동화, -를, 읽었다
	Word	O	O	X	혜미, -가, 동화, -를, 읽, -었다
Morpheme	Morpheme	O	O	O	혜미, -가, 동화, -를, 읽, -었, -다
Character	Eumjeol	-	-	-	혜, -미, -가, 동, -화, -를, 읽, -었, -다
CV	Jamo	-	-	-	ㅎ, -ㅖ, ㅁ, -ㅣ, ㄱ, -ㅏ, ㄷ, -ㅗ, -ㅇ, ㅎ, -ㅘ, ㄹ, -ㅡ, -ㄹ, ㅇ, -ㅣ, -ㄹㄱ, ㅇ, -ㅓ, -ㅆ, ㄷ, -ㅏ

Table 6: Level of word decomposition in Korean, indicating an open discussion about defining a word (Nam et al., 2019).

process. More in-depth architecture is provided in their git page. The model is trained with Sejong Corpus provided by Sejong Project, together with a manually created 6k words. After rooting erroneous sentences out, the size of the corpus reaches about 10.3 million words/Eojeol).

C Tag Sets of Korean Tokenizers

Category			Sejong	Okt	Komoran	MeCab-ko	Kkma	Hannanum	Khaiii	Kiwi
# of tags			*42*	*19*	*42*	*43*	*56*	*22*	*46*	*47*
Substantive	**noun**	**general**	NNG	Noun	NNG	NNG	NNG	NC	NNG	NNG
		proper	NNP		NNP	NNP	NNP	NQ	NNP	NNP
		dependent	NNB		NNB	NNB	NNB	NB	NNB	NNB
		unit				NNBC	NNM			
	pronoun		NP		NP	NP	NP	NP	NP	NP
	numeral		NR		NR	NR	NR	NN	NR	NR
Predicate	**verb**		VV	Verb	VV	VV	VV	PV	VV	VV
	adjective		VA	Adjective	VA	VA	VA	PA	VA	VA
	auxiliary		VX	-	VX	VX	VXV VXA	PX	VX	VX
	copula	**positive**	VCP	-	VCP	VCP	VCP	-	VCP	VCP
		negative	VCN	-	VCN	VCN	VCN	-	VCN	VCN
Modifier	**article**	**determiner**	MM	Determiner	MM	MM	MDT	MM	MM	MM
		numeral					MDN			
	adverb	**general**	MAG	Adverb	MAG	MAG	MAG	MA	MAG	MAG
		connective	MAJ	Conjunction	MAJ	MAJ	MAC		MAJ	MAJ
Interjection	**interjection**		IC	Exclamation	IC	IC	IC	II	IC	IC
Post-positional Particle	**case-marking**	**subjective**	JKS	Josa	JKS	JKS	JKS	JC	JKS	JKS
		complement	JKC		JKC	JKC	JKC		JKC	JKC
		adnominal	JKG		JKG	JKG	JKG		JKG	JKG
		objective	JKO		JKO	JKO	JKO		JKO	JKO
		adverbial	JKB		JKB	JKB	JKM		JKM	JKM
		vocative	JKV		JKV	JKV	JKI		JKI	JKI
		quotation	JKQ		JKQ	JKQ	JKQ		JKQ	JKQ
	auxiliary		JX		JX	JX	JX	JX	JX	JX
	conjunctive		JC		JC	JC	JC		JC	JC
	predicative		-		-	-	-	JP	-	-
Dependent	**pre-final ending**	**honorific**	EP	PreEomi	EP	EP	EPH	EP	EP	EP
		tense					EPT			
		politeness					EPP			
	sentence-closing ending	**declarative**	EF	Eomi	EF	EF	EFN	EF	EF	EF
		interrogative					EFQ			
		imperative					EFO			
		requesting					EFA			
		interjective					EFI			
		honorific					EFR			
	connective ending	**equal**	EC	EC		EC	ECE	EC	EC	EC
		auxiliary					ECS			
		dependent					ECD			
	transformative ending	**nominal**	ETN		ETN	ETN	ETN	ET	ETN	ETN
		adnominal	ETM		ETM	ETM	ETD		ETD	ETD
	prefix	**substantive**	XPN	-	XPN	XPN	XPN	XP	XPN	XPN
		predicative	-	-	-	-	XPV		-	-
	suffix	**derived noun**	XSN	Suffix	XSN	XSN	XSN	XS	XSN	XSN
		derived verb	XSV		XSV	XSV	XSV		XSV	XSV
		derived adverb	XSA		XSA	XSA	XSA		XSA	XSA
	root	**root**	XR	-	XR	XR	XR	-	XR	XR
Punctuation	**. ? !**		SF	Punctuation	SF	SF	SF	S	SF	SF
	…		SE		SE	SE	SE		SE	SE
	“ ” ‘ ’ ( )		SS		SS	SSO SSC	SS		SS	SS
	∼- _		SP		SP	SC	SP		SP	SP
	others		SO		SO	SY	SO		SO	SO
Etc.	**Chinese character**		SW	Foreign	SW		SW		SW	SW
	foreign word		SH		SH	SH	OH	F	SH	SH
	number		SL	Alpha	SL	SL	OL	-	SL	SL
	unknown noun		SN	Number	SN	SN	ON	-	SN	SN
	unknown verb		NF	Unknown	NF	-	UN	-	ZN	UN
	unknown		NV		NV	-		-	ZV	
	unknown		NA		NA	-		-	ZZ	
	consonant/vowel		-	KoreanParticle	-	-	-	-	SWK	-
	hashtag		-	Hashtag	-	-	-	-	-	W_HASHTAG
	user name		-	ScreenName	-	-	-	-	-	W_MENTION
	email		-	Email	-	-	-	-	-	W_EMAIL
	url		-	URL	-	-	-	-	-	W_URL

Table 7: Tag sets of Sejong Project and seven Korean tokenizers.

D Meta-Evaluation

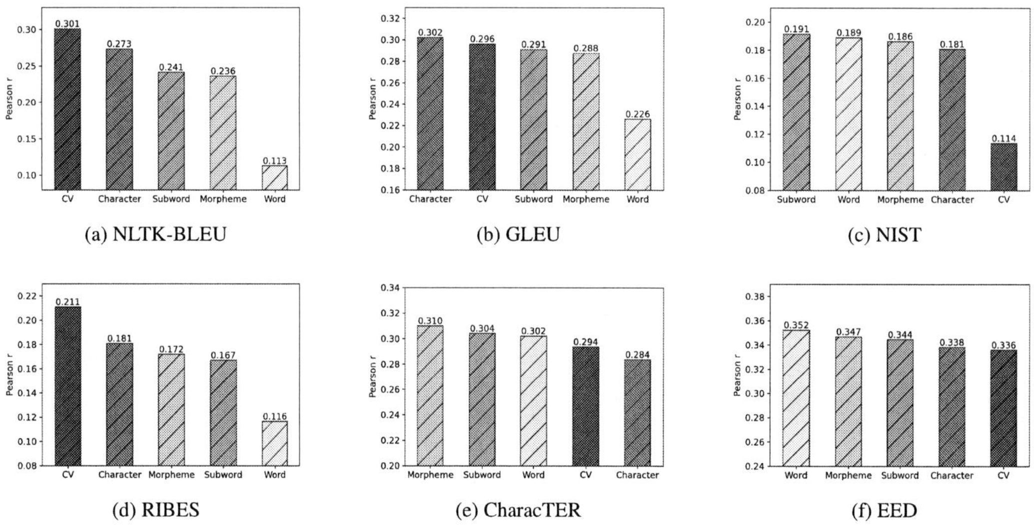

(a) NLTK-BLEU (b) GLEU (c) NIST

(d) RIBES (e) CharacTER (f) EED

Figure 5: The Pearson correlation on the segment level: concerning the meta-level

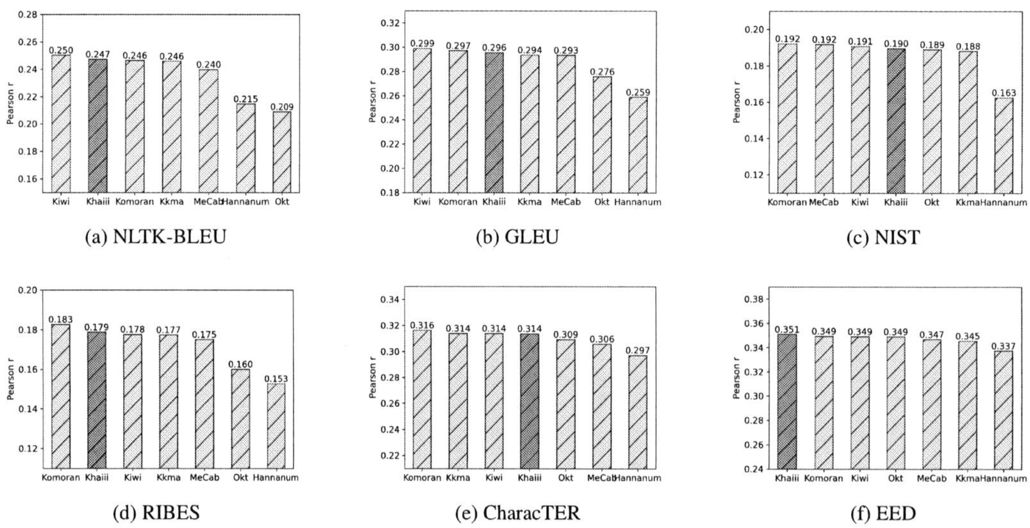

(a) NLTK-BLEU (b) GLEU (c) NIST

(d) RIBES (e) CharacTER (f) EED

Figure 6: The Pearson correlation on the segment level: concerning the morpheme level

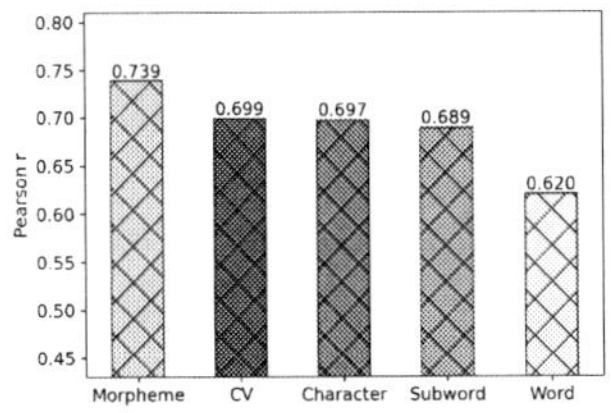

(a) NLTK-BLEU

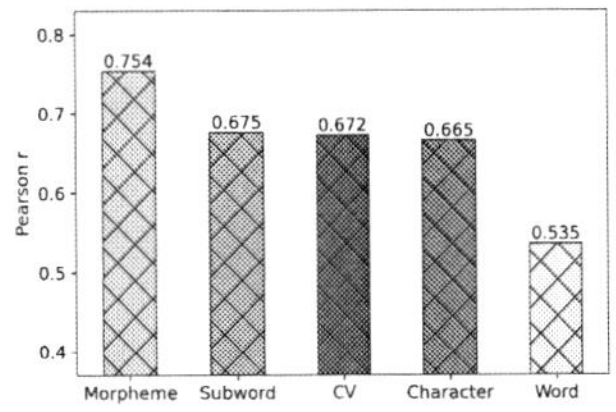

(b) GLEU

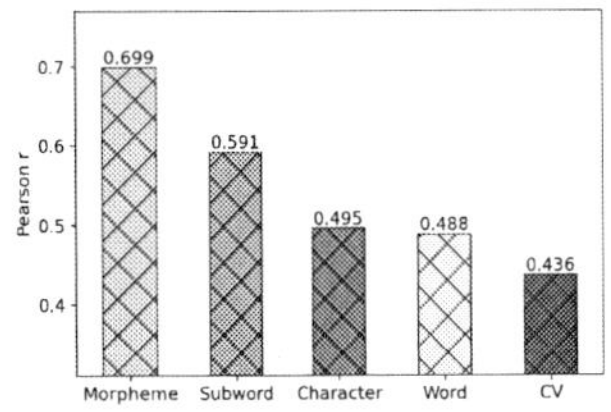

(c) NIST

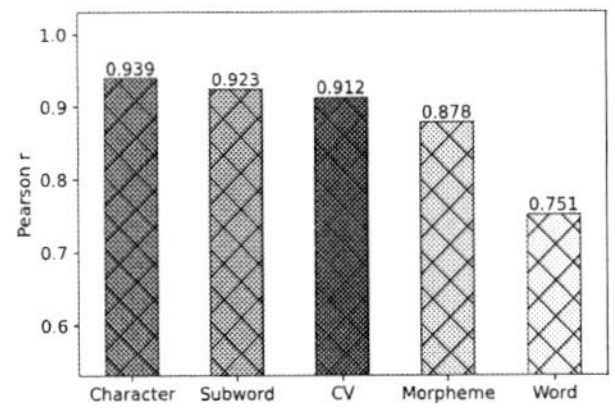

(d) RIBES

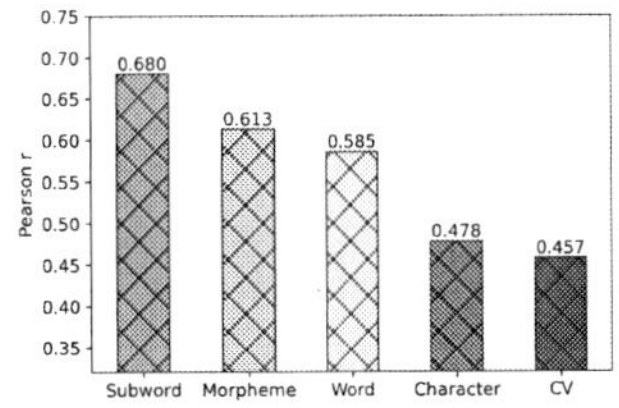

(e) CharacTER

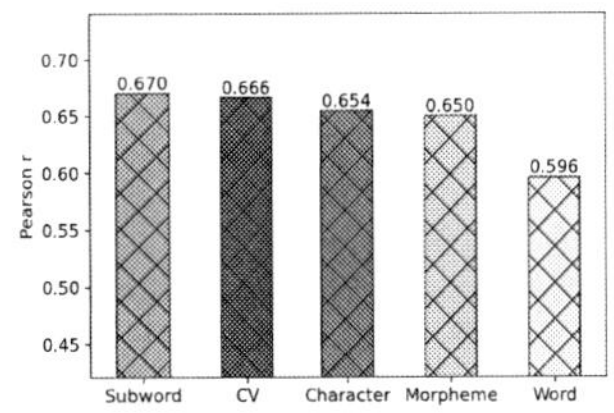

(f) EED

Figure 7: The Pearson correlation on the corpus level: concerning the meta-level

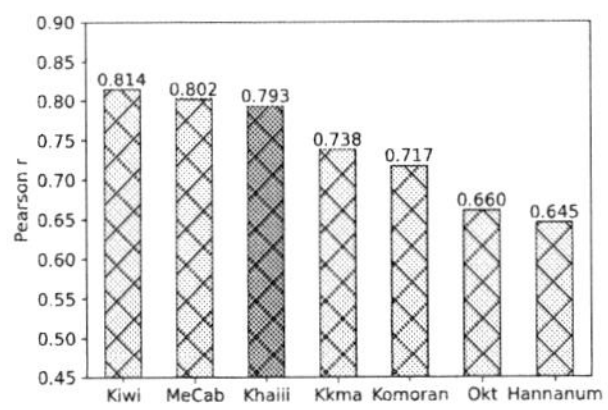

(a) NLTK-BLEU

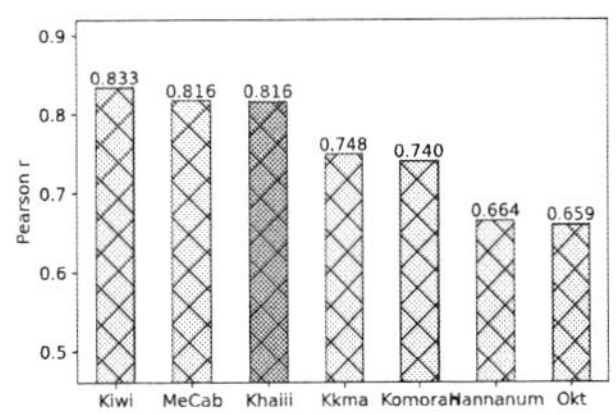

(b) GLEU

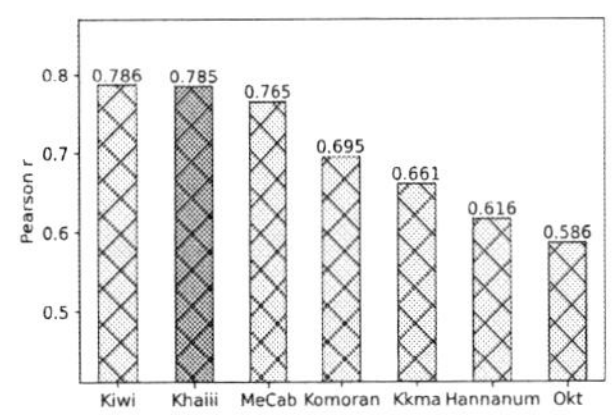

(c) NIST

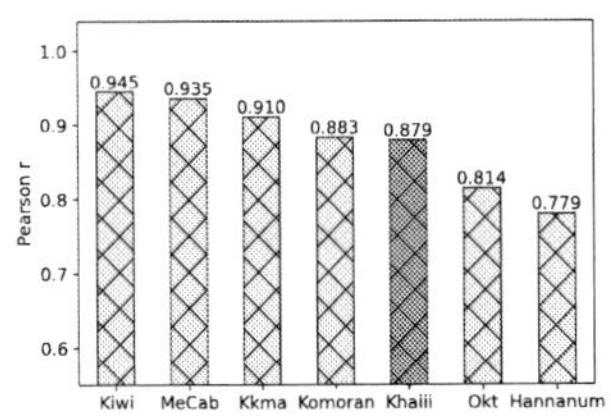

(d) RIBES

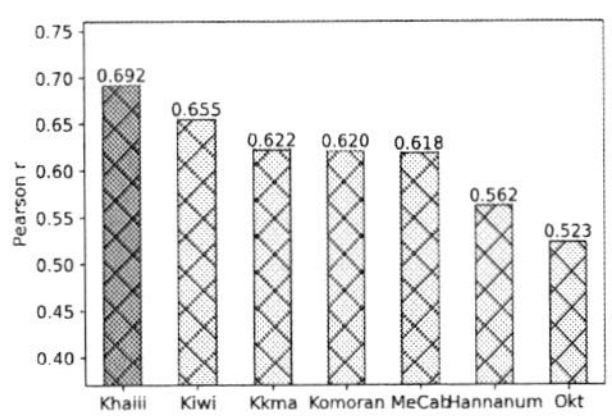

(e) CharacTER

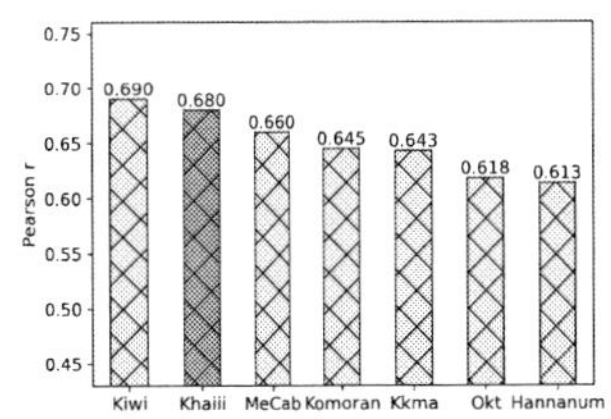

(f) EED

Figure 8: The Pearson correlation on the corpus level: concerning the morpheme level

A Methodology for the Comparison of Human Judgments With Metrics for Coreference Resolution

Mariya Borovikova[1,2] **Loïc Grobol**[2,3] **Anaïs Lefeuvre-Halftermeyer**[2] **Sylvie Billot**[2]

[1]ILPGA, Université Sorbonne Nouvelle
[2]LIFO, Université d'Orléans
[3]Modyco, CNRS et Université Paris Nanterre

mariya.borovikova@sorbonne-nouvelle.fr
lgrobol@parisnanterre.fr
{anais.halftermeyer,sylvie.billot}@univ-orleans.fr

Abstract

We propose a method for investigating the interpretability of metrics used for the coreference resolution task through comparisons with human judgments. We provide a corpus with annotations of different error types and human evaluations of their gravity. Our preliminary analysis shows that metrics considerably overlook several error types and overlook errors in general in comparison to humans. This study is conducted on French texts, but the methodology should be language-independent.

1 Introduction

Coreference resolution is still one of the most challenging tasks in Natural Language Processing. Several metrics have been proposed to evaluate the task, each of them meant to rectify the weaknesses of the previous ones. However, neither their correctness nor their ability to reflect the real quality of algorithms is easily be provable from their mathematical definition. Consequently, some additional tests should be conducted in order to confirm their pertinence. This work aims to compare the evaluation measures used for coreference resolution task with human judgments, i.e. to study them in terms of interpretability. More precisely, B-CUBED (Bagga and Baldwin, 1998), LEA (Moosavi and Strube, 2016), CEAFe and CEAFm (Luo, 2005), CoNLL-2012 (MELA) (Denis and Baldridge, 2009), BLANC (Recasens and Hovy, 2011) and MUC (Vilain et al., 1995) metrics will be analysed.

2 Related work

Although some properties of coreference resolution quality measures have already been studied in Lion-Bouton et al. (2020), Moosavi (2020), Kummerfeld and Klein (2013) and others, to the best of our knowledge, there are no works dedicated to the comparison between automatic measurements and human evaluation of performance for this task. However, very few similar studies were conducted in other domains.

Doshi-Velez and Kim (2017) study the interpretability of machine learning models, in general, using application-grounded, human-grounded, and functionally-grounded approaches.

Foster (2008) describes an experience of evaluating a non-verbal behaviour of an embodied conversational agent. People were asked to choose the most appropriate talking head among the two generated using different strategies. Then β inter-annotator agreement measure (Artstein and Poesio, 2008) was calculated.

In Plank et al. (2015), the correlation between metrics for the dependency parsing task and human judgments was examined. Several models were tested for different languages. The annotators had to choose the best of the two annotations predicted by two different models without knowing the correct option. The obtained results were normalised using Spearman's ρ and compared with standard metrics.

Novikova et al. (2017) explore Natural Language Generation (NLG) evaluation measures. The annotation process is organised as follows: an annotator should score an example using three Likert scales from 0 to 6 based on informativeness, naturalness and quality criteria. The obtained results were normalised using Spearman and intra-class correlation coefficients and compared with NLG metrics.

Considering these studies, for the present research, we will use an approach similar to Novikova et al. (2017), where the annotators evaluate a system on a Likert scale. Despite possible difficulties with the Likert scale treatment (too many mid-point answers, a broad spectrum of responses for one question, etc.), this method seems more appropriate for our purposes.

Proceedings of the 2nd Workshop on Human Evaluation of NLP Systems (HumEval), pages 16 - 23
May 27, 2022 ©2022 Association for Computational Linguistics

Two main reasons make us choose this approach: (1) we do not test particular systems and, therefore, have no alternative annotations and (2) a scaled approach is more accurate and exact while evaluating a system.

3 Methodology

This section is dedicated to the theoretical description of the methods used in the experiments within the scope of this study.

3.1 Errors typology

In order to correctly evaluate the quality of the algorithm, it is necessary to consider all the types of errors it can produce and, therefore, to define those types.

For our purposes, we have chosen the typology of Landragin and Oberle (2018):

1. **Border errors** occur when limits of referential expressions are marked inaccurately;
2. **Type errors** occur when a referential expression is assigned to a false chain;
3. **Noise errors** occur when irrelevant linguistic expressions are marked as a part of a coreference chain;
4. **Silence errors** occur when a system ignores referential expressions which are included in a relevant coreference chain;
5. **Tendency of irrelevant coreference chains construction** occurs when a system composes a new chain from several unrelated mentions.

We use this typology because it is more comprehensive than others and reflects the semantic aspect of the problem. However, we need to introduce an additional error type which we call "chain absence". This error may be regarded as a form of the "silence" error, and it occurs when the whole coreference chain (entity) is missing. The necessity of introducing a new error type arose after the experimentation phase of this study as it allowed to explain some patterns in the behaviour of the metrics. You can find the examples for each error type in the appendix section 1.

3.2 Corpus creation

Our corpus consists of a series of texts, each with two coreference annotations: one is a manual gold annotation, and the other is a purposefully erroneous annotation, one or more manually introduced errors of one of the types defined in section 3.1. There are also a few examples with errors of different types. Two existing coreference resolution corpora for French were used as a basis for the corpus. 52 texts were taken from the DEMOCRAT corpus (Landragin, 2018) and 4 examples - from the ANCOR corpus (Muzerelle et al., 2014). More precisely, we have selected the self-standing passages that are understandable out of context. The corpora are collected in the CoNLL-2012 format (Pradhan et al., 2012)[1]. The final dataset consists of 127 passages of 90-130 words each. 108 examples contain only one error, allowing us to analyse to what extent each error reduces the overall system quality. The rest of the samples are needed to adjust the annotations . Coreference chains lengths vary from 2 to 20 mentions. The mentions to contain an error were chosen at random. The total number of each error in the 108 samples varies between 16 and 28. The total number of each error varies between 44 and 97.

3.3 Evaluation scale

As the primary goal of this study is to evaluate the interpretability of the metrics, it is necessary to compare them to humans opinions about the correctness of the system's responses. Even though the metrics' output values are between 0 and 1, we will not use this range as it is more natural for people to evaluate the quality on an integer scale.

For our study, we use a Likert scale (Likert, 1932) with an even number of choices in order to avoid too many mid-point answers. Usually, coreference resolution is only a part of a pipeline of a more complex system, and the way of evaluation depends on the resolved task. In this study, an information retrieval task has been chosen as a global framework. These conditions require some changes in the classic scale; namely, we introduce a notion of the "importance" of an element. We distinguish two types of elements: peripheral elements and key elements. Peripheral elements can be removed from a text without severe consequences in its general sense. Key elements constitute the core of a text, so their removal will lead to the total loss of meaning. Thus, the gravity of an error and the importance of an element with an error is taken into account.

This scale also contains two points to allow differentiation between similar examples with little nuances: (0) The presumed system's annotation contains significant errors on key elements; (1-2) The presumed system's annotation contains significant

[1] https://github.com/boberle/coreference_databases.git

errors on peripheral elements; (3-4) The presumed system's annotation contains insignificant errors on key elements; (5-6) The presumed system's annotation contains insignificant errors on peripheral elements; (7) The presumed system's annotation does not contain any errors.

3.4 Annotation

Every annotation sample contains a correct annotation and an annotation with mistakes. In order to detect inconsistent annotators, three samples appear twice. The objective given to the annotators is to evaluate coreference resolution samples as a part of an information retrieval system using the Likert scale described in section 3.3. General instructions given before the annotations explain all the necessary concepts[2].

As an inter-annotator agreement measure, Krippendorff's alpha (Krippendorff, 1970) has been chosen and used to identify annotators whose answers differ much from the others using a new algorithm (see algorithm 1 in the appendix). The Krippendorff's alpha is computed for all the possible annotators combinations. Then, these combinations and their scores are sorted by ascending alpha score. We assume that those annotators whose rank is below the others are more important. In order to consider the differences between the alpha scores, the ranks are multiplied by their corresponding alpha scores. The final score is the sum of obtained values for each annotator. These values allow us to understand the annotators' ranking as better annotators have a higher score, but even with these values it remains unclear how to detect the outliers. In order to do this, we divide all the scores by the maximal value.

The coefficients obtained by the algorithm (hereinafter the trust coefficients) allow us to detect outliers (an annotator is considered an outlier if their score is less than or equal to 0.5).

In order to interpret the reasoning of each respondent, regressors have been trained to imitate the annotators' and metrics' behaviours. Each model should predict a score having the number of occurrences of each error type as input features. We have trained one model for each annotator and metric. Once the models are trained, the weights assigned to each feature (error type) are extracted and used for further interpretation.

4 Experiments and results

Human evaluation analysis. Since participation in this study was not rewarded and contained many questions, it involved only 12 participants, 9 of whom were linguists and 8 of whom have already worked with coreference. The analysis of the three duplicated questions showed that no one answered at random among the annotators. Krippendorff's alpha is rather low, so we supposed that some questions in our questionnaire raised more confusion among the respondents than others. Therefore we eliminated the questions that contained more than three different answers from the annotators and computed the results only for the remaining *simple* questions. The total number of questions used in the main analysis is 97. We also decided to compute the inter-annotator agreement on a reduced scale from 0 to 4 points (0 $\rightarrow$ 0, 1 and 2 $\rightarrow$ 1, 3 and 4 $\rightarrow$ 2, 5 and 6 $\rightarrow$ 3, 7 $\rightarrow$ 4) and on the gravity (no errors - insignificant error(s) - significant error(s)) and elements importance (no errors - error(s) on peripheral element - error(s) on key element) scales. These agreements are presented in table 1.

Scale	All examples	*Simple* examples
Standard	0.11	0.25 $\rightarrow$ 0.27
Reduced	0.16	0.34
Gravity	0.24	0.48
Importance	0.16	0.34 $\rightarrow$ 0.42

Table 1: Krippendorff's alphas. An arrow shows that there are outlier annotators on the particular scale and set of examples. A value on the right of an arrow is an alpha after removing outlier annotators.

Human-machine correlation analysis. In order to compare the obtained scores with human judgments, we calculated an average and a mode of human evaluations having previously transformed to a scale from 0 to 1. Every metric was compared with the annotators' assessment on the standard scale, on the reduced scale and on the scale with errors gravity evaluation only. According to the data distributions, in general, the difference between a metric and humans is about 0.33. The averages of differences for all the examples are given in table 2.

Analysis by error type. In order to analyse the influence of a particular error type on a score, we train a linear regression model with the number of errors of each type as the input features and the reversed scores[3] as the outputs. All the input features were centered and reduced in order to obtain more stable results. The coefficients that were assigned to each input feature (and which correspond to one of the error types) during the training have been used as a

[2] You can find the google form with the instructions at `https://forms.gle/cgpsfZvKg5zasnqd6`.

[3] We replaced 7 by 0, 6 by 1, 5 by 2, etc.

Scale	Method	MUC	B-CUBED	CEAFm	CEAFe	BLANC	LEA	CoNLL
Standard	Average	0.289	0.321	0.308	0.269	0.281	0.231	0.291
	Mode	0.294	0.326	0.313	0.283	0.285	0.24	0.299
Reduced	Average	0.314	0.346	0.333	0.29	0.305	0.253	0.315
	Mode	0.312	0.347	0.333	0.292	0.304	0.255	0.316
Gravity	Average	0.43	0.463	0.45	0.405	0.422	0.368	0.432
	Mode	0.43	0.464	0.451	0.408	0.422	0.369	0.434

Table 2: Differences between humans evaluations and metrics on the scale from 0 to 1.

Name	Border	Type	Noise	Silence	Irrelevant chains	Chain absence
MUC	−0.242	−0.249	−0.121	−0.58	−0.345	−0.076
B-CUBED	−0.662	−0.15	—	−0.889	—	−0.264
CEAFm	−0.325	−0.34	−0.139	−0.408	−0.353	−0.101
CEAFe	−0.458	−0.283	−0.322	−0.447	−0.222	—
CoNLL	−0.382	−0.217	−0.083	−0.556	−0.179	−0.187
BLANC	−0.174	−0.385	−0.233	−0.973	−0.074	−0.56
LEA	−0.425	−0.22	−0.207	0.73	−0.432	—
Humans	−0.343	−0.629	−0.598	−0.513	−0.467	−0.727

Table 3: Coefficients of errors importances. "*Humans*" is the average of all the coefficients of models trained on humans' evaluations. See a more detailed version in the appendix (table 4).

measure of the importance of an error in the process of deciding the example's score (see tables 3 and 4).

5 Discussion

Human evaluation analysis. Table 1 reports the inter-annotator agreement on different scales, with several interesting properties about the task. Firstly, we may observe that the reduced scale results are better than those on the standard scale. It can be explained by the fact that even if people agree on the characteristics of the suggested categories, all of them have their own bias about the task, so they pay attention to different annotation nuances. Secondly, the inter-annotator agreement increased when we eliminated the annotators indicated as outliers by the trust coefficient.

Human-machine correlation analysis. One may notice that the average scores of all annotators are relatively high (see table 2). The average difference between all metrics and the annotators is usually above 0 and varies from 0.2 to 0.4 after normalisation, which shows that, generally, metrics tend to overestimate the actual quality of a model significantly.

Analysis by error type. In order to perform the analysis regarding the error types, we modified the table 4 by removing all positive and null coefficients as they mean either the absence of answers considering a particular error type or insufficient training quality of some models. These modifications can be justified by the fact that every coefficient of the model should be negative. Otherwise, it would mean that the presence of an error improves a score.

As our analysis shows, the **border**, **silence** and **irrelevant chains construction** errors are treated correctly. It could be proven by the fact that metrics coefficients are similar to the human ones. The **type**, **noise** and **chain absence** errors are underestimated by the metrics, as their scores are usually higher for the metrics than for the humans coefficients (see correspondent columns of the table 3).

We can analyse each metric separately as well. Firstly, we have noticed that the **MUC** metric considerably underestimates all types of errors except for the "silence" and the "irrelevant chains" ones. Secondly, the **B-CUBED** measure put relevant scores only to the examples which contain "border" and "silence" errors. The **CEAFe** score estimates correctly only the examples with "border" and "irrelevant chains" errors. Similarly, the **CEAFm** metric also underestimates all examples where any errors except for "border" and "irrelevant chains" ones were made. The **BLANC** measure treats properly only texts with "silence" errors. We observe that the **CoNLL-2012** metric tends to overstate the results of a model when the examples contain any errors except for "border" errors. Likewise, the **LEA** metric considerably underestimates all error types except for "border", "silence" and "irrelevant chains" errors (see correspondent lines of the table 3).

6 Conclusion

This study aims to investigate the extent to which we may understand the results produced by the coreference resolution metrics. The preliminary results on the limited corpus show that metrics underestimate errors gravity compared to humans and add approximately 0.33 points to the final score on the scale from 0 to 1. However, these results need to be proven on a more significant number of annotators.

This work's contribution consists in creating the corpus with various errors types and its annotation with the human judgments about the gravity of these errors, the proposal of the new automatic outlying annotator identification algorithm and the suggestion of a methodology of comparison of human evaluations with automatic metrics. All the code and corpus are available at `https://github.com/project178/coref-metrics-vs-humans`.

Possible future work directions may consist in involving more people in the annotation process of the proposed corpus in order to verify the obtained results and in the development of a new metric that will take into consideration the identified shortcomings of the existing measures.

7 Acknowledgements

This work was funded by Région Centre-Val-de-Loire through the RTR DIAMS.

References

Ron Artstein and Massimo Poesio. 2008. Inter-coder Agreement for Computational Linguistics. *Computational Linguistics*, 34(4):555–596.

Amit Bagga and Breck Baldwin. 1998. Algorithms for scoring coreference chains. In *The first international conference on language resources and evaluation workshop on linguistics coreference*, volume 1, pages 563–566. Citeseer.

Pascal Denis and Jason Baldridge. 2009. Global joint models for coreference resolution and named entity classification. *Procesamiento del lenguaje natural*, 42.

Finale Doshi-Velez and Been Kim. 2017. Towards a rigorous science of interpretable machine learning. *arXiv preprint arXiv:1702.08608*.

Mary Ellen Foster. 2008. Automated metrics that agree with human judgements on generated output for an embodied conversational agent. In *Proceedings of the Fifth International Natural Language Generation Conference*, pages 95–103, Salt Fork, Ohio, USA. Association for Computational Linguistics.

Klaus Krippendorff. 1970. Bivariate agreement coefficients for reliability of data. *Sociological methodology*, 2:139–150.

Jonathan K. Kummerfeld and Dan Klein. 2013. Error-driven analysis of challenges in coreference resolution. In *Proceedings of the 2013 Conference on Empirical Methods in Natural Language Processing*, pages 265–277, Seattle, Washington, USA. Association for Computational Linguistics.

Frédéric Landragin and Bruno Oberle. 2018. Identification automatique de chaînes de coréférences : vers une analyse des erreurs pour mieux cibler l'apprentissage. In *Journée commune AFIA-ATALA sur le Traitement Automatique des Langues et l'Intelligence Artificielle pendant la onzième édition de la plate-forme Intelligence Artificielle (PFIA 2018)*, Nancy, France.

Frédéric Landragin. 2018. LIVRABLE L2 "Manuel d'annotation du corpus et organisation de formations sur l'annotation" du projet DEMOCRAT. Research report, Lattice and LiLPa and ICAR and IHRIM.

Rensis Likert. 1932. A technique for the measurement of attitudes. *Archives of psychology*.

Adam Lion-Bouton, Loïc Grobol, Jean-Yves Antoine, Sylvie Billot, and Anaïs Lefeuvre-Halftermeyer. 2020. Comment arpenter sans mètre : les scores de résolution de chaînes de coréférences sont-ils des métriques ? (do the standard scores of evaluation of coreference resolution constitute metrics ?). In *Actes de la 6e conférence conjointe Journées d'Études sur la Parole (JEP, 33e édition), Traitement Automatique des Langues Naturelles (TALN, 27e édition), Rencontre des Étudiants Chercheurs en Informatique pour le Traitement Automatique des Langues (RÉCITAL, 22e édition). 2e atelier Éthique et TRaitemeNt Automatique des Langues (ETeRNAL)*, pages 10–18, Nancy, France. ATALA et AFCP.

Xiaoqiang Luo. 2005. On coreference resolution performance metrics. In *Proceedings of Human Language Technology Conference and Conference on Empirical Methods in Natural Language Processing*, pages 25–32, Vancouver, British Columbia, Canada. Association for Computational Linguistics.

Nafise Sadat Moosavi. 2020. *Robustness in Coreference Resolution*. Ph.D. thesis.

Nafise Sadat Moosavi and Michael Strube. 2016. Which coreference evaluation metric do you trust? a proposal for a link-based entity aware metric. In *Proceedings of the 54th Annual Meeting of the Association for Computational Linguistics (Volume 1: Long Papers)*, pages 632–642, Berlin, Germany. Association for Computational Linguistics.

Judith Muzerelle, Anaïs Lefeuvre, Emmanuel Schang, Jean-Yves Antoine, Aurore Pelletier, Denis Maurel, Iris Eshkol, and Jeanne Villaneau. 2014. ANCOR_Centre, a large free spoken French coreference corpus: description of the resource and reliability measures. In *Proceedings of the Ninth International Conference on Language Resources and Evaluation (LREC'14)*, pages 843–847, Reykjavik, Iceland. European Language Resources Association (ELRA).

Jekaterina Novikova, Ondřej Dušek, Amanda Cercas Curry, and Verena Rieser. 2017. Why we need new evaluation metrics for NLG. In *Proceedings of the 2017*

Conference on Empirical Methods in Natural Language Processing, pages 2241–2252, Copenhagen, Denmark. Association for Computational Linguistics.

Barbara Plank, Héctor Martínez Alonso, Željko Agić, Danijela Merkler, and Anders Søgaard. 2015. Do dependency parsing metrics correlate with human judgments? In *Proceedings of the Nineteenth Conference on Computational Natural Language Learning*, pages 315–320, Beijing, China. Association for Computational Linguistics.

Sameer Pradhan, Alessandro Moschitti, Nianwen Xue, Olga Uryupina, and Yuchen Zhang. 2012. CoNLL-2012 shared task: Modeling multilingual unrestricted coreference in OntoNotes. In *Joint Conference on EMNLP and CoNLL - Shared Task*, pages 1–40, Jeju Island, Korea. Association for Computational Linguistics.

Marta Recasens and Eduard Hovy. 2011. BLANC: Implementing the Rand index for coreference evaluation. *Natural Language Engineering*, 17(4):485.

Marc Vilain, John D Burger, John Aberdeen, Dennis Connolly, and Lynette Hirschman. 1995. A model-theoretic coreference scoring scheme. In *Sixth Message Understanding Conference (MUC-6): Proceedings of a Conference Held in Columbia, Maryland, November 6-8, 1995.*

A Appendix

1. **Borders errors.** *Whales are marine mammals*. instead of *Whales are marine mammals*.
2. **Type errors.** *John likes his brother because he is funny* instead of *John likes his brother because he is funny.*
3. **Noise errors.** *The dog barked. It's time to go.* instead of *The dog barked. It's time to go.*
4. **Silence errors.** *A phone is on the table. It rings. I pick it up* instead of *A phone is on the table. It rings. I pick it up.*
5. **Tendency of irrelevant coreference chains construction.** *A cat and a dog are playing together* instead of *A cat and a dog are playing together.*
6. **Chain absence.** *A phone is on the table. It rings. I pick it up* instead of *A phone is on the table. It rings. I pick it up.*

Figure 1: Error types examples.

Name	Border	Name	Type	Name	Noise	Name	Silence	Name	Irrelevant chains	Name	Chain absence
REDUCED_A6	-0,033	**B-CUBED**	**-0,15**	**CoNLL-2012**	**-0,083**	GRAVITY_A6	-0,011	GRAVITY_A6	-0,018	**MUC**	**-0,076**
GRAVITY_A10	-0,057	**CoNLL-2012**	**-0,217**	GRAVITY_A7	-0,105	STANDARD_A12	-0,262	**BLANC**	**-0,074**	STANDARD_A10	-0,099
STANDARD_A7	-0,097	**LEA**	**-0,22**	**MUC**	**-0,121**	GRAVITY_A8	-0,265	STANDARD_A11	-0,08	**CEAFm**	**-0,101**
GRAVITY_A7	-0,118	GRAVITY_A7	-0,239	REDUCED_A1	-0,122	STANDARD_A11	-0,274	REDUCED_MEAN	-0,097	GRAVITY_A11	-0,124
GRAVITY_A11	-0,152	GRAVITY_A8	-0,24	**CEAFm**	**-0,139**	STANDARD_A9	-0,329	GRAVITY_A11	-0,164	STANDARD_A7	-0,17
STANDARD_A10	-0,166	**MUC**	**-0,249**	STANDARD_A9	-0,146	GRAVITY_A11	-0,391	STANDARD_A4	-0,167	**CoNLL-2012**	**-0,187**
BLANC	**-0,174**	**CEAFe**	**-0,283**	GRAVITY_A11	-0,167	STANDARD_A10	-0,406	**CoNLL-2012**	**-0,179**	GRAVITY_A7	-0,247
STANDARD_A6	-0,182	STANDARD_A10	-0,31	**LEA**	**-0,207**	**CEAFm**	**-0,408**	**CEAFe**	**-0,222**	**B-CUBED**	**-0,264**
STANDARD_A8	-0,212	**CEAFm**	**-0,34**	**BLANC**	**-0,233**	**CEAFe**	**-0,447**	*GRAVITY_MEAN*	*-0,319*	GRAVITY_A8	-0,265
MUC	**-0,242**	STANDARD_A12	-0,362	STANDARD_A7	-0,316	GRAVITY_A1	-0,49	STANDARD_A8	-0,335	STANDARD_A6	-0,283
CEAFm	**-0,325**	GRAVITY_A3	-0,372	**CEAFe**	**-0,322**	GRAVITY_A7	-0,547	**MUC**	**-0,345**	STANDARD_A11	-0,289
CoNLL-2012	**-0,382**	**BLANC**	**-0,385**	STANDARD_MEAN	-0,356	STANDARD_A6	-0,548	**CEAFm**	**-0,353**	STANDARD_A12	-0,411
GRAVITY_A3	-0,388	STANDARD_A8	-0,458	STANDARD_A11	-0,364	**CoNLL-2012**	**-0,556**	GRAVITY_A7	-0,375	**BLANC**	**-0,56**
LEA	**-0,425**	GRAVITY_A11	-0,507	STANDARD_A10	-0,532	**MUC**	**-0,58**	STANDARD_A6	-0,407	STANDARD_A8	-0,634
CEAFe	**-0,458**	STANDARD_A9	-0,563	GRAVITY_A3	-0,566	GRAVITY_A10	-0,586	GRAVITY_A8	-0,409	GRAVITY_A1	-0,737
B-CUBED	**-0,662**	STANDARD_MEAN	-0,607	GRAVITY_A1	-0,691	STANDARD_A7	-0,629	**LEA**	**-0,432**	STANDARD_A9	-0,756
GRAVITY_MEAN	*-0,848*	STANDARD_A11	-0,625	REDUCED_MEAN	-0,712	**LEA**	**-0,73**	GRAVITY_A3	-0,453	STANDARD_A4	-0,919
REDUCED_A1	-1,529	GRAVITY_A1	-0,663	GRAVITY_A4	-0,911	REDUCED_MEAN	-0,883	STANDARD_A9	-0,491	GRAVITY_A10	-0,932
		STANDARD_A7	-0,686	GRAVITY_A10	-0,954	**B-CUBED**	**-0,889**	STANDARD_A7	-0,64	REDUCED_MEAN	-0,943
		STANDARD_A6	-0,741	*GRAVITY_MEAN*	*-1,184*	**BLANC**	**-0,973**	REDUCED_A6	-0,819	GRAVITY_A6	-1,149
		GRAVITY_A6	-0,741	GRAVITY_A6	-1,197	GRAVITY_MEAN	-1,565	STANDARD_A12	-0,859	REDUCED_A1	-1,419
		STANDARD_A4	-0,818	STANDARD_A6	-1,238			STANDARD_MEAN	-0,904	REDUCED_A6	-1,473
		GRAVITY_A4	-0,869					GRAVITY_A4	-0,911	*GRAVITY_MEAN*	*-2,23*
		GRAVITY_MEAN	*-1,027*					GRAVITY_A1	-0,961		
		REDUCED_MEAN	-1,5								

Table 4: Coefficients of error importances obtained during the regressors training for all metrics and annotators. Values in bold are reported by metrics' regressors. Values in italic are reported by a regressor trained on a mean answer on the gravity scale.

Algorithm 1 Calculate trust coefficients

Input: annotated corpus with k annotators

```
alphas ← empty dictionary
for n = 2 To k+1 do
    for each combination ∈ COMBINATIONS(n,k) do
        alphas[combination] ← KRIPPENDORFFSALPHA(corpus[combination])
    end for
end for
SORT alphas BY alphas.values
coefs ← empty dictionary
coef ← 1
score ← 0
for each annotators_comb,alpha ∈ alphas do
    if score < alpha then
        coef ← coef + 1
        score ← alpha
    end if
    for each annotator ∈ annotators_comb do
        coefs[annotator] ← coefs[annotator] + coef × alpha
    end for
end for
coefs.values ← coefs.values/max(coefs.values)
```

Output: coefs

Perceptual Quality Dimensions of Machine-Generated Text with a Focus on Machine Translation

Vivien Macketanz
German Research Center for AI
vivien.macketanz@dfki.de

Babak Naderi
Quality and Usability Lab, TU Berlin
babak.naderi@tu-berlin.de

Steven Schmidt
Quality and Usability Lab, TU Berlin
steven.schmidt@tu-berlin.de

Sebastian Möller
Quality and Usability Lab, TU Berlin
sebastian.moeller@tu-berlin.de

Abstract

The quality of machine-generated text is a complex construct consisting of various aspects and dimensions. We present a study that aims to uncover relevant perceptual quality dimensions for one type of machine-generated text, that is, Machine Translation. We conducted a crowdsourcing survey in the style of a Semantic Differential to collect attribute ratings for German MT outputs. An Exploratory Factor Analysis revealed the underlying perceptual dimensions. As a result, we extracted four factors that operate as relevant dimensions for the Quality of Experience of MT outputs: precision, complexity, grammaticality, and transparency.

1 Introduction

In recent years, automatically generated text has increasingly gained importance, e.g., chatbots, automatic summarizations, or machine translations. Although the quality of such texts has greatly improved over time, it has not yet reached human parity (Toral et al., 2018). Therefore, the quality of machine-generated text is of ongoing interest to the research community and is further important for gaining acceptance in different applications.

The Quality of Experience (QoE) is defined as "the degree of delight or annoyance of the user of an application or service" (Le Callet et al., 2012). This means that the QoE is a subjective perception that needs to be quantified in empirical studies (Möller and Raake, 2014). While there are standardized methods for auditory and visual media, such as ITU P.800, P.910, or BT.500, the QoE of text has been mostly disregarded until now.

The perceptual quality of machine-generated text is a highly complex construct. Many aspects and dimensions play a crucial role; hence, it is the object of investigation of various research areas. We suggest that a multi-dimensional prediction model covering a wide variety of aspects is the best approach to assess the quality of machine-generated text. To the best of our knowledge, no such model exists. Therefore, we are developing a prediction model for the quality of German machine-generated text, specifically, Machine Translation (MT). We aim to create our model based on a combination of linguistic data and automatically extractable factors that can predict the QoE of MT outputs. Our first milestone is identifying relevant perceptual quality dimensions, the foundation of our model. We achieved this milestone by conducting a crowdsourcing study in the style of a Semantic Differential and subsequently extracting the quality dimensions through an Exploratory Factor Analysis.

2 Related Work

This section provides an overview of the existing metrics for capturing the performance or quality of MT systems. The first category of metrics is automatic methods, which have the advantage of being fast, low-cost, and reproducible. The most commonly used metrics are BLEU (Papineni et al., 2002), METEOR (Banerjee and Lavie, 2005), COMET (Rei et al., 2020), and PRISM (Thompson and Post, 2020). Metrics like TER (Snover et al., 2009) measure the translation edit rate, and quality estimation methods (Blatz et al., 2004; Specia et al., 2009) can predict the quality without access to the reference translation(s). However, one shared shortcoming of all these automatic metrics is that, as opposed to our approach, they are not based on relevant quality dimensions and thus lack diagnostic power.

The second category of metrics is subjective methods for directly measuring quality that are more costly yet more reliable. There are large-scale human rankings that are often conducted in international conferences in order to compare the performance and/or quality of several MT systems (Callison-Burch et al., 2007; Bojar et al., 2015). The Multidimensional Quality Metrics (MQM) is a framework for the manual assessment of translation

Proceedings of the 2nd Workshop on Human Evaluation of NLP Systems (HumEval), pages 24 - 31
May 27, 2022

quality (Lommel et al., 2014b). Additionally, test suites have recently regained more importance. A test suite is a challenge set created to systematically analyze the behavior of MT systems in different aspects, e.g., (Guillou and Hardmeier, 2016), (Isabelle et al., 2017), or (Burchardt et al., 2017).

While the mentioned techniques focus on capturing the performance or quality of MT systems, they cannot sufficiently capture the QoE by users of MT output as QoE is the only technique that is not measured by pre-defined criteria. Instead, QoE is based on identifying relevant criteria (i.e., quality dimensions) in a real-world scenario.

3 Experimental Setup

We conducted a study to identify relevant dimensions for the quality of machine-generated text, specifically German MT outputs. We did so by utilizing a crowdsourcing survey in which participants had to rate MT outputs. Our corpus contained English to German translations from the submissions to the News translation task of the Fourth Conference on Machine Translation (WMT19)[1]. We chose this data for our corpus as we needed test sentences from several MT systems with varying translation quality. Furthermore, the data is freely available for research purposes[2]. We extracted a set of translations from six submitted systems that appeared at the top, the middle, and the bottom of the ranking of WMT19 systems (Barrault et al., 2019), resulting in a corpus of 11,922 sentences. A linguistic expert created a sub-corpus for the survey, dedicating around 15 hours to carefully extract translations varying in length, quality, and error types. The sub-corpus consists of 45 sentences.[3]

The survey was conducted as a Semantic Differential (SD) (Osgood et al., 1957). An SD is a rating scale that measures a person's attitude towards an entity, here: our test sentences. The participants were asked to rate their perception of the test items on a scale between two polar adjectives, e.g., "grammatical – ungrammatical". All adjective pairs used in the study can be found in Table 2 in the Appendix. The adjective pairs were carefully selected by a linguist who is experienced in MT evaluation and thereafter discussed with another linguist to cover all potentially relevant aspects for the perceptual quality of the test sentences.

We would like to emphasize that while we are using MT as an example text type, the focus of our study lies on the quality of *machine-generated text*. Therefore, we solely work with the MT outputs and do not take the source sentences and concomitant quality aspects into account (as opposed to approaches that focus on the quality of MT).

3.1 Antonym pair identification study

We first ran a small-scale preliminary study with 14 participants to confirm our antonym pairs. The participants were colleagues and mostly linguistic experts. Our test set comprised 15 sentences from the sub-corpus. The first part of the study consisted of the SD; the participants were instructed to rate the quality of each sentence based on 38 adjective pairs serving as endpoints of a 7-point Likert scale ranging from -3 to +3. As we are solely focusing on the intrinsic quality, they were instructed to rate only the quality of the language but not of the translation itself. The adjective pairs were hand-selected by a linguistic expert, experienced in the evaluation of MT, to cover as many aspects of machine-translated text as possible. In the second part, the participants had to rate each adjective pair on its suitability to evaluate language on a 5-point scale. In addition, they were also encouraged to provide feedback regarding the suitability and to suggest other potential adjective pairs. Based on the rating of the adjective pairs, we removed all adjective pairs with a mean value of less than 3.2 and a standard deviation of more than 1.2. As a result, we reduced the number of adjective pairs to 20.

3.2 Crowdsourcing study

The main study was conducted as a crowdsourcing survey with Crowdee[4]. 141 crowdworkers participated in the study. The survey followed the IRB guidelines of our institution, and participants were paid according to the minimum wage law. Crowdworkers stayed anonymous, no personal information was collected in the survey[5]. The study was accessible to native speakers only as a good knowledge of German was required. As we wanted the participants to evaluate the language itself (and not the content of the test sentences), they were instructed to base their ratings exclusively on the

[1] `http://www.statmt.org/wmt19/index.html`

[2] cf. Licensing of Data `https://www.statmt.org/wmt19/translation-task.html`

[3] `https://github.com/DFKI-NLP/TextQ`

[4] `https://www.crowdee.com/`

[5] Crowdee's privacy Statement can be found here: `https://www.crowdee.com/privacy-statement`

language of the sentences and ignore the meaning of the sentences as best as they could. They were only informed that the sentences might contain errors, but not that the sentences were outputs of English to German MT. The full instructions can be found in Table 3 in the Appendix.

The adjective pairs were randomized per participant, and so was the order of the polarity. All 45 sentences from the sub-corpus were used. While this is a comparably small number of test items, we argue that we can still draw significant conclusions as the items were hand-picked by an expert to cover as many different linguistic aspects as possible. Based on the feedback we received from the preliminary study, we decided to present only three test sentences to each participant, as the rating is very time-consuming. Each sentence had to be rated based on all 20 antonym pairs. Completing the full survey was expected to take around 10 minutes.

Following (Naderi et al., 2015), we incorporated a test condition for the majority of the sentences[6]. The test condition is based on calculating an Inconsistency Score (IS) (Naderi, 2018) on repeated adjective pairs. Altogether, we collected up to 30 ratings of all adjective pairs per sentence. The average working time amounted to 392.1 seconds.

4 Multidimensional Analysis

QoE can be formalized as a multidimensional perceptual space where the defining parameters function as dimensions. It is the aim of the multidimensional analysis to identify those dimensions for the QoE of MT output.

4.1 Data cleansing

While crowdsourcing studies have many benefits, one shortcoming is that there might be crowdworkers who do not work thoroughly, eventually leading to noisy data (Naderi et al., 2015). Thus, we had to cleanse the data to filter out invalid ratings. [7] We did so in three steps: First, we eliminated ratings of participants that completed the survey in 40% or less of the expected 10 minutes. Thus, participants who finished the questionnaire in 240 seconds or less were excluded from the analysis. Second, we excluded all ratings of participants who provided the same value for every adjective pair for every sentence, assuming they were not reading the test material. Lastly, we calculated the IS (Naderi, 2018). While it is known that the degree of variance in human evaluation of translation is high (Lommel et al., 2014a), the IS allows filtering out outliers that show a higher degree of variance than expected under normal conditions. The IS calculation is based on the test conditions of the repeated adjective pairs. For details of the calculation, the interested reader is referred to Naderi (2018).

The data cleansing removed 6,800 ratings, resulting in 14,200 ratings. The average working time after the data cleansing amounted to 473.31 sec.

4.2 Exploratory Factor Analysis

We conducted an Exploratory Factor Analysis (EFA) in SPSS (IBM Corp.). Factor analysis is a technique for identifying common factors (i.e., latent variables) that explain the correlation among a set of observed variables. The extraction method used was Maximum Likelihood; The rotation method was PROMAX with Kaiser Normalization, leading to non-orthogonal dimensions.

It is important to balance the statistical goodness-of-fit and the interpretability of the resulting dimensions (Wältermann et al., 2010). Our data contained several adjective pairs with low communalities and/or cross-loadings differing by less than 0.2. Our interpretation is that these pairs are not specific enough or are related to other, irrelevant aspects. Thus, we removed those attributes for the sake of interpretability. The dimension reduction revealed four factors for eight polar adjective pairs. Pearson's chi-squared test for the goodness of fit was $p = 0.36$ ($\chi^2 = 2.06$, $df = 2$). The Kaiser-Meyer-Olkin value was quite high at 0.901, indicating that the data is adequate for a factor analysis.

The distribution of the adjective pairs on the four factors and the explained percentage of variance can be seen in Table 1. Note that the adjectives are translated into English for better understanding. The four adjective pairs *unambiguous – ambiguous* (German: eindeutig – mehrdeutig), *precise – vague* (präzise – ungenau), *complete – incomplete* (vollständig – lückenhaft), and *clear – chaotic* (klar – wirr) are loading on factor 1 (F1). F1 explains 53.2% of the variance. Factor 2 (F2) is loaded by the two adjective pairs *direct – ponderous* (direkt – umständlich) and *simple – complicated* (einfach – kompliziert) and explains an additional 8.4% of the variance. Only one adjective pair is loading on Fac-

[6] 30 of the 45 test sentences were rated with the test condition, as we ran the survey in two batches and included the test condition only in the second batch.

[7] Crowdworkers were paid regardless of their ratings.

	F1	F2	F3	F4
unambiguous – ambiguous	.757			
precise – vague	.947			
complete – incomplete	.822			
clear – chaotic	.580			
direct – ponderous		.806		
simple – complicated		.923		
grammatical – ungrammatical			.958	
neat – confusing				.915
% of variance	53.2	8.4	10.5	8.0

Table 1: Loadings of the adjective pairs (English translations) on the factors and % of explained variance.

tor 3 (F3): *grammatical – ungrammatical* (grammatisch – ungrammatisch) and another 10.5% of the variance is explained by F3. The fourth factor (F4) is also loaded by one adjective pair only, namely *neat – confusing* (übersichtlich – verwirrend), and it explains an additional 8.0% of the variance.

The adjective pairs loading on F1 are all describing characteristics related to precision; hence, this factor is labeled *precision*. The adjective pairs loading on F2 are related to complexity; thus, F2 is labeled *complexity*. F3 is labeled *grammaticality*, and F4 is labeled *transparency*. The *precision* and *transparency* factors seem to overlap while the remaining factors are more easily separable in their meaning.

4.3 Quality dimensions

Former commonly used quality aspects for MT were *fluency* and *adequacy* (cf., e.g., the MQM metrics mentioned in Section 2). While our study has not tested for extrinsic *adequacy*, as we only presented the MT outputs and not the source sentences, other authors have already stated that *fluency* is not the central problem in MT nowadays (Bentivogli et al., 2016). Neural MT has become more fluent, with MT errors being more subtle and thus harder to spot. Our study confirms this claim as the analysis has brought out four other relevant quality dimensions: *precision*, *complexity*, *grammaticality*, and *transparency*. Interestingly, our 20 antonym pairs did include the adjective pair *fluent – non-fluent*, as we covered a wide variety of translation issues. However, we had to eliminate this pair during the EFA due to discriminant validity issues.

Looking at our four dimensions, the factor *precision* seems to refer to the clarity and completeness of the text. The factor *complexity* presumably refers to the textual complexity, and sentences with a high rating for the adjectives *complicated* and *ponderous* in our study generally tend to be longer. More interesting findings arise when looking further into our data: Sentences with a high rating for the factor *grammaticality* tend to miss words, contain spelling or punctuation errors, or hold mistranslations. Interestingly though, these sentences tend to be shorter rather than longer. Our theory is that the longer and therefore more convoluted a sentence is, the more difficult it is to spot grammar errors, and, consequently, other factors like *complexity* become more relevant. Our last dimension, *transparency*, seems less tangible than the other dimensions. We theorize that it refers to the lucidity of the text. It seems similar to *precision*, and there is indeed a higher correlation (0.748).

As a final remark, we would like to point out that the identification of the dimensions in the multidimensional analysis is strongly dependent on the data (Wältermann et al., 2010), i.e., the choice of test sentences and antonym pairs. While we collected a large number of data points, validating these is the subject of future work. Hence, we cannot guarantee that the identified quality dimensions cover all potential perceptions completely. Furthermore, as the survey was conducted with German native speakers, the majority of the participants can be assumed to be WEIRD participants[8] (Henrich et al., 2010) which leads to a demographic bias. Our findings cannot be assumed to be valid for other languages and/or participant groups.

5 Conclusion and Outlook

We present a study exploring the relevant quality dimensions for MT outputs. We identified antonym pairs of a Semantic Differential in a preliminary study and used these attributes to rate 45 German test sentences. We then carried out an Exploratory Factor Analysis that resulted in the extraction of four relevant quality dimensions: *precision*, *complexity*, *grammaticality*, and *transparency*. According to our study, these are the quality dimensions that are relevant for the QoE, i.e., the subjective perception of a user of a text.

Our ultimate goal is to develop a prediction model to assess the quality of machine-generated text. We focus on two text types: Machine Translation and Automatic Text Summarization (ATS). Our next step is to identify the relevant quality dimensions for ATS. To do so, we are currently

[8]WEIRD stands for **w**estern, **e**ducated, **i**ndustrialized, **r**ich, and **d**emocratic participants

conducting another crowdsourcing study with an adapted set of adjective pairs. The focus on two different types of machine-generated texts allows us to compare the (potential) differences in the perceptive quality dimensions and enables us to draw generalizations for other text types.

Simultaneously, we are working on the quantification of the quality dimensions for MT. As the factor analysis conducted in the study at hand is highly complex, we are developing a simplified survey in which we present only one representative antonym pair per dimension. If the result of the follow-up study verifies our current study, we can assume our dimensions to be accurate.

Further steps will involve correlating automatically extractable text parameters and quality dimensions, and building and testing various prediction models. These efforts should ultimately result in a quality prediction model for MT, ATS, and potentially other types of machine-generated text.

Other potential future work includes analyzing the possible overlap between the four dimensions at hand and other existing quality metrics, e.g., MQM. Furthermore, it would be of interest to expand the analysis to other languages, as it might also counteract the WEIRD bias.

Acknowledgements

The present study was funded by the Deutsche Forschungsgemeinschaft (DFG) through the project “Analyse und automatische Abschätzung der Qualität maschinell generierter Texte”, project number 436813723. We thank all colleagues who participated in our preliminary study.

References

Satanjeev Banerjee and Alon Lavie. 2005. Meteor: An automatic metric for MT evaluation with improved correlation with human judgments. In *Proceedings of the acl workshop on intrinsic and extrinsic evaluation measures for machine translation and/or summarization*, pages 65–72.

Loïc Barrault, Ondřej Bojar, Marta R. Costa-jussà, Christian Federmann, Mark Fishel, Yvette Graham, Barry Haddow, Matthias Huck, Philipp Koehn, Shervin Malmasi, Christof Monz, Mathias Müller, Santanu Pal, Matt Post, and Marcos Zampieri. 2019. Findings of the 2019 Conference on Machine Translation (WMT19). In *Proceedings of the Fourth Conference on Machine Translation (Volume 2: Shared Task Papers, Day 1)*, pages 1–61, Florence, Italy. Association for Computational Linguistics.

Luisa Bentivogli, Arianna Bisazza, Mauro Cettolo, and Marcello Federico. 2016. Neural versus phrase-based machine translation quality: a case study. *arXiv preprint arXiv:1608.04631*.

John Blatz, Erin Fitzgerald, George Foster, Simona Gandrabur, Cyril Goutte, Alex Kulesza, Alberto Sanchis, and Nicola Ueffing. 2004. Confidence estimation for machine translation. In *Proceedings of the 20th International Conference on Computational Linguistics*, COLING '04, page 315–es, USA. Association for Computational Linguistics.

Ondrej Bojar, Rajen Chatterjee, Christian Federmann, Barry Haddow, Matthias Huck, Chris Hokamp, Philipp Koehn, Varvara Logacheva, Christof Monz, Matteo Negri, et al. 2015. Findings of the 2015 Workshop on Statistical Machine Translation.

Aljoscha Burchardt, Vivien Macketanz, Jon Dehdari, Georg Heigold, Jan-Thorsten Peter, and Philip Williams. 2017. A linguistic evaluation of rule-based, phrase-based, and neural MT engines. *The Prague Bulletin of Mathematical Linguistics*, 108(1):159–170.

Chris Callison-Burch, Cameron Shaw Fordyce, Philipp Koehn, Christof Monz, and Josh Schroeder. 2007. (meta-) evaluation of machine translation. In *Proceedings of the Second Workshop on Statistical Machine Translation*, pages 136–158.

Liane Guillou and Christian Hardmeier. 2016. PROTEST: A Test Suite for Evaluating Pronouns in Machine Translation. In *Proceedings of the Tenth International Conference on Language Resources and Evaluation (LREC'16)*, pages 636–643, Portorož, Slovenia. European Language Resources Association (ELRA).

Joseph Henrich, Steven J Heine, and Ara Norenzayan. 2010. The weirdest people in the world? *Behavioral and brain sciences*, 33(2-3):61–83.

IBM Corp. IBM SPSS Statistics for Macintosh. Version 28.0.

Pierre Isabelle, Colin Cherry, and George Foster. 2017. A Challenge Set Approach to Evaluating Machine Translation.

Patrick Le Callet, Sebastian Möller, Andrew Perkis, et al. 2012. Qualinet white paper on definitions of quality of experience. *European network on quality of experience in multimedia systems and services (COST Action IC 1003)*, 3(2012).

Arle Lommel, Maja Popovic, and Aljoscha Burchardt. 2014a. Assessing inter-annotator agreement for translation error annotation. In *MTE: Workshop on Automatic and Manual Metrics for Operational Translation Evaluation*.

Arle Lommel, Hans Uszkoreit, and Aljoscha Burchardt. 2014b. Multidimensional quality metrics (MQM): A framework for declaring and describing translation quality metrics. *Tradumàtica*, (12):0455–463.

Sebastian Möller and Alexander Raake. 2014. *Quality of experience: advanced concepts, applications and methods*. Springer.

Babak Naderi. 2018. *Motivation of workers on micro-task crowdsourcing platforms*. Springer.

Babak Naderi, Ina Wechsung, and Sebastian Möller. 2015. Effect of being observed on the reliability of responses in crowdsourcing micro-task platforms. In *2015 Seventh International Workshop on Quality of Multimedia Experience (QoMEX)*, pages 1–2. IEEE.

Charles Egerton Osgood, George J Suci, and Percy H Tannenbaum. 1957. *The measurement of meaning*. 47. University of Illinois press.

Kishore Papineni, Salim Roukos, Todd Ward, and Wei-Jing Zhu. 2002. BLEU: A Method for Automatic Evaluation of Machine Translation. In *Proceedings of the 40th Annual Meeting on Association for Computational Linguistics*, ACL '02, page 311–318, USA. Association for Computational Linguistics.

Ricardo Rei, Craig Stewart, Ana C Farinha, and Alon Lavie. 2020. Unbabel's participation in the WMT20 metrics shared task. In *Proceedings of the Fifth Conference on Machine Translation*, pages 911–920, Online. Association for Computational Linguistics.

Matthew Snover, Nitin Madnani, Bonnie Dorr, and Richard Schwartz. 2009. Fluency, adequacy, or HTER? Exploring different human judgments with a tunable MT metric. In *Proceedings of the Fourth Workshop on Statistical Machine Translation*, pages 259–268, Athens, Greece. Association for Computational Linguistics.

Lucia Specia, Craig Saunders, Marco Turchi, Zhuoran Wang, and John Shawe-Taylor. 2009. Improving the confidence of machine translation quality estimates.

Brian Thompson and Matt Post. 2020. Automatic machine translation evaluation in many languages via zero-shot paraphrasing. In *Proceedings of the 2020 Conference on Empirical Methods in Natural Language Processing (EMNLP)*, pages 90–121, Online. Association for Computational Linguistics.

Antonio Toral, Sheila Castilho, Ke Hu, and Andy Way. 2018. Attaining the Unattainable? Reassessing Claims of Human Parity in Neural Machine Translation.

Marcel Wältermann, Alexander Raake, and Sebastian Möller. 2010. Quality dimensions of narrowband and wideband speech transmission. *Acta Acustica united with Acustica*, 96(6):1090–1103.

A Appendix

	German original	English translation
Group 1: final list of adjective pairs that are loading on the underlying factors	direkt – umständlich	direct – ponderous
	eindeutig – mehrdeutig	unambiguous – ambiguous
	einfach – kompliziert	simple – complicated
	grammatisch – ungrammatisch	grammatical – ungrammatical
	klar – wirr	clear – chaotic
	präzise – ungenau	precise – vague
	übersichtlich – verwirrend	neat – confusing
	vollständig – lückenhaft	complete – incomplete
Group 2: list of adjective pairs that were removed during the factor analysis for the sake of interpretability	flüssig – holprig	fluent – non-fluent
	formell – informell	formal – informal
	geordnet – durcheinander	orderly – messy
	geschrieben – gesprochen	written – spoken
	höflich – unhöflich	polite – impolite
	kongruent – inkongruent	congruent – incongruent
	konsistent – inkonsistent	consistent – inconsistent
	logisch – unlogisch	logical – illogical
	menschlich – technisch	human – technical
	muttersprachlich – fremdprachlich	native – foreign-language
	persönlich – unpersönlich	personal – impersonal
	professionell – laienhaft	professional – unprofessional
Group 3: list of adjective pairs that were removed after the preliminary study	aktiv – passiv	active – passive
	angemessen – unangemessen	appropriate – inappropriate
	angenehm – unangenehm	pleasant – unpleasant
	bedeutungsvoll – bedeutungslos	meaningful – meaningless
	bekannt – unbekannt	known – unknown
	förmlich – lässig	formal – casual
	gebildet – ungebildet	educated – uneducated
	gut – schlecht	good - bad
	hochwertig – minderwertig	valuable – poor
	informativ – nichtssagend	informative – bland
	kreativ – simpel	creative – simple
	lustig – ernst	funny – serious
	optimal – suboptimal	optimal – suboptimal
	praktisch – unpraktisch	practical – impractical
	stilvoll – stillos	classy – unclassy
	vertraut – fremd	familiar – foreign
	vorhersehbar – unberechenbar	predictable – unpredictable
	warm – kalt	warm – cold
	weich – hart	soft – hard
	zweckorientiert – zweckfrei	purposeful – purposeless

Table 2: Complete list of polar adjective pairs used in the study in the German original and translated into English for better understanding.

German original
Willkommen zur Umfrage In dieser Umfrage sollst du die Sprache von verschiedenen Sätzen anhand einer Adjektivliste bewerten. Hierzu werden dir insgesamt 3 Sätze auf je 4 Seiten gezeigt. Die Sätze können fehlerhaft sein, müssen aber nicht. Bitte bewerte jeden dieser 3 Sätze in Hinblick auf die verwendete Sprache (inklusive Satzzeichen) mit Hilfe der Adjektivliste. Die Adjektivliste enthält 22 gegesätzliche Adjektivpaare, die an den beiden Enden einer Skala von -3 bis +3 stehen. Bitte schiebe für jedes Adjektivpaar den Slider auf der Skala dorthin, wo der Wert deiner Meinung nach die Sprache des jeweiligen Satzes am besten beschreibt. Versuche, den Inhalt der Sätze nicht in deine Bewertung miteinfließen zu lassen. Alle deine Antworten aus dem folgenden Fragebogen werden anonym behandelt und dienen ausschließlich dem Zweck dieser wissenschaftlichen Arbeit. Achtung: Das Ergebnis dieser Umfrage ist sehr wichtig für uns und andere Wissenschaftler, die in diesem Bereich arbeiten. Wir verfügen über Methoden um die Einheitlichkeit deiner Antworten zu überprüfen. Wir werden diese Methoden nutzen, um die Qualität der abgeschickten Aufgaben zu bewerten. Crowdworker, die qualitativ hochwertige Antworten geben, werden zu weiteren Untersuchungen eingeladen, zu denen sie exklusiven Zugang erhalten. Auf der nächsten Seite wirst du zunächst ein Beispiel sehen, bevor es losgeht.
English translation
Welcome to the survey In this survey, you are supposed to evaluate the language of different sentences with the help of an adjective list. You will be shown 3 sentences altogether, distributed over 4 pages each. Die sentences might, but don't have to, contain errors. Please evaluate each of the 3 sentences with regard to the language used (including punctuation) with the help of the adjective list. The adjective list contains 22 polar adjective pairs which are located on both ends of a scale from -3 to +3. Please move the slider for each adjective pair to the point on the scale where the value describes the language of the respective sentence best in your opinion. Try to not let the content of the sentences influence your evaluation. All your answers in the following survey will be handled anonymously and exclusively serve the aim of this scientific work. Note: The result of this survey is very important for us and other scientists working in this area. We are equipped with methods to check your answers for consistency. We will use these methods to evaluate the quality of the completed task. Crowdworkers that provide high-quality answers will be invited to further surveys to which they will receive exclusive access. On the next page, you will first see an example before the survey starts.

Table 3: Instructions for the crowdsourcing survey in the German original and translated into English for better understanding.

Human evaluation of web-crawled parallel corpora for machine translation

Gema Ramírez-Sánchez, Marta Bañón
Jaume Zaragoza-Bernabeu, Sergio Ortiz-Rojas
Prompsit Language Engineering, Spain
{gramirez, mbanon, jzaragoza, sortiz}@prompsit.com

Abstract

Quality assessment has been an ongoing activity of the series of ParaCrawl efforts to crawl massive amounts of parallel data from multilingual websites for 29 languages. The goal of ParaCrawl is to get parallel data that is good for machine translation. To prove so, both, automatic (extrinsic) and human (intrinsic and extrinsic) evaluation tasks have been included as part of the quality assessment activity of the project. We sum up the various methods followed to address these evaluation tasks for the web-crawled corpora produced and their results. We review their advantages and disadvantages for the final goal of the ParaCrawl project and the related ongoing project MaCoCu.

1 Introduction

Machine translation and particularly neural machine translation is a data hungry process. Data, ideally in the form of parallel texts, is many times scarce for many languages, poorly varied for others or very low quality. Multilingual websites are a great source of parallel data to complement these poor data scenarios, enabling the use and usefulness of machine translation for many use cases. But the web is wild and automatic harvesting of parallel data is not exempt of errors.

Web-crawled parallel content, usually noisy, can be then filtered for quality. The final parallel sentences that make it to a web-crawled parallel corpus will have gone through a complex pipeline before they are compiled and released in the form of a parallel corpus.

Once produced, how good are these parallel sentences? How good is the corpus as a whole? What kind of errors does it contain? Are these errors problematic for building machine translation? What type of evaluation process can help us to identify action points to improve the production pipeline?

These are the questions that we were trying to answer when designing the tasks that would be carried out as part of the quality assessment activity in the ParaCrawl project. (Bañón et al., 2020) provides a full description of the project, methods to gather corpora and a description of released corpora and their usefulness to create machine translation systems. ParaCrawl goal was the release of the largest collection of parallel corpora harvested from multilingual websites to advance machine translation. Initially targeting 23 co-official European languages paired with English, the final version contains also Norwegian Nynorsk, Norwegian Bokmål and Icelandic paired with English and 3 corpora for co-official languages in Spain paired with Spanish. Version 9 accounts for 1.457 million unique sentence pairs across 29 language pairs.[1] Additionally, 17 corpora for other language combinations have been released as bonus corpora.

In the following sections, we review related work and focus on the human evaluation methods. We also report about extrinsic automatic evaluation experiments through machine translation. We try to analyse how human and automatic evaluation methods relate and discuss their usefulness to to answer our questions.

2 Related work

Besides ParaCrawl, there have been a number of past and recent efforts to compile parallel corpora from web-crawled content. Among the recent ones, we find, for example, WikiMatrix (Schwenk et al., 2021), CCAligned (El-Kishky et al., 2020) or OSCAR (Ortiz Suárez et al., 2019).

Many of these parallel corpora are usually evaluated through machine translation (Khayrallah and Koehn, 2018) where automatic filtering of corpora and its impact on machine translation quality has gained interest in the last years (Koehn et al., 2018,

[1] See `https://paracrawl.eu/` for a breakdown of corpus size by language.

Proceedings of the 2nd Workshop on Human Evaluation of NLP Systems (HumEval), pages 32 - 41

2019, 2020). Some other recent work like (Caswell et al., 2021) has, in contrast, put the focus on human evaluation and recommend techniques to evaluate and improve multilingual corpora to avoid low-quality data releases.

3 Human Evaluation

Human evaluation of the corpora in ParaCrawl was done in 3 different ways depending on the version of the corpus: a) based on error annotation of parallel sentences, b) based on post-editing (PE) of the output of MT systems trained with the crawled parallel corpora and c) based on manual searches over the parallel sentences using a concordancer.

We detail each of these methods in the following subsections.

3.1 Error annotation-based evaluation

Error annotation of parallel sentences was done following ELRC guidelines as compulsory required by the project call.[2] These guidelines define a set of labels to annotate sentences following a hierarchical error typology. They literally read as follows:

1. Wrong language identification (L): means the crawler tools failed in identifying the right language.
2. Incorrect alignment (A): refers to segments having a different content due to wrong alignment.
3. Wrong tokenization (T): means the text has not been tokenized properly by the crawler tools (no separator between words).
4. MT translation (MT): refers to content identified as having been translated through a Machine Translation system. A few hints to detect if this is the case:
    - grammar errors such as gender and number agreement;
    - words that are not to be translated (trademarks for instance Nike Air => if 'Air' is translated in the target language instead of being kept unmodified);
    - inconsistencies (use of different words for referring to the same object/person);
    - translation errors showing there is no human behind.
5. Translation error refers to (E):
    - Lexical errors (omitted/added words or wrong choice of lexical item, due to misinterpretation or mistranslation),
    - Syntactic error (grammatical errors such as problems with verb tense, coreference and inflection, misinterpretation of the grammatical relationships among the words in the text).
    - Poor usage of language (awkward, unidiomatic usage of the target language and failure to use commonly recognized titles and terms). It could be due to MT translation.
6. Free translation (F): means a non-literal translation in the sense of having the content completely reformulated in one language (for editorial purposes for instance). This is a correct translation but in a different style or form. This includes figures of speech such as metaphors, anaphors, etc.

If none of these errors applied, the sentence pair should be labelled as Valid.

When more than one issue appeared in the evaluated sentences, annotators were asked to choose the first one according to the above referred error typology (1 to 6). Selecting a label was compulsory to consider the sentence evaluated and be able to complete the task, although during evaluation, if no label was selected, the sentence pair was labeled as pending.

Besides this, extra information was asked after the first evaluation campaign out of the 3 carried out to clarify some of the errors:

- Wrong language identification: whether the source, the target or both texts are wrongly identified.
- MT Translation: whether the source, the target or both text are MT-translated.
- Free translation: whether the translation should be kept, even though it is freely translated.

Moreover, after the first evaluation campaign, we asked evaluators to flag sentences which contained personal data or inappropriate language by using the check boxes on the bottom right of the screen.

[2] Seehttps://www.lr-coordination.eu/sites/default/files/common/Validation_guidelines_CEF-AT_v6.2_20180720.pdf.

3.1.1 Annotators selection and annotation tool

External annotators were selected by a language service provider (LSP). Depending on the campaign, we had 1 or 2 annotators for each language pair and between 23 and 29 language pairs. Annotators were translators and had experience in similar tasks. They were introduced to the task by the LSP project managers and received an extensive support, supervision and material from our side.

The annotation was carried out using Keops,[3] a free/open-source web-based tool to perform manual evaluation of parallel sentences. Keops covers different tasks including annotation of parallel sentences following ELRC criteria. It also supports adequacy, fluency and ranking tasks. The tool was developed inside ParaCrawl and shaped to the purpose of manual evaluation of the corpora to be released. It allows managing corpora, users, roles, projects, tasks and results.

The ELRC-based annotation screen (see figure 1) was designed to focus on a sentence pair and the annotation task itself in a user-friendly way. Annotation guidelines with examples were provided in the annotation screen to avoid users get lost. Besides this, the tool allows evaluators to navigate freely through all sentence pairs in a task, see the progress of the task, leave the task and come back at any point, access the last annotated sentence or get your own annotations or a summary in TSV format. This summary is also plotted in the results screen along with time-tracking details and a form to provide feedback on the tool.

3.1.2 Error annotation campaigns

Three error-annotation evaluation campaigns were organized for different versions of the corpora:

- Campaign 1 included 2,000 randomly sampled sentences for each of the 23 language pairs covered in ParaCrawl version 3 and 1 annotator per language pair
- Campaign 2 included 1,000 randomly sampled sentences for each of the 29 language pairs covered in ParaCrawl version 6 and 2 annotators per language pair
- Campaign 3 included 1,000 randomly sampled sentences for each of the 29 language pairs covered in ParaCrawl version 7 and 1 annotator per language pair

ParaCrawl versions 3, 6 and 7 are very different in size and in which this data was processed specially regarding alignment and cleaning components as explained in (Bañón et al., 2020).

Annotators were given 3 hours to get familiar with the project, the guidelines and the tool and to ask for doubts. They needed to complete the evaluation of 1,000 sentence pairs in 10 hours. They had a week to complete the task, once started.

They were presented the error typology and criteria in different ways: a brief oral introduction, the full guidelines in PDF, a visual help section in the annotation screen and a link to Keops Evaluator Guide[4] with examples.

Extra materials and support were provided during the evaluation campaigns when necessary: more examples and refinement of definition on error typologies, where to include issues out of the error typology, etc.

In some cases, during the course of the annotation period, we were checking actively the annotations and contacting users that were mistaken. Even though, it happened twice that we asked for a second annotator after the full task was completed because there were major issues with the 1,000 annotated sentences.

During the first evaluation campaign, we had to improvise on the fly the redefinition of some of categories to accommodate issues that were not matching any of them in the ELRC error typology that we needed to follow according to the call requirements. Namely:

- encoding issues: strange characters like Ã appeared in the texts, all due to encoding issues derived from automatic processing. We asked annotators to label those as Wrong Language.
- segmentation issues: there were sentences with partially missing text in source or target which did not match any of the categories. We asked annotators to label those as Tokenization errors.
- MT translation definition: annotators were including valid parallel sentences in this category just because they were valid but suspicious of having been produced by machine translation, we asked them not to do so but to label only bad parallel sentences that seemed to be produced by machine translation.

[3]https://github.com/paracrawl/keops

[4]https://github.com/paracrawl/keops/blob/master/evaluators.md

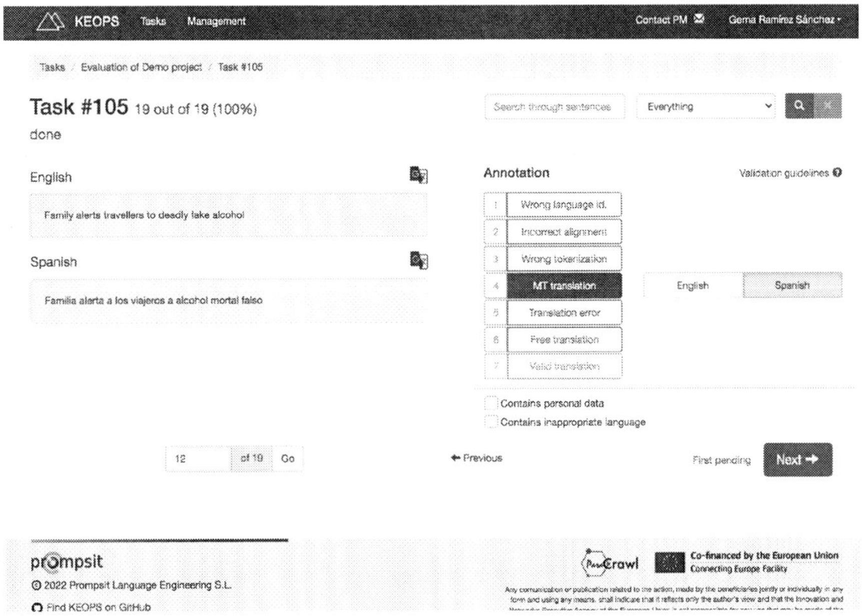

Figure 1: ELRC-based error annotation screen in Keops

3.1.3 Analysis of results for error annotation

Results from the first campaign were extensively reviewed by project team members. Some samples were re-annotated before determining action points on how improve the processing pipeline. We concluded that we needed better language identification, sentence segmenting or encoding fixing. But the annotation numbers themselves were considered distrustful as we observed many mislabeled sentences, mainly by lack of adherence to the hierarchy in the errors and abuse of the machine translation error category.

For example, sentences like "Hotel rooms in Paris - Habitaciones de hotel en Barcelona (Hotel rooms in Barcelona)", annotators were using MT error instead of Bad Alignment as well as for sentences like "Start your day with a good breakfast - No se puede empezar un buen día sin desayunar bien. (One cannot start a good day without a good breakfast)", very unlikely to have been produced by a MT system and probably a Free Translation.

After the first evaluation campaign, we introduced the extra information above described to be able to distinguish if the issues applied to source, target or both sides of the sentence pair or if Free translation-labelled sentences were considered as to be kept or left form the final corpus.

For the second evaluation campaign, for which we improved communication and materials about the error hierarchy adding more examples, we decided to do a second round with a second annotator. The first round results was inconclusive and even very odd for some language pairs. The second round results were very different for many languages, and, indeed, inter-annotator agreement was really low. These results are presented in table1.

For the third evaluation campaign, we tried with early spotting of annotation errors and tighter project management, but results were, again, inconclusive.

Although further annotation-based evaluation campaigns were planned in the project, we decided to replace them with other activities that could give us hints on what to focus to improve the quality of our corpora. We, though, reused the labeled sentences to perform a reassessment with the overlapping sentences from subsequent versions of the corpus.

Labelled data from all campaings is publicly available with a free/open-source licence.[5]

3.2 PE-based evaluation

When arriving at a mature phase of corpora production, and after many experiments showing that automatic metrics were improving with MT systems trained with them (see section 3 for a full explanation), we performed a PE-based evaluation

[5] https://github.com/paracrawl/human-evaluations

	L		A		T		MT		E		F		V		*IAA*
	A	B	A	B	A	B	A	B	A	B	A	B	A	B	*A-B*
Bulgarian	2	7	0	3	7	9	34	35	19	8	1	5	36	33	*0,40*
Croatian	2	1	4	4	7	5	30	23	12	11	12	2	34	53	*0,36*
Czech	3	5	36	0	8	5	17	17	3	9	1	50	31	14	*0,20*
Danish	0	0	0	0	3	0	6	58	63	5	2	0	26	37	*0,15*
Dutch	0	0	4	1	0	5	24	3	6	21	15	1	51	68	*0,22*
Estonian	0	6	5	3	10	1	48	46	17	8	0	4	19	31	*0,44*
Finnish	4	1	0	4	10	14	38	42	11	1	1	23	35	16	*0,38*
French	2	0	2	7	10	8	13	1	10	28	3	1	60	55	*0,27*
German	0	1	8	4	1	6	12	23	6	6	2	8	72	53	*0,30*
Greek	1	2	1	4	10	11	27	31	41	29	4	1	17	23	*0,42*
Hungarian	7	8	1	16	2	3	29	32	24	11	1	5	36	26	*0,41*
Icelandic	0	1	1	2	6	7	36	73	41	2	2	0	15	15	*0,23*
Irish	0	20	1	7	3	8	29	23	26	31	0	0	40	11	*0,21*
Italian	0	0	1	5	3	11	51	13	14	2	17	3	14	65	*0,15*
Latvian	5	1	1	2	8	4	26	49	26	6	2	5	32	32	*0,43*
Lithuanian	3	2	4	2	5	4	42	48	1	7	6	6	38	31	*0,47*
Maltese	0	1	4	2	19	0	51	59	2	15	1	3	23	20	*0,34*
Norwegian B.	3	5	5	10	3	4	21	0	18	28	0	16	51	36	*0,19*
Norwegian N.	1	1	24	34	0	2	1	0	9	5	8	0	57	59	*0,54*
Polish	1	0	6	3	11	1	34	50	5	8	1	5	41	33	*0,38*
Portuguese	6	3	6	6	15	3	14	5	6	1	14	2	39	78	*0,27*
Romanian	1	0	4	1	5	1	18	24	29	26	13	0	30	48	*0,16*
Slovak	3	13	3	7	3	8	27	31	14	14	14	0	36	27	*0,33*
Slovenian	5	6	4	7	8	3	46	34	12	10	6	7	18	32	*0,38*
Spanish	2	1	5	5	6	8	11	42	29	11	0	0	47	33	*0,26*
Swedish	0	1	2	7	1	5	1	19	34	21	5	9	56	39	*0,25*
Basque	0	0	7	0	0	0	15	12	53	33	2	14	23	41	-
Catalan	1	0	10	1	1	4	8	4	4	5	2	2	73	83	-
Galician	1	4	5	15	2	1	15	5	15	18	6	3	56	53	-

Table 1: Error category percentages (see error typology in section 2.1) by the two annotators (A and B) of the second evaluation campaign along with inter-annotator agreement.

experiment to have a broader view of the usefulness of our corpora to improve MT output.

To that aim, we set up an experiment to post-edit the output of the baseline MT systems and baseline + ParaCrawl MT systems created during automatic evaluation for 5 language pairs in just one translation direction (from English into 5 target languages).

3.2.1 Post-editors selection and PE tool

External post-editors were selected by an LSP to carry out the task. They were all professional translators with previous experience in PE.

The post-editing task was done using the free online MateCat CAT tool[6]. This allowed us to manage the task materials as we wanted, to invite post-editors easily and to monitor their work. MateCat makes possible the addition of user's own translation memories and also turning off any other supporting materials like machine translation or their general translation memory. In this way, we could provide the output of our systems in the form of a suggestion from a translation memory. Also for the detailed log in a spreadsheet file that we could use to perform analysis of the results.

[6]Accesible at `https://www.matecat.com/`

3.2.2 PE evaluation campaign

We launched just one campaign for PE-based evaluation for the final version of the corpus as the project reached its end. It was done for 1,000 words, 5 translation directions, 2 different MT systems and 3 post-editors per translation direction.

We compiled the source text to be post-edited from the online multilingual new project The Conversation[7] that publishes articles with a free/open-source licence that allows using them. We compiled the contents from a single article and segmented them while keeping the order. The article[8] was picked from a date that was out of the scope of any of the data used to train the MT systems to be evaluated.

The 15 post-editors were introduced to the tool, the details of the project, the goal of their work, etc. during a one-hour call. Instructions were shared with them also in written, and doubts were double-checked during the call:

- For every source segment, they would have two suggestions in the target language coming from two different translation memories.
- These suggestion were actually the output of machine translation but we would not tell them the particular system they were coming from.
- They needed to pick the most convenient for them to perform edits and deliver an adequate translation.
- Using external resources (dictionaries, searches, etc.) was allowed, if necessary.
- They had three days to complete the task, MateCat would track the actual time spent on it.
- In case of doubt, they should contact their project manager or ourselves.

3.2.3 Analysis of results for PE

Results (see 2) were analysed in two ways: which system was picked most frequently to perform PE and what was the edit distance (character level) from the post-edited sentence to each of the systems.

System 2 was baseline and System 1 was baseline + ParaCrawl. In all cases, the most frequently picked system was baseline + ParaCrawl.

Edit distance confirms that the final translation was closer to the output of baseline + Project-corpora than to the output of baseline. It also shows that the hardest combination to post-edit was English-Latvian, followed by English-German and English-Romanian, being English-Czech and interestingly English-Finnish the pairs with less edits. An interesting observation was that the output for baseline system for English-Czech was not so close to the baseline + Project-corpora as automatic metrics were showing in all versions of the released corpora. We deemed this information very valuable to complement the automatic evaluation based on automatic metrics only (see section 3).

3.3 Search-based evaluation

During the post-editing based campaign, we asked post-editors to use an external tool to perform searches during or after PE time.

This tool, named Corset,[9] was developed to let people perform full-index searches over the project corpora (see 2 . It also allows to select subsets of the corpora that are similar to a query document.

Internally, we had been using Corset to spot errors on the corpus looking for typical processing errors after each step in the pipeline or just doing random searches to inspect the results. This was very useful to refine the production pipeline. Also to order the results from searches on the tool based on quality heuristics.

We wanted, though, to see if professional translators found this tool useful for their work. This would give the corpora released from the project an alternative translation-related use, besides their usefulness as training data for MT.

Search-based evaluation was based on 10 manual searches, 5 language combinations a and 3 linguists per language combination.

Searchers were the same 15 professional translators working on the PE evaluation task. They were asked to perform at least 10 searches and answer a 6-question survey on their experience including usability, quality of results and value of the tool. Only 13 out of the 15 post-editors completed the work and only 11 answered the survey.

Searches were mostly related to the post-editing job content (e-bike, tyre, terrain bicycle, ubiquitous,

[7]https://theconversation.com

[8]https://theconversation.com/are-e-bikes-ruining-mountain-biking-166121

[9]https://corset.paracrawl.eu

By PE job	S1 chosen	S2 chosen	S1=S2	S1 avg ED	S2 avg ED
en-cs-nina	38	8	1	23.65	43.40
en-cs-pinta	28	15	4	40.37	53.13
en-cs-santa	32	15	1	24.18	36.77
en-de-nina	29	20	0	31.47	32.02
en-de-pinta	27	23	1	38.53	37.27
en-de-santa	30	19	0	32.43	34.39
en-fi-nina	44	7	1	30.18	52.02
en-fi-pinta	47	3	0	24.24	61.18
en-fi-santa	43	6	1	28.52	55.56
en-lv-nina	33	16	2	39.71	52.95
en-lv-pinta	32	15	1	45.65	55.76
en-lv-santa	34	13	2	46.16	58.91
en-ro-nina	39	13	1	33.84	46.43
en-ro-pinta	40	12	1	31.37	45.51
en-ro-santa	45	6	2	38.13	53.70
By language	**S1 chosen**	**S2 chosen**	**S1=S2**	**S1 avg ED**	**S2 avg ED**
en-cs	98	38	6	29.37	44.38
en-de	86	62	1	34.20	34.59
en-fi	134	16	2	27.68	56.20
en-lv	99	44	5	43.77	55.84
en-ro	124	31	4	34.44	48.55

Table 2: Post-editing (PE) results by individual jobs and by language for the most frequently chosen MT system (S1 or S2) and edit-distance (ED) from each system to the final translation

outweighs, rubbing other people's noses, mountain bikers, etc.) and a few of their own invention (medical product, disclosure statement, COVID restrictions, etc.). Most in English, and just a few in the target languages. We discovered, though, that many of the searches in English were performed on the target side of the corpus (user needs to indicate source or target) because the target side was the default option. We changed it to source after discovering so many mistaken searches.

Users reported positive feedback on the usability of the tool and the value of being able to perform searches over a parallel corpus. Some of them, though were complaining about the presence of English in the target languages, derived from the user interface mistake above mentioned. After repeating the searches setting the correct side of the corpus they were looking into, most of the negative comments turned into positive feedback about the diversity of examples and translations. Users reported also the presence of MT content and misaligned sentences in some languages.

Their feedback and our own experience showed that this simple method could be easily turned into action points although not being very systematic.

4 Automatic Evaluation

Automatic evaluation was done mainly by the addition of ParaCrawl data to WMT data from the translation shared task (Bojar et al., 2017) as an ongoing experiment carried out since the first version of the corpus released in Januany 2018 up to the final version until present dated from September 2021. MT evaluation based on sub samples of ParaCrawl and the addition to Europarl (Koehn, 2005) was also explored for an early version but was abandoned by lack of resources and time.

4.1 WMT-based evaluation

This experiment was designed to compare the performance of state-of-the-art neural machine translation models trained on WMT datasets (baseline) and adding ParaCrawl corpora (baseline + ParaCrawl) for five language pairs: English-Czech, English-German, English-Romanian, English-Finnish and English-Latvian

Baselines use the data from WMT17 except for English-Romanian for which the data comes from WMT16. The different ParaCrawl versions are added to WMT data to see their effect. Neural

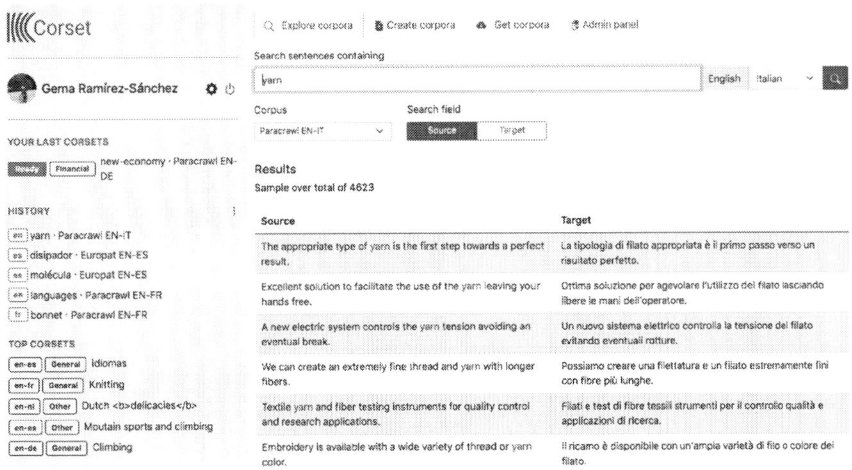

Figure 2: Full-index parallel corpora search screen in Corset.

models are trained using MarianNMT (Junczys-Dowmunt et al., 2018) transformer-base with a 32,000 word SentencePiece (Kudo and Richardson, 2018) vocabulary. BLEU (Papineni et al., 2001) scores for the last four versions of the corpus systems are shown in table 3 and corpora sizes are shown in figure 4.

Further metrics such as chrF (Popović, 2015) and COMET (Rei et al., 2020) were computed. All lead to the same conclusions and even showed that version 9 of the corpus was better than 7 for English-German, contradicting BLEU. We also used a second test set, a shelf-crawled strictly multilingual TED Talks test set, for which results were all positive when adding ParaCrawl corpora to baseline with an exception for English-Czech. For this pair, the baseline was never beaten according to BLEU and chrF, in disagreement with COMET.

Comparing automatic and PE results, we noted that the little improvement in BLEU in the English-Czech baseline + ParaCrawl v9 system was having a much higher positive impact when deciding which system output to pick for PE. In all other cases, improvement in automatic metrics were higher and PE results were consistent.

Although the results show improvement for all language combinations and PE results are accordingly, there is still uncertainty about the reason of the improvement being the addition of new data more than the quality of the corpora themselves. We are also unsure about the suitability of this experiment, covering only 5 pairs, to represent the overall quality of the released corpora, which included 29 languages in its last version. Finally, we are also not convinced about the suitability of the test sets used to show the value of the corpora.

5 Conclusions and future work

We have presented in this paper a summary of the tasks carried out as part o the quality assessment activities of the ParaCrawl project to evaluate the production of web-crawled parallel corpora for machine translation. We have extensively described and discussed how we implemented different human evaluation tasks based on error annotation, post-editing and searches over the corpora and their results. We have also briefly reported about the extrinsic evaluation through machine translation conducted in parallel with human evaluation. Besides describing the methods and experiments, we have discussed their usefulness to meet the goals of the ParaCrawl project and their limitations.

The advantages and disadvantages of these methods are now being discussed in MaCoCu,[10] a similar effort for which quality assessment activities are being planned not only for bilingual corpora but also for monolingual ones. For human evaluation, annotation is probably going to be focused on single issues tasks rather that multiple and hierarchic ones. Searches and post-editing are under discussion as well as the suitability for other tasks like direct assessment, ranking and fluency, this last maybe suitable also for monolingual corpora. For extrinsic automatic evaluation, more balanced corpora sizes or not only concatenation of data but also fine tuning is being considered. Monolingual

[10] https://macocu.eu/

training corpus	cs-en	en-cs	de-en	en-de	fi-en	en-fi	lv-en	en-lv	ro-en	en-ro
WMT	28.1	21.7	33.4	27.2	24.8	21.3	18.1	15.2	33.4	28.3
WMT + PC-6	28.4	22.0	36.3	29.8	31.7	23.7	22.8	19.6	39.3	31.4
WMT + PC-7	28.0	21,9	**36.4**	30.0	32.2	24.8	23.2	19.5	39.4	31.7
WMT + PC-8	**29.0**	22.3	35.3	29.6	32.3	25.7	23.0	20.0	40.2	32.5
WMT + PC-9	**29.0**	**22.9**	36.0	**30.5**	**33.1**	**27.9**	**24.0**	**20.7**	**40.5**	**33.5**

Table 3: BLEU scores for the NMT models trained with WMT16/17 training corpora and adding ParaCrawl versions 6 to 9. Best scores are in bold.

corpus	cs	de	fi	lv	ro
WMT	52.0	5.8	2.6	4.5	0.6
PC-6	17.9	58.8	4.3	2.2	4.2
PC-7	14.0	42.8	7.3	3.7	6.2
PC-8	50.0	261.0	15.0	8.0	13.0
PC-9	50.6	278.0	31.0	13.0	25.0

Table 4: Corpus sizes in million sentences from the WMT (baseline) and ParaCrawl versions 6 to 9.

corpora will probably also be automatically tested on downstream applications or tasks.

Acknowledgements

This work has been supported by the three ParaCrawl projects (paracrawl.eu) funded by the Connecting Europe Facility of the European Union 2014-2020 - CEF Telecom, already finished and an additional ongoing project, MaCoCu (macocu.eu), also funded by the same programme under Grant Agreement No. INEA/CEF/ICT/A2020/2278341. This communication reflects only the author's view.

References

Marta Bañón, Pinzhen Chen, Barry Haddow, Kenneth Heafield, Hieu Hoang, Miquel Esplà-Gomis, Mikel L. Forcada, Amir Kamran, Faheem Kirefu, Philipp Koehn, Sergio Ortiz Rojas, Leopoldo Pla Sempere, Gema Ramírez-Sánchez, Elsa Sarrías, Marek Strelec, Brian Thompson, William Waites, Dion Wiggins, and Jaume Zaragoza. 2020. ParaCrawl: Web-scale acquisition of parallel corpora. In *Proceedings of the 58th Annual Meeting of the Association for Computational Linguistics*, pages 4555–4567, Online. Association for Computational Linguistics.

Ondřej Bojar, Rajen Chatterjee, Christian Federmann, Yvette Graham, Barry Haddow, Shujian Huang, Matthias Huck, Philipp Koehn, Qun Liu, Varvara Logacheva, Christof Monz, Matteo Negri, Matt Post, Raphael Rubino, Lucia Specia, and Marco Turchi. 2017. Findings of the 2017 conference on machine translation (WMT17). In *Proceedings of the Second Conference on Machine Translation*, pages 169–214, Copenhagen, Denmark. Association for Computational Linguistics.

Isaac Caswell, Julia Kreutzer, Lisa Wang, Ahsan Wahab, Daan van Esch, Nasanbayar Ulzii-Orshikh, Allahsera Tapo, Nishant Subramani, Artem Sokolov, Claytone Sikasote, Monang Setyawan, Supheakmungkol Sarin, Sokhar Samb, Benoît Sagot, Clara Rivera, Annette Rios, Isabel Papadimitriou, Salomey Osei, Pedro Javier Ortiz Suárez, Iroro Orife, Kelechi Ogueji, Rubungo Andre Niyongabo, Toan Q. Nguyen, Mathias Müller, André Müller, Shamsuddeen Hassan Muhammad, Nanda Muhammad, Ayanda Mnyakeni, Jamshidbek Mirzakhalov, Tapiwanashe Matangira, Colin Leong, Nze Lawson, Sneha Kudugunta, Yacine Jernite, Mathias Jenny, Orhan Firat, Bonaventure F. P. Dossou, Sakhile Dlamini, Nisansa de Silva, Sakine Çabuk Balli, Stella Biderman, Alessia Battisti, Ahmed Baruwa, Ankur Bapna, Pallavi Baljekar, Israel Abebe Azime, Ayodele Awokoya, Duygu Ataman, Orevaoghene Ahia, Oghenefego Ahia, Sweta Agrawal, and Mofetoluwa Adeyemi. 2021. Quality at a glance: An audit of web-crawled multilingual datasets. *CoRR*, abs/2103.12028.

Ahmed El-Kishky, Vishrav Chaudhary, Francisco Guzmán, and Philipp Koehn. 2020. CCAligned: A massive collection of cross-lingual web-document pairs. In *Proceedings of the 2020 Conference on Empirical Methods in Natural Language Processing (EMNLP)*, pages 5960–5969, Online. Association for Computational Linguistics.

Marcin Junczys-Dowmunt, Roman Grundkiewicz, Tomasz Dwojak, Hieu Hoang, Kenneth Heafield, Tom Neckermann, Frank Seide, Ulrich Germann, Alham Fikri Aji, Nikolay Bogoychev, André F. T. Martins, and Alexandra Birch. 2018. Marian: Fast neural machine translation in C++. In *Proceedings of ACL 2018, System Demonstrations*, pages 116–121, Melbourne, Australia. Association for Computational Linguistics.

Huda Khayrallah and Philipp Koehn. 2018. On the

impact of various types of noise on neural machine translation. In *Proceedings of the 2nd Workshop on Neural Machine Translation and Generation*, pages 74–83, Melbourne, Australia. Association for Computational Linguistics.

Philipp Koehn. 2005. Europarl: A Parallel Corpus for Statistical Machine Translation. In *Conference Proceedings: the tenth Machine Translation Summit*, pages 79–86, Phuket, Thailand. AAMT, AAMT.

Philipp Koehn, Vishrav Chaudhary, Ahmed El-Kishky, Naman Goyal, Peng-Jen Chen, and Francisco Guzmán. 2020. Findings of the WMT 2020 shared task on parallel corpus filtering and alignment. In *Proceedings of the Fifth Conference on Machine Translation*, pages 726–742, Online. Association for Computational Linguistics.

Philipp Koehn, Francisco Guzmán, Vishrav Chaudhary, and Juan Pino. 2019. Findings of the WMT 2019 shared task on parallel corpus filtering for low-resource conditions. In *Proceedings of the Fourth Conference on Machine Translation (Volume 3: Shared Task Papers, Day 2)*, pages 54–72, Florence, Italy. Association for Computational Linguistics.

Philipp Koehn, Huda Khayrallah, Kenneth Heafield, and Mikel L. Forcada. 2018. Findings of the WMT 2018 shared task on parallel corpus filtering. In *Proceedings of the Third Conference on Machine Translation: Shared Task Papers*, pages 726–739, Belgium, Brussels. Association for Computational Linguistics.

Taku Kudo and John Richardson. 2018. SentencePiece: A simple and language independent subword tokenizer and detokenizer for neural text processing. In *Proceedings of the 2018 Conference on Empirical Methods in Natural Language Processing: System Demonstrations*, pages 66–71, Brussels, Belgium. Association for Computational Linguistics.

Pedro Javier Ortiz Suárez, Benoît Sagot, and Laurent Romary. 2019. Asynchronous pipelines for processing huge corpora on medium to low resource infrastructures. Proceedings of the Workshop on Challenges in the Management of Large Corpora (CMLC-7) 2019. Cardiff, 22nd July 2019, pages 9 – 16, Mannheim. Leibniz-Institut für Deutsche Sprache.

Kishore Papineni, Salim Roukos, Todd Ward, and Wei-Jing Zhu. 2001. BLEU: a method for automatic evaluation of machine translation. Technical Report RC22176(W0109-022), IBM Research Report.

Maja Popović. 2015. chrF: character n-gram F-score for automatic MT evaluation. In *Proceedings of the Tenth Workshop on Statistical Machine Translation*, pages 392–395, Lisbon, Portugal. Association for Computational Linguistics.

Ricardo Rei, Craig Stewart, Ana C Farinha, and Alon Lavie. 2020. COMET: A neural framework for MT evaluation. In *Proceedings of the 2020 Conference on Empirical Methods in Natural Language Processing (EMNLP)*, pages 2685–2702, Online. Association for Computational Linguistics.

Holger Schwenk, Vishrav Chaudhary, Shuo Sun, Hongyu Gong, and Francisco Guzmán. 2021. WikiMatrix: Mining 135M parallel sentences in 1620 language pairs from Wikipedia. In *Proceedings of the 16th Conference of the European Chapter of the Association for Computational Linguistics: Main Volume*, pages 1351–1361, Online. Association for Computational Linguistics.

Beyond calories: evaluating how tailored communication reduces emotional load in diet-coaching

Simone Balloccu and Ehud Reiter
University of Aberdeen / United Kingdom
simone.balloccu@abdn.ac.uk
e.reiter@abdn.ac.uk

Abstract

Dieting is a behaviour change task that is difficult for many people to conduct successfully. This is due to many factors, including stress and cost. Mobile applications offer an alternative to traditional coaching. However, previous work on apps evaluation only focused on dietary outcomes, ignoring users' emotional state despite its influence on eating habits. In this work, we introduce a novel evaluation of the effects that tailored communication can have on the emotional load of dieting. We implement this by augmenting a traditional diet-app with affective NLG, text-tailoring and persuasive communication techniques. We then run a short 2-weeks experiment and check dietary outcomes, user feedback of produced text and, most importantly, its impact on emotional state, through PANAS questionnaire. Results show that tailored communication significantly improved users' emotional state, compared to an app-only control group.

1 Introduction

An unhealthy diet poses a serious threat to an individual's health. Research showed that a poor diet kills more people than smoking (Afshin et al., 2019) and that obesity has tripled since 1975.[1] Coaching through human experts is one of the most effective ways to improve diet (Gordon et al., 2017; Schmittdiel et al., 2017), but it can be too expensive for disadvantaged groups, adding to other costs associated with a healthy diet (Aggarwal et al., 2011; Barosh et al., 2014; Morris et al., 2014; Håkansson, 2015).

E-health apps are a cheaper alternative, although there is mixed evidence about their effectiveness (Wang et al., 2016; McCarroll et al., 2017; Lee et al., 2018; Aromatario et al., 2019). Compared to experts, apps often show sub-optimal communication. Typically apps focus on data presentation (e.g.: charts), limiting the use of text to short and fixed messages. This could be the reason why previous apps evaluation focused primarily on diet outcomes. There has been little work on effective communication for dieting tools: this should be addressed as it plays a big role in engagement and adherence (Lee and Cho, 2017). Dieting habits are also known to be influenced by emotional state (Macht and Simons, 2011; Koenders and van Strien, 2011; Klump et al., 2016), yet no prior work on diet-apps investigated communication's role in this.

In this paper, we implement an advanced communication strategy and investigate its effect on emotional state in the context of diet coaching apps. We exploit affective-NLG, text-tailoring and persuasive communication techniques to create weekly diet reports. Reports are implemented as an additional layer on top of a standard diet app, augmenting its communicative capability. We then proceed to evaluate our system in a short experiment. We compare participants that used the report-augmented app, with an app-only control group. Unlike previous work, we do not focus our human evaluation on dietary outcome only. We inspect communication adequacy through user feedback on a variety of measures including readability and accuracy. As a novel contribution we evaluate if our reports improved participant's affective state. We adopt a validated psychometric tool, the PANAS questionnaire (Watson et al., 1988), to analyse the behaviour of both groups on a weekly basis. Participants who received our report experienced significantly more positive emotions and fewer negative ones. We also observe the opposite behaviour in the control group.

In Section 2 we expose the common limits of diet apps under the functional, communication and psychological aspect. We also briefly describe SOTA

[1] https://www.who.int/news-room/fact-sheets/detail/obesity-and-overweight

Proceedings of the 2nd Workshop on Human Evaluation of NLP Systems (HumEval), pages 42 - 53
May 27, 2022

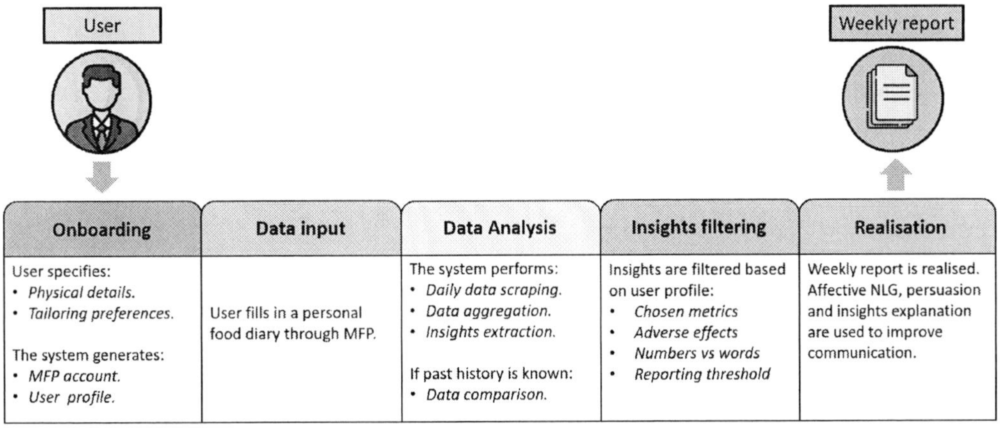

Figure 1: Execution flow, from user subscription to report delivery.

> Hello Dan18777, you told us that you want to gain some weight, so we wrote this report especially for you.
>
> Your calorie intake could use some improvement: there was an occasional lack of food (generally you ate about a third less than your target). It was a bit better the previous time, we're sure you can do it again!
> Friday looks like the most problematic day (you ate about half of your target).
>
> It seems that sodium and protein intake needs a bit of improvement.
>
> Your sodium consumption was about half of your target. Of the foods you ate, "Spinacina" was the highest in sodium. It would be better to correct this as sodium deficiency can lead to cramps.
>
> Also, your protein consumption was about half of your target. Last week it was better and we know you can do it again! "Pizza" was the food you ate which had the most protein. Keep in mind that protein deficiency can be responsible for muscle loss.

Figure 2: Example of a generated weekly report on the second week.

in communication-based systems for diet-coaching. In Section 3 we detail our approach to augmenting diet-coaching apps communication, and describe the implemented features. We present our experiment methodology in Section 4, and discuss the results in Section 5. In Section 6 we sum up our conclusions and present our future research directions. Finally, in Section 7 we detail the procedure through which we ensured ethical compliance for our experiment.

2 Related work

Today people can access lots of diet tools, but both academic and commercial products show some common limits. Some of these are purely functional: missing features that negatively impact on effectiveness. This includes low accuracy (Vasiloglou et al., 2020), fixed suggestions (Lieffers et al., 2018) or the excessive use of humans in the loop (Teeriniemi et al., 2018)[2][3]. Low accuracy is an obvious limit to the app's effectiveness; fixed suggestions overlook customisation and potential dangers (like allergies, user taste and religious food dogmas); major use of human experts nullifies apps' usefulness in the first place. However, these problems can be solved by expanding the tool-set of features and evaluating dietary outcomes.

But if we consider the behavioural component of dieting, we raise different problems, for example at communication and psychological level. Previous research showed that behaviour change benefits more from advanced communication (Van Dorsten and Lindley, 2008; Balloccu et al., 2021; Whitehead and Parkin, 2022) than from factual text. Diet apps (Corcoran, 2014; Evans, 2017; Tredrea et al., 2017), however, do not follow this logic and favour data presentation, through visual features (like charts, color codes and tables) (Eikey, 2021). At communication level, used text is typically short, fixed and lacks informativeness (Vasiloglou et al., 2020).

[2] www.rise.us
[3] https://www.noom.com/

A first way to improve the communication of diet apps could be the use of fine-tuned, domain-specific NLG, combined with text-tailoring (Kreuter and Wray, 2003; Noar et al., 2007) and persuasive communication (Guerini et al., 2011; Duerr and Gloor, 2021; Shabir et al., 2022). This is motivated by the relationship between personalisation and engagement in diet apps (Lieffers et al., 2018; Zmora and Elinav, 2021), and the role of persuasion in behaviour change (Orji and Moffatt, 2018; Balloccu et al., 2021). Additionally, NLG has been used in various healthcare domains (Reiter et al., 2003; Finley et al., 2018; Pauws et al., 2019; Hommes et al., 2019), including some work in nutrition. Shed (Lim-Cheng et al., 2014) is a tailored diet-system that exploits NLG to propose alternative meal plans in real time. Initial inspection of user acceptance showed it as a promising system for further evaluation. A conceptual diet-recommender system has been proposed (Ritschel et al., 2019), focusing on reinforcement learning for linguistic personalisation. Other work (Donadello et al., 2019) presented a NLG-based persuasive reasoner to address dietary guidelines violations. Evaluation showed the appropriateness of presented feedback, and its effectiveness in reducing the amount of violations compared to canned text. MADiMan (Anselma et al., 2018; Anselma and Mazzei, 2020) is a persuasive diet-coaching system, developed to convince the user to opt for an healthier diet. Evaluation in both controlled and uncontrolled scenario revealed that users appreciated the presence of both visualisations and text, and confirmed its persuasiveness. While these works evaluated the use of persuasion and dietary outcomes, we note that tailoring involved only data analysis (e.g.: custom meal plans) and not textual features. Moreover, previous research did not inspect whether the adopted communication techniques had an effect on users' emotional state. This aligns with previous evidence that diet-apps rarely consider this element (Ferrara et al., 2019). We know from nutrition research (Torres and Nowson, 2007; Puddephatt et al., 2020; Riffer et al., 2019) that user's emotional/affective state influences eating habits, causing various issues including calorie excess (Fong et al., 2019), emotional (Macht and Simons, 2011; Van Strien et al., 2012) and binge (Klump et al., 2016) eating. The importance of this factor is also confirmed by previous research of the matter in other domains such as Cognitive Behaviour Therapy (Fitzpatrick et al., 2017), mental well-being (Ly et al., 2017), substance abuse (Prochaska et al., 2021) or emotional support in public speaking (Murali et al., 2021). To the best of our knowledge, this is the first work in NLG for nutrition that investigates the influence of the system on affective state.

3 Augmenting diet apps communication

We implement an NLG report generator for diet-coaching based on our previous work (Balloccu et al., 2020a)[4], and use it to augment the communication strategy of a traditional diet app. We use MyFitnessPal (MFP) (Evans, 2017) as data source. The execution flow can be seen in Figure 1. The report is tailored based on various preferences. Users were asked to specify:

1. A nickname
2. Their motivation for using the system (e.g.: "I want to lose weight")
3. How they wanted to display quantities in reports. The options were pure values (e.g.: "50% of your calorie goal") or fuzzy quantification (e.g.: "half of your calorie goal")
4. Metrics of interest (one or more from: calories, carbohydrates, protein, fat, sodium and sugar)
5. Threshold for intake reporting. This allows the system to ignore small anomalies like 1% calorie excess.
6. Whether or not to see possible adverse effects of their dietary choices (e.g.: consequences of calorie excess/deficit)

Username and motivation are injected in the report, to make it feel more personal, while the other elements are used for content selection and tailoring. Reports are further enriched with the following insights:

1. **Worst day:** the day whose caloric intake was the furthest from the goal.
2. **Nutrients ranking:** nutrients are ranked and only the two furthest ones from the goal are shown.

[4]Code available at: `https://bitbucket.org/uccollab/diet-tailoring/`

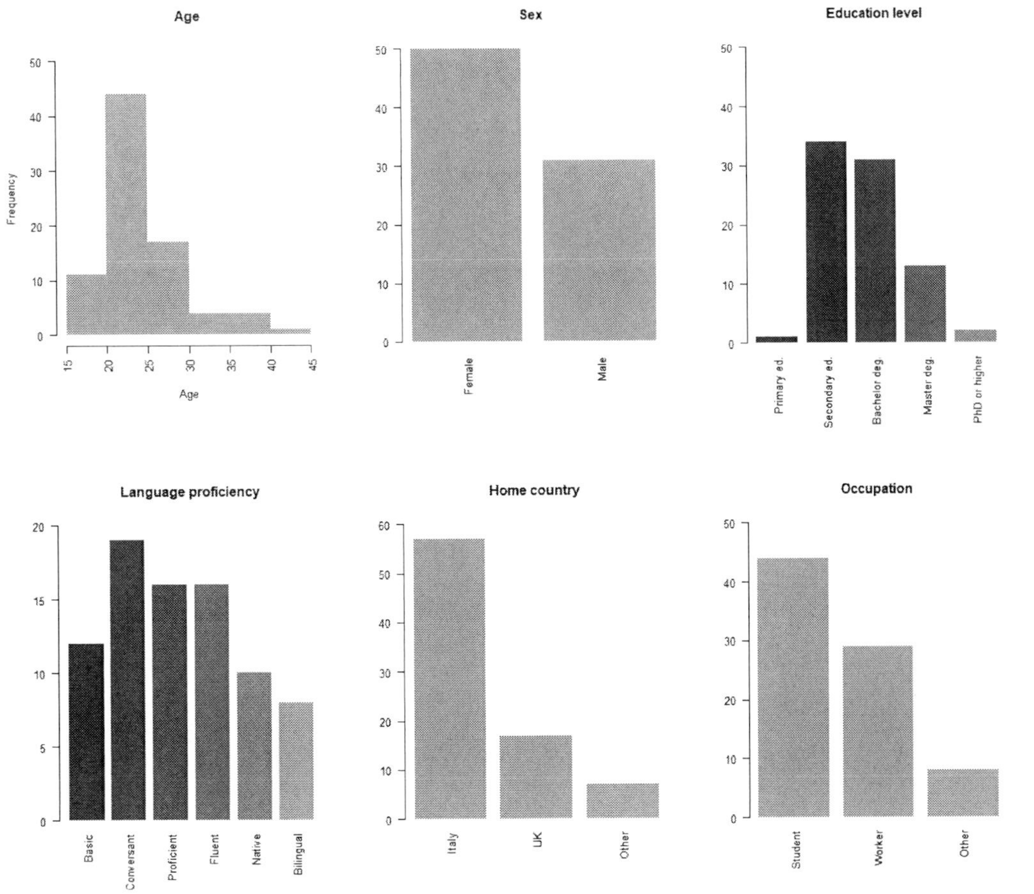

Figure 3: Population demographics. For language proficiency we adopt the scale proposed at `https://csb.uncw.edu/`. The process was supervised in order to avoid erroneous self-assessments.

3. **Food analysis:** for each nutrients, the food which provided most of it is listed.

4. **Comparisons:** if previous week data are present, intakes are compared and the eventual improvement/worsening is shown.

Finally, we adopt Affective NLG (de Rosis and Grasso, 2000; Mahamood and Reiter, 2011; Piwek, 2002), framing the document as positive-toned. This includes expressing comfort in case of negative developments and congratulations for positive ones (e.g.: calorie intake improved/worsened). Each report referred to the past week. An output example can be seen in Figure 2.

4 Experiment setup

We evaluated the effect of our reports on the diet and emotional state of users in a 2-weeks experiment. A total of 81 participants were recruited (see Section 7 for details). Population demographics can be seen in Figure 3.

Participants were trained in using MFP and asked to log their meals through the app for the following 2 weeks. They were then randomly split into two groups: "Report group" ($n = 43$) and "Control group" ($n = 38$). Participants in report group received one report at the end of each week, while control group could only see the insights provided in MFP.

About 60% of the participants (from both groups) agreed to fill-in a weekly PANAS questionnaire (Watson et al., 1988) that we used to monitor their emotional/affective state. PANAS consists of 20 mixed positive (e..g: "Attentive", "Proud", "Strong" etc...) and negative (e.g.: "Hostile", "Guilty", "Scared" etc...) words. Users score

Positive and Negative Affect Schedule (PANAS-SF)

Indicate the extent you have felt this way over the past week.		Very slightly or not at all	A little	Moderately	Quite a bit	Extremely
PANAS 1	Interested	☐ 1	☐ 2	☐ 3	☐ 4	☐ 5
PANAS 2	Distressed	☐ 1	☐ 2	☐ 3	☐ 4	☐ 5
PANAS 3	Excited	☐ 1	☐ 2	☐ 3	☐ 4	☐ 5
PANAS 4	Upset	☐ 1	☐ 2	☐ 3	☐ 4	☐ 5
PANAS 5	Strong	☐ 1	☐ 2	☐ 3	☐ 4	☐ 5
PANAS 6	Guilty	☐ 1	☐ 2	☐ 3	☐ 4	☐ 5
PANAS 7	Scared	☐ 1	☐ 2	☐ 3	☐ 4	☐ 5
PANAS 8	Hostile	☐ 1	☐ 2	☐ 3	☐ 4	☐ 5
PANAS 9	Enthusiastic	☐ 1	☐ 2	☐ 3	☐ 4	☐ 5
PANAS 10	Proud	☐ 1	☐ 2	☐ 3	☐ 4	☐ 5
PANAS 11	Irritable	☐ 1	☐ 2	☐ 3	☐ 4	☐ 5
PANAS 12	Alert	☐ 1	☐ 2	☐ 3	☐ 4	☐ 5
PANAS 13	Ashamed	☐ 1	☐ 2	☐ 3	☐ 4	☐ 5
PANAS 14	Inspired	☐ 1	☐ 2	☐ 3	☐ 4	☐ 5
PANAS 15	Nervous	☐ 1	☐ 2	☐ 3	☐ 4	☐ 5
PANAS 16	Determined	☐ 1	☐ 2	☐ 3	☐ 4	☐ 5
PANAS 17	Attentive	☐ 1	☐ 2	☐ 3	☐ 4	☐ 5
PANAS 18	Jittery	☐ 1	☐ 2	☐ 3	☐ 4	☐ 5
PANAS 19	Active	☐ 1	☐ 2	☐ 3	☐ 4	☐ 5
PANAS 20	Afraid	☐ 1	☐ 2	☐ 3	☐ 4	☐ 5

Figure 4: Weekly PANAS questionnaire, as it was administered during the experiment

	Participants that improved (%)		
Goal	Report group	Control group	p-value (χ^2)
Calories	42%	23%	≈ 0.23
Nutrient 1	56%	33%	≈ 0.16
Nutrient 2	40%	42%	≈ 0.43

Table 1: Diet outcomes per group (after two weeks). For each group, we report how many participants got closer to their dietary goals.

	Improvement (distance from goal)		
Goal	Report group	Control Group	p-value (t-test)
Calories	+1.78%	+6.53%	≈ 0.14
Nutrient 1	-25.92%	-29.60%	≈ 0.17
Nutrient 2	-10.74%	-17.36%	≈ 0.76

Table 2: Diet outcomes per group (after two weeks): we report participants average improvement in terms of distance from dietary goals (for calories and the nutrients that were mentioned in the report). For distance from goal, a decrease is considered and improvement.

each word on a 5-points scale, based on what extent they felt that way during the past week. An example of the questionnaire can be seen in Figure 4. PANAS generates a pair of independent scores: Positive Affect (PA) and Negative Affect (NA). Each score refers to what degree the participant experienced positive (for PA) or negative (for NA) emotions. PANAS improvement is expressed as an increase in PA, a decrease in NA or both. Participants were given PANAS before the experiment and at the end of each week, and always before report delivery to avoid any influence. We note this implies that, at the end of the first week, neither the report or control group had seen a report when filling out the form. We chose PANAS as a measuring tool because its scores are generalised across multiple aspects of the affective state. Both scores include the cumulative contribution a wide range of emotions. Other tools such as SPSS (Cohen et al., 1994) or HAM-A (Hamilton, 1959) would have been too focused on specific aspects. We also avoided combining multiple tools as this could have been too tiring for participants, leading to inaccurate results. Finally, at the end of the experiment, participants were asked to evaluate the report by scoring eight Likert-7 questions that can be seen in Figure 6. Participants were also given the chance to express an open comment about the system. We let participants from the control group read one single report at the end of the experiment to let them express their feedback as well.

Through this setup, we inspected the following research hypotheses:

Hypothesis 1 (H1): *Participants in report group improved their diet (in terms of caloric and nutritional intakes) more than control group.*

Hypothesis 2 (H2): *Participants in report group improved their positive affect score more than control group.*

Hypothesis 3 (H3): *Participants in report group improved their negative affect score more than control group.*

While H1 is comparable to classic diet-coaching evaluation, we introduce H2 and H3 as a novel investigation of the communicative potential of these tools, related to users' emotional state. For H1 we check the initial distance between MFP goals (for calories and nutrients) and user intake. Then, we verify if, at the end of week 1 and week 2, participants got closer to said goals. For nutrients, we consider the two most unbalanced ones (those that could be seen in the report). For H2 and H3 we monitor weekly PANAS scores (PA and NA) for each group. Since no group had access to reports when completing PANAS at the end of the first week, we use this value as a starting point. Then, we check differences at the end of week 2 and overall (from the start of the experiment).

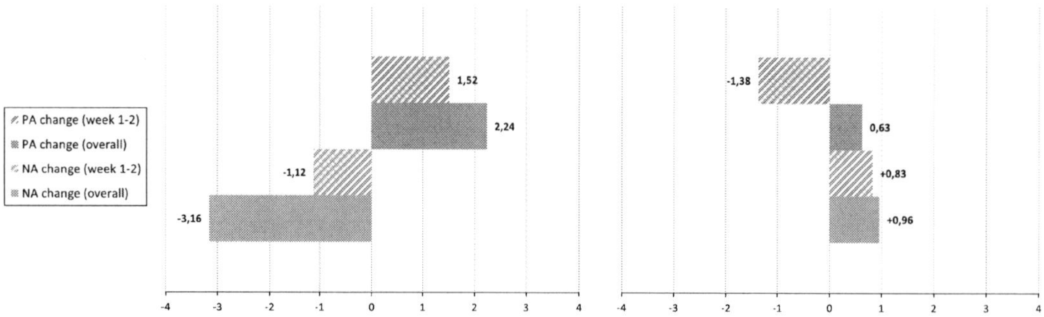

(a) **Report Group** (b) **Control group**

Figure 5: Results from PANAS analysis for both groups. We report Positive Affect (**PA**) and Negative Affect (**NA**) change from week 1 to week 2, and overall (from the start of the experiment). For PA higher is better; for NA lower is better.

5 Results and discussion

In terms of dietary outcomes, we obtained mixed results, but none of these were significant. In fact, the majority of participants improving calories and the first most unbalanced nutrient were in report group, but a chi-squared test revealed no significance (see Table 1). Both groups worsened their calories intake and we saw the biggest improvement in control group for nutrients (see Table 2). Again, a t-test revealed that none of these results is statistically significant. People in the report group were more likely to improve, while people in control group showed the biggest improvements, but a longer experiment is needed to assess whether reports (or their absence) played a role in this. With these results, we reject H1. However, it is safe to assume that reports didn't worsen the effectiveness of MyFitnessPal.

On the other hand, PANAS analysis gave us more interesting results. Initially, we verified through a t-test that the two groups shared similar initial PA (average difference = 0.1, $p = 0.96$) and NA (average difference = 1.7, $p = 0.51$). Then, we checked how scores changed for both groups. PA and NA were checked at week 1, week 2 and across the whole experiment. The report group showed bigger improvements, both in terms of PA and NA (see Figure 5).

The report group showed (through t-test and Sidak's p-value adjustment) a significantly bigger improvement for PA on the second week ($p = 0.04$) and for NA across the whole experiment ($p = 0.04$). Generally, the report group improved both scores more than the control group in any other situation, but only in these two cases the p-values were statistically significant. These results tell us that the report group tended to experience significantly:

1. More positive feelings during the second week
2. Fewer negative feelings across the whole experiment

than the control group. It is interesting to see PA significantly improving during second week. Since PANAS was administered before each report delivery, that was the first time that the report group could express their emotional state after reading a report.

The control group generally showed worse behaviour: PA greatly worsened during second week, while there was a slight improvement across the whole experiment (but much lower than the one experienced from the report group). NA consistently worsened in both cases. This tells us that the control group experienced a heavier emotional load during the experiment. We hypothesise that this is related to the cognitive load: the control group had to figure out how to interpret MFP charts and numerical data, while the report group was helped by the explanation provided in the generated text. Moreover, nutrients ranking helped participants from the report to focus on a limited amount of elements. In contrast, participants from the control group had to pay attention to calories and each nutrient. We also checked whether we could find some differences in the emotional state during the first week, when no group had access to the report. We observed a bigger PA improvement in control

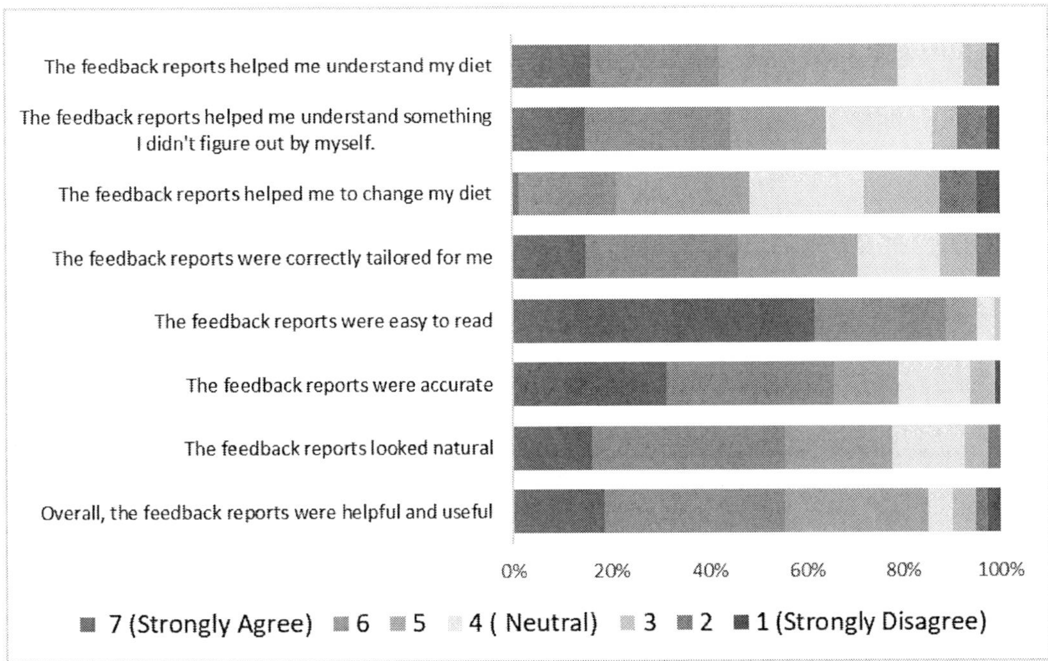

Figure 6: Overview of feedback from participants.

group ($\Delta = 2$) than in report group ($\Delta = 0.72$). The opposite happened for NA, with the report group improving it ($\Delta = -2.04$) and control group slightly worsening it ($\Delta = 0.13$). None of these was statistically significant. Considering the lack of reports, in this case, we can assume that the cognitive load was similar. Overall, we could see a significant improvement in emotional state for the report group (PA in the second week, NA overall). With these results we confirm H2 and H3.

Final feedback (Figure 6) was mostly positive. The lowest scores belong to the help in changing diet, which could also be related to the experiment duration. When given the chance to express a comment on the system, many participants asked for charts and graphical elements which could have improved understanding. This result aligns with previous research (Law et al., 2005; Molina et al., 2011; Gkatzia et al., 2017), suggesting that a combination of visual features and textual communication could be the most effective approach.

6 Conclusion

In this paper we evaluated the effects of augmented communication in diet-apps using Affective NLG, tailoring and persuasive communication techniques. Unlike previous work in evaluating diet-coaching systems, we did not look only at dietary outcomes. Since diet is influenced by psychological factors we introduced a novel evaluation by adopting a validated psychometric tool (PANAS). We inspected whether our reports could play a role in improving users' affective state.

Our hypotheses were confirmed, as we found that participants who read the report experienced more positive emotions and fewer negative ones. We also saw the opposite in most cases for the control group. Our work has shown that improved communication can reduce the impact of emotional load on dieting. Most importantly, we showed how important it is to consider the psychological component when designing, developing and evaluating communication systems, in diet-coaching and other domains. We could not see an effect on diet itself, which encourages us to run a longer trial (one month or more) in future, to further assess the effectiveness of our communication strategy. However, we ran just a basic assessment on the psychological side. We plan to expand our evaluation procedure by combining multiple tools and scales. As our previous work pointed out, stress is one particular factor that could be worth monitoring (Balloccu et al., 2020b), so this is one of the main directions we intend to follow. We also could not run any kind of ablation test. This leaves us with the conclusion that our approach did work, but without any insights on how different elements (affective NLG, persuasion or text tailoring) contributed.

Based on the feedback from users, more than just text is required to improve the system. We leave this as future work. Still feedback was largely positive with regards to textual features and comprehension. We note that the questions were not accompanied by rigorous definitions of "readability", "accuracy" and others. Users expressed feedback based on their own personal idea of these concepts and this raises questions regarding the reliability of the results. We consider the overall uniformity of ratings as an indicator that all participants had a "common" definition of the proposed concepts. Still this uncertainty contributes to a well-known problem in human evaluation (Howcroft et al., 2020), so we commit to more rigorous and uniform metric definitions in future.

7 Ethical considerations

This section sums up the procedure we adopted to ensure the ethical compliance of our experiment.

7.1 Preliminary review

Before starting the experiment, procedure and materials were carefully reviewed by the University of Aberdeen Ethics Board. Our experiment proposal was accepted without major revisions.

7.2 Recruitment

Participants were recruited through physical interaction on campus (by flyer distribution), department mailing list or social media public posts. No recruitment qualification was specified, beside the lack of health conditions that are known to affect individuals diet. This includes pregnancy, suffering from eating disorders or psychological treatments. This was done since our system has been developed to work in "standard" situations, while the aforementioned cases would have pose high risks for participants. Participants were showed a consent form containing all the information regarding the experiment procedure. All participants had to confirm their acceptance of these conditions (through check-boxes and signature) in order to proceed with the experiment. Participants were given an email contact in case of problems during the experiment.

7.3 Pay and workload

Each participants received £20 (or 20€ for participants outside of UK) at the end of the experiment, as a token of gratitude for their contribution. Access to the token of gratitude was bound to the compliance of the following condition:

1. To complete the experiment (that is, using MFP for two weeks; giving the final feedback)

2. To provide, to the best of their capabilities, the most complete and accurate food diaries they could.

Requirement 1) also included PANAS forms for those participants who agreed to do so. For 2) participants were supervised and given support about meal logging and eventual missing entries. Participants were also informed of the possibility of abandoning the experiment (up to the point of data analysis), which would result in exclusion from receiving the token of gratitude.

7.4 Data protection and storage

A MFP account for each participant was generated through temporary email that was in no way linked to their identity. Following the experiment conclusion, all accounts have been blocked. Data have been safely stored and anonymised.

References

Ashkan Afshin, Patrick John Sur, Kairsten A Fay, Leslie Cornaby, Giannina Ferrara, Joseph S Salama, Erin C Mullany, Kalkidan Hassen Abate, Cristiana Abbafati, Zegeye Abebe, et al. 2019. Health effects of dietary risks in 195 countries, 1990–2017: a systematic analysis for the global burden of disease study 2017. *The Lancet*, 393(10184):1958–1972.

Anju Aggarwal, Pablo Monsivais, Andrea J Cook, and Adam Drewnowski. 2011. Does diet cost mediate the relation between socioeconomic position and diet quality? *European journal of clinical nutrition*, 65(9):1059–1066.

Luca Anselma, Simone Donetti, Alessandro Mazzei, and Andrea Pirone. 2018. CheckYourMeal!: diet management with NLG. In *Proceedings of the Workshop on Intelligent Interactive Systems and Language Generation (2IS&NLG)*, pages 45–47, Tilburg, the Netherlands. Association for Computational Linguistics.

Luca Anselma and Alessandro Mazzei. 2020. Building a persuasive virtual dietitian. In *Informatics*, volume 7, page 27. Multidisciplinary Digital Publishing Institute.

O Aromatario, A Van Hoye, A Vuillemin, A-M Foucaut, C Crozet, J Pommier, and L Cambon. 2019. How do mobile health applications support behaviour changes? a scoping review of mobile health applications relating to physical activity and eating behaviours. *Public health*, 175:8–18.

Simone Balloccu, Steffen Pauws, and Ehud Reiter. 2020a. A nlg framework for user tailoring and profiling in healthcare. In *SmartPhil@ IUI*, pages 13–32.

Simone Balloccu, Ehud Reiter, Matteo G Collu, Federico Sanna, Manuela Sanguinetti, and Maurizio Atzori. 2021. Unaddressed challenges in persuasive dieting chatbots. In *Adjunct Proceedings of the 29th ACM Conference on User Modeling, Adaptation and Personalization*, pages 392–395.

Simone Balloccu, Ehud Reiter, Alexandra Johnstone, and Claire Fyfe. 2020b. How are you? introducing stress-based text tailoring. In *Proceedings of the Workshop on Intelligent Information Processing and Natural Language Generation*, pages 62–70, Santiago de Compostela, Spain. Association for Computational Lingustics.

Laurel Barosh, Sharon Friel, Katrin Engelhardt, and Lilian Chan. 2014. The cost of a healthy and sustainable diet–who can afford it? *Australian and New Zealand journal of public health*, 38(1):7–12.

Sheldon Cohen, Tom Kamarck, Robin Mermelstein, et al. 1994. Perceived stress scale. *Measuring stress: A guide for health and social scientists*, 10(2):1–2.

Kathleen Corcoran. 2014. Fooducate.

Fiorella de Rosis and Floriana Grasso. 2000. *Affective Natural Language Generation*, pages 204–218. Springer Berlin Heidelberg, Berlin, Heidelberg.

Ivan Donadello, Mauro Dragoni, and Claudio Eccher. 2019. Persuasive explanation of reasoning inferences on dietary data. In *PROFILES/SEMEX@ ISWC*.

Sebastian Duerr and Peter A Gloor. 2021. Persuasive natural language generation–a literature review. *arXiv preprint arXiv:2101.05786*.

Elizabeth V Eikey. 2021. Effects of diet and fitness apps on eating disorder behaviours: qualitative study. *BJPsych Open*, 7(5).

Daniel Evans. 2017. Myfitnesspal. *British Journal of Sports Medicine*, 51(14):1101–1102.

Giannina Ferrara, Jenna Kim, Shuhao Lin, Jenna Hua, and Edmund Seto. 2019. A focused review of smartphone diet-tracking apps: usability, functionality, coherence with behavior change theory, and comparative validity of nutrient intake and energy estimates. *JMIR mHealth and uHealth*, 7(5):e9232.

Gregory Finley, Erik Edwards, Amanda Robinson, Michael Brenndoerfer, Najmeh Sadoughi, James Fone, Nico Axtmann, Mark Miller, and David Suendermann-Oeft. 2018. An automated medical scribe for documenting clinical encounters. In *Proceedings of the 2018 Conference of the North American Chapter of the Association for Computational Linguistics: Demonstrations*, pages 11–15, New Orleans, Louisiana. Association for Computational Linguistics.

Kathleen Kara Fitzpatrick, Alison Darcy, and Molly Vierhile. 2017. Delivering cognitive behavior therapy to young adults with symptoms of depression and anxiety using a fully automated conversational agent (woebot): a randomized controlled trial. *JMIR mental health*, 4(2):e7785.

Mackenzie Fong, Ang Li, Andrew J Hill, Michelle Cunich, Michael R Skilton, Claire D Madigan, and Ian D Caterson. 2019. Mood and appetite: Their relationship with discretionary and total daily energy intake. *Physiology & behavior*, 207:122–131.

Dimitra Gkatzia, Oliver Lemon, and Verena Rieser. 2017. Data-to-text generation improves decision-making under uncertainty. *IEEE Computational Intelligence Magazine*, 12(3):10–17.

Neil F. Gordon, Richard D. Salmon, Brenda S. Wright, George C. Faircloth, Kevin S. Reid, and Terri L. Gordon. 2017. Clinical effectiveness of lifestyle health coaching: Case study of an evidence-based program. *American Journal of Lifestyle Medicine*, 11(2):153–166.

Marco Guerini, Oliviero Stock, Massimo Zancanaro, Daniel J O'Keefe, Irene Mazzotta, Fiorella de Rosis, Isabella Poggi, Meiyii Y Lim, and Ruth Aylett. 2011. Approaches to verbal persuasion in intelligent user interfaces. In *Emotion-Oriented Systems*, pages 559–584. Springer.

Andreas Håkansson. 2015. Has it become increasingly expensive to follow a nutritious diet? insights from a new price index for nutritious diets in sweden 1980–2012. *Food & Nutrition Research*, 59(1):26932.

M Hamilton. 1959. Hamilton anxiety scale. *Group*, 1(4):10–1037.

Saar Hommes, Chris van der Lee, Felix Clouth, Jeroen Vermunt, Xander Verbeek, and Emiel Krahmer. 2019. A personalized data-to-text support tool for cancer patients. In *Proceedings of the 12th International Conference on Natural Language Generation*, pages 443–452, Tokyo, Japan. Association for Computational Linguistics.

David M. Howcroft, Anya Belz, Miruna-Adriana Clinciu, Dimitra Gkatzia, Sadid A. Hasan, Saad Mahamood, Simon Mille, Emiel van Miltenburg, Sashank Santhanam, and Verena Rieser. 2020. Twenty years of confusion in human evaluation: NLG needs evaluation sheets and standardised definitions. In *Proceedings of the 13th International Conference on Natural Language Generation*, pages 169–182, Dublin, Ireland. Association for Computational Linguistics.

Kelly L Klump, Shannon M O'Connor, Britny A Hildebrandt, Pamela K Keel, Michael Neale, Cheryl L Sisk, Steven Boker, and S Alexandra Burt. 2016.

Differential effects of estrogen and progesterone on genetic and environmental risk for emotional eating in women. *Clinical Psychological Science*, 4(5):895–908.

Paul G Koenders and Tatjana van Strien. 2011. Emotional eating, rather than lifestyle behavior, drives weight gain in a prospective study in 1562 employees. *Journal of Occupational and Environmental Medicine*, 53(11):1287–1293.

Matthew W Kreuter and Ricardo J Wray. 2003. Tailored and targeted health communication: strategies for enhancing information relevance. *American journal of health behavior*, 27(1):S227–S232.

Anna S Law, Yvonne Freer, Jim Hunter, Robert H Logie, Neil McIntosh, and John Quinn. 2005. A comparison of graphical and textual presentations of time series data to support medical decision making in the neonatal intensive care unit. *Journal of clinical monitoring and computing*, 19(3):183–194.

H Erin Lee and Jaehee Cho. 2017. What motivates users to continue using diet and fitness apps? application of the uses and gratifications approach. *Health communication*, 32(12):1445–1453.

Mikyung Lee, Hyeonkyeong Lee, Youlim Kim, Junghee Kim, Mikyeong Cho, Jaeun Jang, and Hyoeun Jang. 2018. Mobile app-based health promotion programs: a systematic review of the literature. *International journal of environmental research and public health*, 15(12):2838.

Jessica R. L. Lieffers, José F. Arocha, Kelly Anne Grindrod, and Rhona M. Hanning. 2018. Experiences and perceptions of adults accessing publicly available nutrition behavior-change mobile apps for weight management. *Journal of the Academy of Nutrition and Dietetics*, 118 2:229–239.e3.

Nathalie Rose Lim-Cheng, Gabriel Isidro G Fabia, Marco Emil G Quebral, and Miguelito T Yu. 2014. Shed: An online diet counselling system. In *DLSU research congress*, pages 1–7.

Kien Hoa Ly, Ann-Marie Ly, and Gerhard Andersson. 2017. A fully automated conversational agent for promoting mental well-being: A pilot rct using mixed methods. *Internet interventions*, 10:39–46.

Michael Macht and Gwenda Simons. 2011. https://doi.org/10.1016/j.appet.2011.10.005. In *Emotion regulation and well-being*, pages 281–295. Springer.

Saad Mahamood and Ehud Reiter. 2011. Generating affective natural language for parents of neonatal infants. In *Proceedings of the 13th European Workshop on Natural Language Generation*, pages 12–21.

Rebecca McCarroll, Helen Eyles, and Cliona Ni Mhurchu. 2017. Effectiveness of mobile health (mhealth) interventions for promoting healthy eating in adults: A systematic review. *Preventive Medicine*, 105:156–168.

Martin Molina, Amanda Stent, and Enrique Parodi. 2011. Generating automated news to explain the meaning of sensor data. In *International Symposium on Intelligent Data Analysis*, pages 282–293. Springer.

Michelle A Morris, Claire Hulme, Graham P Clarke, Kimberley L Edwards, and Janet E Cade. 2014. What is the cost of a healthy diet? using diet data from the uk women's cohort study. *Journal of Epidemiology & Community Health*, 68(11):1043–1049.

Prasanth Murali, Ha Trinh, Lazlo Ring, and Timothy Bickmore. 2021. A friendly face in the crowd: Reducing public speaking anxiety with an emotional support agent in the audience. In *Proceedings of the 21st ACM International Conference on Intelligent Virtual Agents*, pages 156–163.

Seth M Noar, Christina N Benac, and Melissa S Harris. 2007. Does tailoring matter? meta-analytic review of tailored print health behavior change interventions. *Psychological bulletin*, 133(4):673.

Rita Orji and Karyn Moffatt. 2018. Persuasive technology for health and wellness: State-of-the-art and emerging trends. *Health informatics journal*, 24(1):66–91.

Steffen Pauws, Albert Gatt, Emiel Krahmer, and Ehud Reiter. 2019. Making effective use of healthcare data using data-to-text technology. In *Data Science for Healthcare*, pages 119–145. Springer.

Paul Piwek. 2002. An annotated bibliography of affective natural language generation. *Information Technology Research Institute (ITRI), University of Brighton, ITRI-02-02*.

Judith J Prochaska, Erin A Vogel, Amy Chieng, Matthew Kendra, Michael Baiocchi, Sarah Pajarito, and Athena Robinson. 2021. A therapeutic relational agent for reducing problematic substance use (woebot): development and usability study. *Journal of Medical Internet Research*, 23(3):e24850.

Jo-Anne Puddephatt, Gregory S Keenan, Amy Fielden, Danielle L Reaves, Jason CG Halford, and Charlotte A Hardman. 2020. 'eating to survive': A qualitative analysis of factors influencing food choice and eating behaviour in a food-insecure population. *Appetite*, 147:104547.

Ehud Reiter, Roma Robertson, and Liesl M Osman. 2003. Lessons from a failure: Generating tailored smoking cessation letters. *Artificial Intelligence*, 144(1-2):41–58.

Friedrich Riffer, Manuel Sprung, Hannah Münch, Elmar Kaiser, Lore Streibl, Kathrin Heneis, and Alexandra Kautzky-Willer. 2019. Relationship between psychological stress and metabolism in morbidly obese individuals. *Wiener klinische Wochenschrift*, pages 1–11.

Hannes Ritschel, Kathrin Janowski, Andreas Seiderer, and Elisabeth André. 2019. Towards a robotic dietitian with adaptive linguistic style.

Julie A. Schmittdiel, Sara R. Adams, Nancy Goler, Rashel S. Sanna, Mindy Boccio, David J. Bellamy, Susan D. Brown, Romain S. Neugebauer, and Assiamira Ferrara. 2017. The impact of telephonic wellness coaching on weight loss: A "natural experiments for translation in diabetes (next-d)" study. *Obesity*, 25(2):352–356.

Habiba Shabir, Matthew D'Costa, Zain Mohiaddin, Zaeem Moti, Hamza Rashid, Daria Sadowska, Benyamin Alam, and Benita Cox. 2022. The barriers and facilitators to the use of lifestyle apps: A systematic review of qualitative studies. *European journal of investigation in health, psychology and education*, 12(2):144–165.

A-M Teeriniemi, T Salonurmi, T Jokelainen, H Vähänikkilä, T Alahäivälä, P Karppinen, H Enwald, M-L Huotari, J Laitinen, H Oinas-Kukkonen, et al. 2018. A randomized clinical trial of the effectiveness of a web-based health behaviour change support system and group lifestyle counselling on body weight loss in overweight and obese subjects: 2-year outcomes. *Journal of internal medicine*, 284(5):534–545.

Susan J Torres and Caryl A Nowson. 2007. Relationship between stress, eating behavior, and obesity. *Nutrition*, 23(11-12):887–894.

Matthew S Tredrea, Vincent J Dalbo, and Aaron T Scanlan. 2017. Lifesum: easy and effective dietary and activity monitoring. *British Journal of Sports Medicine*, 51(13):1042–1043.

Brent Van Dorsten and Emily M Lindley. 2008. Cognitive and behavioral approaches in the treatment of obesity. *Endocrinology and metabolism clinics of North America*, 37(4):905–922.

Tatjana Van Strien, C Peter Herman, Doeschka J Anschutz, Rutger CME Engels, and Carolina de Weerth. 2012. Moderation of distress-induced eating by emotional eating scores. *Appetite*, 58(1):277–284.

Maria F Vasiloglou, Stergios Christodoulidis, Emilie Reber, Thomai Stathopoulou, Ya Lu, Zeno Stanga, and Stavroula Mougiakakou. 2020. What healthcare professionals think of "nutrition & diet" apps: An international survey. *Nutrients*, 12(8):2214.

Qing Wang, Bjørg Egelandsdal, Gro V Amdam, Valerie L Almli, and Marije Oostindjer. 2016. Diet and physical activity apps: perceived effectiveness by app users. *JMIR mHealth and uHealth*, 4(2):e33.

David Watson, Lee Anna Clark, and Auke Tellegen. 1988. Development and validation of brief measures of positive and negative affect: the panas scales. *Journal of personality and social psychology*, 54(6):1063.

Kirsten Whitehead and Tracey Parkin. 2022. Uk dietitians' views on communication skills for behaviour change: A 10 year follow-up survey. *Journal of Human Nutrition and Dietetics*, 35(1):112–123.

Niv Zmora and Eran Elinav. 2021. Harnessing smartphones to personalize nutrition in a time of global pandemic. *Nutrients*, 13(2):422.

The Human Evaluation Datasheet: A Template for Recording Details of Human Evaluation Experiments in NLP

Anastasia Shimorina
Orange
Lannion, France
anastasia.shimorina@orange.com

Anya Belz
ADAPT Research Centre, DCU, Ireland
University of Aberdeen, UK
anya.belz@adaptcentre.ie

Abstract

This paper presents the Human Evaluation Datasheet (HEDS), a template for recording the details of individual human evaluation experiments in Natural Language Processing (NLP), and reports on first experience of researchers using HEDS sheets in practice. Originally taking inspiration from seminal papers by Bender and Friedman (2018), Mitchell et al. (2019), and Gebru et al. (2020), HEDS facilitates the recording of properties of human evaluations in sufficient detail, and with sufficient standardisation, to support comparability, meta-evaluation, and reproducibility assessments for human evaluations. These are crucial for scientifically principled evaluation, but the overhead of completing a detailed datasheet is substantial, and we discuss possible ways of addressing this and other issues observed in practice.

1 Introduction

Human evaluation plays a special role in NLP and NLG in particular as it is generally seen as the most reliable form of evaluation (Reiter and Belz, 2009; Novikova et al., 2017; Reiter, 2018). Comparability and reproducibility of evaluations (both human and automatic) are gaining in recognition and importance across NLP, as the field develops towards scientific maturity. For both reasons, it is of concern that there continues to be little consensus or standard practice across all aspects of human evaluation in NLP. Other efforts are aimed at standardisation of evaluation methods and quality criteria (van der Lee et al., 2021; Gehrmann et al., 2021). With the Human Evaluation Datasheet (HEDS) we wish to provide simply a way of recording properties of human evaluations in a standard hence comparable form (regardless of the level of standardisation of the deployed methods themselves).

HEDS is a template for recording properties of single human evaluation experiments. It uses multiple-choice questions where possible, for increased standardisation and automatic comparability. HEDS is designed to be generally applicable to human evaluations across NLP. It consists of 29 experiment-level questions plus 17 for each quality criterion, available as an online form which also contains explanations and guidance for completing it. The idea is that researchers use completed forms for preregistration of experiments and for archiving their details, to aid in comparability of evaluations across experiments, meta-evaluation of evaluation methods, and reproducibility of results.

Our intention is that HEDS should be suitable for all human evaluation experiments in NLP. Human evaluations in NLP typically get participants to assess system outputs or to interact with systems, but the HEDS sheet also accommodates what we call 'human-authored stand-ins' below, i.e. manually created 'system outputs' (e.g. in a wizard-of-oz scenario or when reference outputs are included in an evaluation) evaluated in a way that can at least in principle be used to evaluate actual system outputs.

The sheet is completed for a *single human evaluation experiment* by which we mean an experiment that evaluates a single set of directly comparable systems in a single experimental design, but may assess multiple quality criteria. This is the intended meaning when we refer to 'the evaluation experiment' in questions below.

2 Relationship to Existing Work

A first version of the datasheet (HEDS 1.0) was reported via a non-archival pre-print (Shimorina and Belz, 2021). In this paper, we present HEDS in its next revision (v2.0) alongside a summary of what we learnt from observing the datasheet being used in practice since its first publication. We focus discussion in this paper on Questions 4.1.1–4.2.3 (Sections 5 and 6) relating to quality criteria and their operationalisation: these caused some difficulty to users in practice, and were revised more substantively than other questions. The full

Proceedings of the 2nd Workshop on Human Evaluation of NLP Systems (HumEval), pages 54 - 75
May 27, 2022 ©2022 Association for Computational Linguistics

datasheet is provided in the appendix for reference.

HEDS directly benefited from several papers and resources. Questions 2.1–2.5 relating to evaluated system, and 4.3.1–4.3.8 relating to response elicitation, are based on Howcroft et al. (2020), with some significant changes. Questions 4.1.1–4.2.3 relating to quality criteria, and some of the questions about system outputs, evaluators, and experimental design (3.1.1–3.2.3, 4.3.5, 4.3.6, 4.3.9–4.3.11) are based on Belz et al. (2020). HEDS was also informed by van der Lee et al. (2019, 2021) and by Gehrmann et al. (2021)'s[1] data card guide.

More generally, the original inspiration for creating a 'datasheet' for describing human evaluation experiments of course comes from seminal papers by Bender and Friedman (2018), Mitchell et al. (2019) and Gebru et al. (2020).

HEDS is related to other efforts in the NLP community related to reproducibility and ethics. Different NLP checklists have been introduced in recent years, e.g. the Reproducibility Checklist (Dodge et al., 2019) adopted by many conferences, and the ACL Rolling Review's Responsible NLP checklist.[2] These checklists mainly deal with the recreatability of computational experiments, details of used datasets and models, and risks and limitations of research studies and applications. The focus of HEDS is recording properties of human evaluation experiments, which are not covered by the above checklists.

3 HEDS Structure and Resources

The Human Evaluation Datasheet package consists of the following three resources:

1. The HEDS template: available at `https://forms.gle/MgWiKVu7i5UHeMNQ9`;
2. Description and completion guidance: this document;
3. Scripts for automatically converting between the HEDS online form and alternative Markdown and LaTeX template formats: available at `https://github.com/Shimorina/human-evaluation-datasheet`.

A collection of completed HEDS datasheets is also available at the HEDS GitHub repository.

The full HEDS sheet can be found in Appendix A. In its template form as well as in this paper, HEDS is divided into five sections, addressing topics and containing questions as follows:

1. Paper and Resources: HEDS Questions 1.1–1.3, listed in Appendix Section A.1;
2. Evaluated System: HEDS Questions 2.1–2.5, Section A.2;
3. Output Sample, Evaluators and Experimental Design: HEDS Questions 3.1.1–3.3.8, Section A.3;
4. Quality Criteria: HEDS Questions 4.1.1–4.3.11, listed in Section 6 of the paper and, for completeness also in Section A.4 in the Appendix—this section is completed separately for each quality criterion used as part of the same evaluation experiment;
5. Ethics: HEDS Questions 5.1–5.4, Section A.5.

Section A.1 records bibliographic information: link to the paper reporting the evaluation experiment, shared evaluation resources (e.g., a webpage, repository), contact author details.

Section A.2 describes information about outputs that are evaluated in the evaluation experiment and how they were produced. For example, it records the task performed by the system, types of system input and output, input and output language.

Section A.3 collects information about the evaluated sample (size, selection process, statistical power), the evaluators participating in the experiment, and experimental design (collection method, quality assurance, conditions for evaluators).

Section A.4 captures information about quality criteria assessed in the human evaluation experiment. We discuss this section in the main body of the paper in Section 6.

Section A.5 relates to ethical aspects of the evaluation: approval by ethics committees, and collection of personal and other sensitive data.

4 Insights from Use of HEDS 1.0 in Practice

HEDS 1.0 was used in the 2021 ReproGen Shared Task on Reproducibility of Evaluations in NLG[3] (Belz et al., 2021). All shared task participants, as well as the authors of the original papers up for

[1] `https://gem-benchmark.com/data_cards/guide`

[2] `https://aclrollingreview.org/responsibleNLPresearch/`

[3] `https://reprogen.github.io/2021/`

reproduction in Track A, completed the HEDS 1.0 form. Moreover, the HEDS 1.0 sheet was completed another three times outside of the shared task context.

General feedback from users was that the HEDS 1.0 sheet was for the most part straightforward to complete, but that completion still represented a considerable overhead. This is the general conundrum of initiatives such as HEDS: what is the incentive for researchers to complete the sheet when (i) it is merely good scientific hygiene rather than a component of the work without which it could not be carried out, and (ii) it mainly benefits follow on research rather than the paper it is completed for? Unless it is a requirement for submission to a particular event, or it is generally expected practice, the tendency may always be to avoid the overhead. To address this, we are in the process of preparing a shorter version of the sheet, with the aim of cutting the effort involved in half, for use in contexts where less detail is acceptable.

We also observed that there were a number of questions in HEDS 1.0 that users found difficult to complete for different reasons. Question 3.1.3 (*What is the statistical power of the sample size?*) posed difficulties partly because power calculations are a relatively new tool in NLP. We address this in this paper with additional information, and in the future by providing a new resource to support calculation.

A more fundamental issue was caused by how HEDS 1.0 captured information about quality criteria, and the use of duplicate subsections for multiple quality criteria. We believe that this was due largely to insufficient context, motivation and explanation being provided in the documentation and form about quality criteria and their properties, and we seek to provide the latter in version 2.0 (in this paper as well as in the form).

Using HEDS as part of the ReproGen shared task demonstrated the utility of having information about original studies and reproduction studies available in the same standard format: it meant it was straightforward for organisers to capture and analyse the similarities and differences between original and reproduction studies, e.g. to identify sources of variation in results for the results report (Belz et al., 2021). It also gave participants (authors of reproduction papers) a tool with which to verify whether their reproduction study of human evaluation was the same as the original study in all important respects, at a fine-grained level of detail.

5 Concepts Underlying Quality Criterion Questions 4.1.1–4.3.11 in HEDS

The overall aim of human evaluations in NLP is generally to assess some aspect of the quality of a system or component. Researchers use terms such as *Fluency* and *Informativeness* to refer to different aspects of quality. However, as discussed in detail by Howcroft et al. (2020) and Belz et al. (2020), just because two studies used the same term (e.g. Fluency) it does not mean they evaluated the same aspect of quality. In order to establish what was evaluated, we need to know the term and definition used, but also how it was 'operationalised,' i.e. what was presented to evaluators and how their assessments were recorded.

This is why HEDS, picking up from the two publications above, records properties relating to evaluation criteria and their operationalisation separately for each quality criterion. Because within the same experiment different quality criteria are often assessed in similar ways (e.g. using the same rating instrument), this can result in some repetition when completing a HEDS sheet, albeit unfortunately not in predictable ways.

Following Belz et al. (2020), properties relating to quality criteria and their operationalisation in HEDS fall into three groups: *quality criteria*, *evaluation mode*, and *experimental design*. A **quality criterion** is a criterion in terms of which the quality of system outputs is assessed, and is in itself entirely agnostic about how it is evaluated. **Evaluation modes** are properties that need to be specified to turn a quality criterion into an **evaluation measure** that can be implemented, and are orthogonal to quality criteria, i.e. any given quality criterion can be combined with any mode. **Experimental design** is the full specification of how to obtain a quantitative or qualitative *response value* for a given evaluation measure, yielding a fully specified **evaluation method**. In sum:

- Quality criterion + evaluation mode = evaluation measure;
- Evaluation measure + experimental design = evaluation method.

Each of the above concepts is covered by one or more questions in HEDS. Three HEDS questions capture properties of *quality criteria* in terms of (i) what type of quality is being assessed (Question 4.1.1); (ii) what aspect of the system output is being assessed (Question 4.1.2); and (iii) whether system outputs are assessed in their own right or with reference to some system-internal or system-external frame of reference (Question 4.1.3).

Three questions capture *evaluation mode*: (i) subjective vs. objective (Question 4.2.1), (ii) absolute vs. relative (Question 4.2.2), and (iii) intrinsic vs. extrinsic (Question 4.2.3). *Experimental design* is covered by Questions 4.3.1–11 (operationalisation of quality criteria assessment), and Questions 3.* (other aspects).

We present, explain and discuss each of the above questions in the following section.

6 HEDS Questions about Properties of Quality Criteria and their Operationalisation

In this section, we present, verbatim, the questions referred to in the last section relating to properties of quality criteria and their operationalisation. All questions in this section need to be completed once for each quality criterion assessed in the single evaluation experiment that a HEDS sheet is being completed for. E.g. if an evaluation assesses *Fluency* and *Grammaticality*, then the questions below need to be filled in, separately, for each.

We refer below to 'output' as shorthand for that which is being assessed by evaluators. The latter is most often some form of language output assessed at different lengths (phrase, sentence, document), but it can also be a more complete form of system behaviour (e.g. language displayed along with audio and/or visual elements, on interfaces, etc.). It is in this more general sense that we intend the term 'output' to be understood in the present context.

6.1 Quality criterion properties (Questions 4.1.1–4.1.3)

Questions 4.1.1–4.1.3 capture the aspect of quality that is assessed by a given quality criterion, in terms of three orthogonal properties. They help determine whether or not the same aspect of quality is being evaluated in different evaluation experiments. The three properties characterise quality criteria in terms of (i) what type of quality is being assessed; (ii) what aspect of the system output is being assessed; and (iii) whether system outputs are assessed in their own right or with reference to some system-internal or system-external frame of reference. For full explanations see Belz et al. (2020).

Note that if NLP had a generally accepted standard set of quality criteria with common names, definitions and operationalisations, then most of the questions in this section could be replaced by a much smaller set capturing criterion name and operationalising techniques. The reason there are so many questions is precisely because we do not have such a standard nomenclature.

Question 4.1.1: What type of quality is assessed by the quality criterion?

Multiple-choice options (select one):

- ○ ***Correctness***: Select this option if it is possible to state, generally for all outputs, the conditions under which outputs are maximally correct (hence of maximal quality). E.g. for *Grammaticality*,[4] outputs are (maximally) correct if they contain no grammatical errors; for *Semantic Completeness*, outputs are correct if they express all the content in the input.
- ○ ***Goodness***: Select this option if, in contrast to correctness criteria, there is no single, general mechanism for deciding when outputs are maximally good, only for deciding for any two outputs which is better and which is worse. E.g. for *Fluency*, even if outputs contain no disfluencies, there may be other ways in which any given output could be more fluent.
- ○ ***Feature***: Choose this option if, in terms of property X captured by the criterion, outputs are not generally better if they are more X, but instead, depending on evaluation context, more X may be either better or worse. E.g. for *Specificity*, outputs can be more specific or less specific, but it's not the case that outputs are, in the general case, better when they are more specific.

Question 4.1.2: Which aspect of system outputs is assessed by the quality criterion?

Multiple-choice options (select one):

[4] We take all examples of quality criteria from published reports of evaluations, via the annotated database compiled by Howcroft et al. (2020).

- *Form of output*: Choose this option if the criterion assesses the form of outputs alone, e.g. *Grammaticality* is only about the form, a sentence can be grammatical yet be wrong or nonsensical in terms of content.
- *Content of output*: Select this option if the criterion assesses the content/meaning of the output alone, e.g. *Meaning Preservation* only assesses content; two sentences can be considered to have the same meaning, but differ in form.
- *Both form and content of output*: Choose this option if the criterion assesses outputs as a whole, not just form or just content. E.g. *Coherence* is a property of outputs as a whole, either form or meaning can detract from it. Inherently extrinsic criteria such as *Usefulness* or *Task Completion* also fall in this category.

Question 4.1.3: Is each output assessed for quality in its own right, or with reference to a system-internal or external frame of reference?

Multiple-choice options (select one):

- *Quality of output in its own right*: Select this option if output quality is assessed without referring to anything other than the output itself, i.e. no system-internal or external frame of reference. E.g. *Poeticness* is assessed by considering (just) the output and how poetic it is.
- *Quality of output relative to the input*: Choose this option if output quality is assessed relative to the input. E.g. *Answerability* is the degree to which the output question can be answered from information in the input.
- *Quality of output relative to a system-external frame of reference*: Choose this option if output quality is assessed with reference to system-external information, such as a knowledge base, a person's individual writing style, or the performance of an embedding system. E.g. *Factual Accuracy* assesses outputs relative to a source of real-world knowledge.

6.2 Evaluation mode properties (Questions 4.2.1–4.2.3)

Questions 4.2.1–4.2.3 record properties that are orthogonal to quality criteria (covered by questions in the preceding section), i.e. any given quality criterion can in principle be combined with any of the modes (although some combinations are more common than others).

Question 4.2.1: Does an individual assessment involve an objective or a subjective judgment?

Multiple-choice options (select one):

- *Objective*: Choose this option if the evaluation uses objective assessment, e.g. any automatically counted or otherwise quantified measurements such as mouse-clicks, occurrences in text, etc. Repeated assessments of the same output with an objective-mode evaluation method always yield the same score/result.
- *Subjective*: Choose this option in all other cases. Subjective assessments involve ratings, opinions and preferences by evaluators. Some criteria lend themselves more readily to subjective assessments, e.g. *Friendliness* of a conversational agent, but an objective measure e.g. based on lexical markers is also conceivable.

Question 4.2.2: Are outputs assessed in absolute or relative terms?

Multiple-choice options (select one):

- *Absolute*: Select this option if evaluators are shown outputs from a single system during each individual assessment.
- *Relative*: Choose this option if evaluators are shown outputs from multiple systems at the same time during assessments, typically ranking or preference-judging them.

Question 4.2.3: Is the evaluation intrinsic or extrinsic?

Multiple-choice options (select one):

- *Intrinsic*: Choose this option if quality of outputs is assessed *without* considering their *effect* on something external to the system, e.g. the performance of an embedding system or of a user at a task.

○ ***Extrinsic***: Choose this option if quality of outputs is assessed in terms of their *effect* on something external to the system such as the performance of an embedding system or of a user at a task.

6.3 Response elicitation (Questions 4.3.1–4.3.11)

The questions in this section concern response elicitation, by which we mean how the ratings or other measurements that represent assessments for the quality criterion in question are obtained, covering what is presented to evaluators, how they select response and via what type of tool, etc. The eleven questions (4.3.1–4.3.11) are based on the information annotated in the large scale survey of human evaluation methods in NLG by Howcroft et al. (2020).

Question 4.3.1: What do you call the quality criterion in explanations/interfaces to evaluators? Enter 'N/A' if criterion not named.

What to enter in the text box: the name you use to refer to the quality criterion in explanations and/or interfaces created for evaluators. Examples of quality criterion names include Fluency, Clarity, Meaning Preservation. If no name is used, state 'N/A'.

Question 4.3.2: What definition do you give for the quality criterion in explanations/interfaces to evaluators? Enter 'N/A' if no definition given.

What to enter in the text box: Copy and past the verbatim definition you give to evaluators to explain the quality criterion they're assessing. If you don't explicitly call it a definition, enter the nearest thing to a definition you give them. If you don't give any definition, state 'N/A'.

Question 4.3.3: Size of scale or other rating instrument (i.e. how many different possible values there are). Answer should be an integer or 'continuous' (if it's not possible to state how many possible responses there are). Enter 'N/A' if there is no rating instrument.

What to enter in the text box: The number of different response values for this quality criterion. E.g. for a 5-point Likert scale, the size to enter is 5. For two-way forced-choice preference judgments, it is 2; if there's also a no-preference option, enter 3. For a slider that is mapped to 100 different values for the purpose of recording assessments, the size to enter is 100. If no rating instrument is used (e.g. when evaluation gathers post-edits or qualitative feedback only), enter 'N/A'.

Question 4.3.4: List or range of possible values of the scale or other rating instrument. Enter 'N/A', if there is no rating instrument.

What to enter in the text box: list, or give the range of, the possible values of the rating instrument. The list or range should be of the size specified in Question 4.3.3. If there are too many to list, use a range. E.g. for two-way forced-choice preference judgments, the list entered might be *A better, B better*; if there's also a no-preference option, the list might be *A better, B better, neither*. For a slider that is mapped to 100 different values for the purpose of recording assessments, the range *1–100* might be entered. If no rating instrument is used (e.g. when evaluation gathers post-edits or qualitative feedback only), enter 'N/A'.

Question 4.3.5: How is the scale or other rating instrument presented to evaluators? If none match, select 'Other' and describe.

Multiple-choice options (select one):

○ ***Multiple-choice options***: choose this option if evaluators select exactly one of multiple options.

- ○ ***Check-boxes***: choose this option if evaluators select any number of options from multiple given options.
- ○ ***Slider***: choose this option if evaluators move a pointer on a slider scale to the position corresponding to their assessment.
- ○ ***N/A (there is no rating instrument)***: choose this option if there is no rating instrument.
- ○ ***Other (please specify)***: choose this option if there is a rating instrument, but none of the above adequately describe the way you present it to evaluators. Use the text box to describe the rating instrument and link to a screenshot.

Question 4.3.6: If there is no rating instrument, describe briefly what task the evaluators perform (e.g. ranking multiple outputs, finding information, playing a game, etc.), and what information is recorded. Enter 'N/A' if there is a rating instrument.

What to enter in the text box: If (and only if) there is no rating instrument, i.e. you entered 'N/A' for Questions 4.3.3–4.3.5, describe the task evaluators perform in this space. Otherwise, here enter 'N/A' if there *is* a rating instrument.

Question 4.3.7: What is the verbatim question, prompt or instruction given to evaluators (visible to them during each individual assessment)?

What to enter in the text box: Copy and paste the verbatim text that evaluators see during each assessment, that is intended to convey the evaluation task to them. E.g. *Which of these texts do you prefer?* Or *Make any corrections to this text that you think are necessary in order to improve it to the point where you would be happy to provide it to a client.*

Question 4.3.8: Form of response elicitation. If none match, select 'Other' and describe.

Multiple-choice options (select one):[5]

[5]Explanations adapted from Howcroft et al. (2020).

- ○ ***(dis)agreement with quality statement***: Participants specify the degree to which they agree with a given quality statement by indicating their agreement on a rating instrument. The rating instrument is labelled with degrees of agreement and can additionally have numerical labels. E.g. *This text is fluent — 1=strongly disagree...5=strongly agree.*
- ○ ***direct quality estimation***: Participants are asked to provide a rating using a rating instrument, which typically (but not always) mentions the quality criterion explicitly. E.g. *How fluent is this text? — 1=not at all fluent...5=very fluent.*
- ○ ***relative quality estimation (including ranking)***: Participants evaluate two or more items in terms of which is better. E.g. *Rank these texts in terms of fluency*; *Which of these texts is more fluent?*; *Which of these items do you prefer?*.
- ○ ***counting occurrences in text***: Evaluators are asked to count how many times some type of phenomenon occurs, e.g. the number of facts contained in the output that are inconsistent with the input.
- ○ ***qualitative feedback (e.g. via comments entered in a text box)***: Typically, these are responses to open-ended questions in a survey or interview.
- ○ ***evaluation through post-editing/annotation***: Choose this option if the evaluators' task consists of editing or inserting annotations in text. E.g. evaluators may perform error correction and edits are then automatically measured to yield a numerical score.
- ○ ***output classification or labelling***: Choose this option if evaluators assign outputs to categories. E.g. *What is the overall sentiment of this piece of text? — Positive/neutral/negative.*
- ○ ***user-text interaction measurements***: choose this option if participants in the evaluation experiment interact with a text in some way, and measurements are taken of their interaction. E.g. reading speed, eye movement tracking, comprehension questions, etc. Excludes situations where participants are given a task to solve and their performance is measured which comes under the next option.
- ○ ***task performance measurements***: choose this option if participants in the evaluation experiment are given a task to perform, and measure-

ments are taken of their performance at the task. E.g. task is finding information, and task performance measurement is task completion speed and success rate.

○ ***user-system interaction measurements***: choose this option if participants in the evaluation experiment interact with a system in some way, while measurements are taken of their interaction. E.g. duration of interaction, hyperlinks followed, number of likes, or completed sales.

○ ***Other (please specify)***: Use the text box to describe the form of response elicitation used in assessing the quality criterion if it doesn't fall in any of the above categories.

Question 4.3.9: How are raw responses from participants aggregated or otherwise processed to obtain reported scores for this quality criterion? State if no scores reported.

What to enter in the text box: normally a set of separate assessments is collected from evaluators and is converted to the results as reported. Describe here the method(s) used in the conversion(s). E.g. macro-averages or micro-averages are computed from numerical scores to provide summary, per-system results.

Question 4.3.10: Method(s) used for determining effect size and significance of findings for this quality criterion.

What to enter in the text box: A list of methods used for calculating the effect size and significance of any results, both as reported in the paper given in Question 1.1, for this quality criterion. If none calculated, state 'None'.

Question 4.3.11: Has the inter-annotator and intra-annotator agreement between evaluators for this quality criterion been measured? If yes, what method was used, and what are the agreement scores?

What to enter in the text box: the methods used to compute, and results obtained from, any measures of inter-annotator and intra-annotator agreement obtained for the quality criterion.

7 Conclusion

In this paper we have presented the Human Evaluation Datasheet (HEDS), intended as a way of recording properties of human evaluations in NLP in a sufficiently standardised way to support comparability between evaluation experiments, meta-evaluation of evaluation methods, and reproducibility assessments of evaluation results.

We have reported insights from observing HEDS 1.0 being used in practice, and have described improvements we have made in response to these insights. In particular, we have provided additional context, motivation and explanation to the HEDS questions relating to evaluation criteria assessed in evaluation experiments and their operationalisation. Moreover, we are currently developing a shorter version of HEDS, a version with reduced effort for use in certain contexts.

We view HEDS as continuing to develop in response to feedback received and insights gathered through use in practice. We continue to welcome feedback on any aspect of HEDS, and hope the growing repository of completed sheets will prove useful for future comparisons, meta-evaluation and reproducibility assessments, as demonstrated in the ReproGen shared task.

References

Laura Banarescu, Claire Bonial, Shu Cai, Madalina Georgescu, Kira Griffitt, Ulf Hermjakob, Kevin Knight, Philipp Koehn, Martha Palmer, and Nathan Schneider. 2013. Abstract Meaning Representation for sembanking. In *Proceedings of the 7th Linguistic Annotation Workshop and Interoperability with Discourse*, pages 178–186, Sofia, Bulgaria. Association for Computational Linguistics.

Anya Belz, Simon Mille, and David M. Howcroft. 2020. Disentangling the properties of human evaluation methods: A classification system to support comparability, meta-evaluation and reproducibility testing. In *Proceedings of the 13th International Conference on Natural Language Generation*, pages 183–194, Dublin, Ireland. Association for Computational Linguistics.

Anya Belz, Anastasia Shimorina, Shubham Agarwal, and Ehud Reiter. 2021. The ReproGen shared task on reproducibility of human evaluations in NLG: Overview and results. In *The 14th International Conference on Natural Language Generation*.

Emily M. Bender and Batya Friedman. 2018. Data statements for natural language processing: Toward mitigating system bias and enabling better science. *Transactions of the Association for Computational Linguistics*, 6:587–604.

Dallas Card, Peter Henderson, Urvashi Khandelwal, Robin Jia, Kyle Mahowald, and Dan Jurafsky. 2020. With little power comes great responsibility. In *Proceedings of the 2020 Conference on Empirical Methods in Natural Language Processing (EMNLP)*, pages 9263–9274, Online. Association for Computational Linguistics.

Jesse Dodge, Suchin Gururangan, Dallas Card, Roy Schwartz, and Noah A. Smith. 2019. Show your work: Improved reporting of experimental results. In *Proceedings of the 2019 Conference on Empirical Methods in Natural Language Processing and the 9th International Joint Conference on Natural Language Processing (EMNLP-IJCNLP)*, pages 2185–2194, Hong Kong, China. Association for Computational Linguistics.

Timnit Gebru, Jamie Morgenstern, Briana Vecchione, Jennifer Wortman Vaughan, Hanna Wallach, Hal Daumé III, and Kate Crawford. 2020. Datasheets for datasets.

Sebastian Gehrmann, Tosin Adewumi, Karmanya Aggarwal, Pawan Sasanka Ammanamanchi, Anuoluwapo Aremu, Antoine Bosselut, Khyathi Raghavi Chandu, Miruna-Adriana Clinciu, Dipanjan Das, Kaustubh Dhole, Wanyu Du, Esin Durmus, Ondřej Dušek, Chris Chinenye Emezue, Varun Gangal, Cristina Garbacea, Tatsunori Hashimoto, Yufang Hou, Yacine Jernite, Harsh Jhamtani, Yangfeng Ji, Shailza Jolly, Mihir Kale, Dhruv Kumar, Faisal Ladhak, Aman Madaan, Mounica Maddela, Khyati Mahajan, Saad Mahamood, Bodhisattwa Prasad Majumder, Pedro Henrique Martins, Angelina McMillan-Major, Simon Mille, Emiel van Miltenburg, Moin Nadeem, Shashi Narayan, Vitaly Nikolaev, Andre Niyongabo Rubungo, Salomey Osei, Ankur Parikh, Laura Perez-Beltrachini, Niranjan Ramesh Rao, Vikas Raunak, Juan Diego Rodriguez, Sashank Santhanam, João Sedoc, Thibault Sellam, Samira Shaikh, Anastasia Shimorina, Marco Antonio Sobrevilla Cabezudo, Hendrik Strobelt, Nishant Subramani, Wei Xu, Diyi Yang, Akhila Yerukola, and Jiawei Zhou. 2021. The GEM benchmark: Natural language generation, its evaluation and metrics. In *Proceedings of the 1st Workshop on Natural Language Generation, Evaluation, and Metrics (GEM 2021)*, pages 96–120, Online. Association for Computational Linguistics.

David M. Howcroft, Anya Belz, Miruna-Adriana Clinciu, Dimitra Gkatzia, Sadid A. Hasan, Saad Mahamood, Simon Mille, Emiel van Miltenburg, Sashank Santhanam, and Verena Rieser. 2020. Twenty years of confusion in human evaluation: NLG needs evaluation sheets and standardised definitions. In *Proceedings of the 13th International Conference on Natural Language Generation*, pages 169–182, Dublin, Ireland. Association for Computational Linguistics.

David M. Howcroft and Verena Rieser. 2021. What happens if you treat ordinal ratings as interval data? human evaluations in NLP are even more underpowered than you think. In *Proceedings of the 2021 Conference on Empirical Methods in Natural Language Processing*, pages 8932–8939, Online and Punta Cana, Dominican Republic. Association for Computational Linguistics.

Hans Kamp and Uwe Reyle. 2013. *From discourse to logic: Introduction to modeltheoretic semantics of natural language, formal logic and discourse representation theory*, volume 42. Springer Science & Business Media.

Margaret Mitchell, Simone Wu, Andrew Zaldivar, Parker Barnes, Lucy Vasserman, Ben Hutchinson, Elena Spitzer, Inioluwa Deborah Raji, and Timnit Gebru. 2019. Model cards for model reporting. In *Proceedings of the Conference on Fairness, Accountability, and Transparency*, FAT* '19, page 220–229, New York, NY, USA. Association for Computing Machinery.

Jekaterina Novikova, Ondřej Dušek, Amanda Cercas Curry, and Verena Rieser. 2017. Why we need new evaluation metrics for NLG. In *Proceedings of the 2017 Conference on Empirical Methods in Natural Language Processing*, pages 2241–2252.

Ehud Reiter. 2018. A structured review of the validity of BLEU. *Computational Linguistics*, 44(3):393–401.

Ehud Reiter and Anya Belz. 2009. An investigation into the validity of some metrics for automatically evaluating natural language generation systems. *Computational Linguistics*, 35(4):529–558.

Anastasia Shimorina and Anya Belz. 2021. The human evaluation datasheet 1.0: A template for recording details of human evaluation experiments in NLP. ArXiv preprint arXiv:2103.09710v1.

Chris van der Lee, Albert Gatt, Emiel van Miltenburg, and Emiel Krahmer. 2021. Human evaluation of automatically generated text: Current trends and best practice guidelines. *Computer Speech & Language*, 67:101151.

Chris van der Lee, Albert Gatt, Emiel van Miltenburg, Sander Wubben, and Emiel Krahmer. 2019. Best practices for the human evaluation of automatically generated text. In *Proceedings of the 12th International Conference on Natural Language Generation*, pages 355–368.

A Appendix: Full HEDS 2.0 Data Sheet

A.1 Questions about Paper and Supplementary Resources (Questions 1.1–1.3)

Questions 1.1–1.3 record bibliographic and related information. These are straightforward and don't warrant much in-depth explanation.

Question 1.1: Link to paper reporting the evaluation experiment. If the paper reports more than one experiment, state which experiment you're completing this sheet for. Or, if applicable, enter 'for preregistration.'

What to enter in the text box: a link to an online copy of the main reference for the human evaluation experiment, identifying which of the experiments the form is being completed for if there are several. If the experiment hasn't been run yet, and the form is being completed for the purpose of submitting it for preregistration, simply enter 'for preregistration'.

Question 1.2: Link to website providing resources used in the evaluation experiment (e.g. system outputs, evaluation tools, etc.). If there isn't one, enter 'N/A'.

What to enter in the text box: link(s) to any resources used in the evaluation experiment, such as system outputs, evaluation tools, etc. If there aren't any publicly shared resources (yet), enter 'N/A'.

Question 1.3: Name, affiliation and email address of person completing this sheet, and of contact author if different.

What to enter in the text box: names, affiliations and email addresses as appropriate.

A.2 System Questions 2.1–2.5

Questions 2.1–2.5 record information about the system(s) (or human-authored stand-ins) whose outputs are evaluated in the Evaluation experiment that this sheet is being completed for.

The input, output, and task questions in this section are closely interrelated: the value for one partially determines the others, as indicated for some combinations in Question 2.3.

Question 2.1: What type of input do the evaluated system(s) take? Select all that apply. If none match, select 'Other' and describe.

Describe the type of input, where input refers to the representations and/or data structures shared by all evaluated systems.

This question is about input type, regardless of number. E.g. if the input is a set of documents, you would still select *text: document* below.

Check-box options (select all that apply):

- □ ***raw/structured data***: numerical, symbolic, and other data, possibly structured into trees, graphs, graphical models, etc. May be the input e.g. to Referring Expression Generation (REG), end-to-end text generation, etc. NB: excludes linguistic structures.
- □ ***deep linguistic representation (DLR)***: any of a variety of deep, underspecified, semantic representations, such as abstract meaning representations (AMRs; Banarescu et al., 2013) or discourse representation structures (DRSs; Kamp and Reyle, 2013).
- □ ***shallow linguistic representation (SLR)***: any of a variety of shallow, syntactic representations, e.g. Universal Dependency (UD) structures; typically the input to surface realisation.
- □ ***text: subsentential unit of text***: a unit of text shorter than a sentence, e.g. Referring Expressions (REs), verb phrase, text fragment of any length; includes titles/headlines.
- □ ***text: sentence***: a single sentence (or set of sentences).
- □ ***text: multiple sentences***: a sequence of multiple sentences, without any document structure (or a set of such sequences).
- □ ***text: document***: a text with document structure, such as a title, paragraph breaks or sections, e.g. a set of news reports for summarisation.
- □ ***text: dialogue***: a dialogue of any length, excluding a single turn which would come under one of the other text types.

□ ***text: other***: input is text but doesn't match any of the above *text:** categories.

□ ***speech***: a recording of speech.

□ ***visual***: an image or video.

□ ***multi-modal***: catch-all value for any combination of data and/or linguistic representation and/or visual data etc.

□ ***control feature***: a feature or parameter specifically present to control a property of the output text, e.g. positive stance, formality, author style.

□ ***no input (human generation)***: human generation[6], therefore no system inputs.

□ ***other (please specify)***: if input is none of the above, choose this option and describe it.

Question 2.2: What type of output do the evaluated system(s) generate? Select all that apply. If none match, select 'Other' and describe.

Describe the type of output, where output refers to the representations and/or data structures shared by all evaluated systems.

This question is about output type, regardless of number. E.g. if the output is a set of documents, you would still select *text: document* below.

Note that the options for outputs are the same as for inputs except that the *no input (human generation) option* is replaced with *human-generated 'outputs'*, and the *control feature* option is removed.

Check-box options (select all that apply):

□ ***raw/structured data***: numerical, symbolic, and other data, possibly structured into trees, graphs, graphical models, etc. May be the input e.g. to Referring Expression Generation (REG), end-to-end text generation, etc. NB: excludes linguistic structures.

□ ***deep linguistic representation (DLR)***: any of a variety of deep, underspecified, semantic representations, such as abstract meaning representations (AMRs; Banarescu et al., 2013) or discourse representation structures (DRSs; Kamp and Reyle, 2013).

□ ***shallow linguistic representation (SLR)***: any of a variety of shallow, syntactic representations, e.g. Universal Dependency (UD) structures; typically the input to surface realisation.

□ ***text: subsentential unit of text***: a unit of text shorter than a sentence, e.g. Referring Expressions (REs), verb phrase, text fragment of any length; includes titles/headlines.

□ ***text: sentence***: a single sentence (or set of sentences).

□ ***text: multiple sentences***: a sequence of multiple sentences, without any document structure (or a set of such sequences).

□ ***text: document***: a text with document structure, such as a title, paragraph breaks or sections, e.g. a set of news reports for summarisation.

□ ***text: dialogue***: a dialogue of any length, excluding a single turn which would come under one of the other text types.

□ ***text: other***: select if output is text but doesn't match any of the above *text:** categories.

□ ***speech***: a recording of speech.

□ ***visual***: an image or video.

□ ***multi-modal***: catch-all value for any combination of data and/or linguistic representation and/or visual data etc.

□ ***human-generated 'outputs'***: manually created stand-ins exemplifying outputs.[6]

□ ***other (please specify)***: if output is none of the above, choose this option and describe it.

Question 2.3: How would you describe the task that the evaluated system(s) perform in mapping the inputs in Q2.1 to the outputs in Q2.2? Occasionally, more than one of the options below may apply. If none match, select 'Other' and describe.

This field records the task performed by the system(s) being evaluated. This is independent of the application domain (financial reporting, weather forecasting, etc.), or the specific method (rule-based, neural, etc.) implemented in the system. We indicate mutual constraints between inputs, outputs and task for some of the options below.

Check-box options (select all that apply):

[6]We use the term 'human generation' where the items being evaluated have been created manually, rather than generated by an automatic system.

□ ***content selection/determination***: selecting the specific content that will be expressed in the generated text from a representation of possible content. This could be attribute selection for REG (without the surface realisation step). Note that the output here is not text.

□ ***content ordering/structuring***: assigning an order and/or structure to content to be included in generated text. Note that the output here is not text.

□ ***aggregation***: converting inputs (typically *deep linguistic representations* or *shallow linguistic representations*) in some way in order to reduce redundancy (e.g. representations for 'they like swimming', 'they like running' $\rightarrow$ representation for 'they like swimming and running').

□ ***referring expression generation***: generating *text* to refer to a given referent, typically represented in the input as a set of attributes or a linguistic representation.

□ ***lexicalisation***: associating (parts of) an input representation with specific lexical items to be used in their realisation.

□ ***deep generation***: one-step text generation from *raw/structured data* or *deep linguistic representations*. One-step means that no intermediate representations are passed from one independently run module to another.

□ ***surface realisation (SLR to text)***: one-step text generation from *shallow linguistic representations*. One-step means that no intermediate representations are passed from one independently run module to another.

□ ***feature-controlled text generation***: generation of text that varies along specific dimensions where the variation is controlled via *control features* specified as part of the input. Input is a non-textual representation (for feature-controlled text-to-text generation select the matching text-to-text task).

□ ***data-to-text generation***: generation from *raw/structured data* which may or may not include some amount of content selection as part of the generation process. Output is likely to be *text:** or *multi-modal*.

□ ***dialogue turn generation***: generating a dialogue turn (can be a greeting or closing) from a representation of dialogue state and/or last turn(s), etc.

□ ***question generation***: generation of questions from given input text and/or knowledge base such that the question can be answered from the input.

□ ***question answering***: input is a question plus optionally a set of reference texts and/or knowledge base, and the output is the answer to the question.

□ ***paraphrasing/lossless simplification***: text-to-text generation where the aim is to preserve the meaning of the input while changing its wording. This can include the aim of changing the text on a given dimension, e.g. making it simpler, changing its stance or sentiment, etc., which may be controllable via input features. Note that this task type includes meaning-preserving text simplification (non-meaning preserving simplification comes under *compression/lossy simplification* below).

□ ***compression/lossy simplification***: text-to-text generation that has the aim to generate a shorter, or shorter and simpler, version of the input text. This will normally affect meaning to some extent, but as a side effect, rather than the primary aim, as is the case in *summarisation*.

□ ***machine translation***: translating text in a source language to text in a target language while maximally preserving the meaning.

□ ***summarisation (text-to-text)***: output is an extractive or abstractive summary of the important/relevant/salient content of the input document(s).

□ ***end-to-end text generation***: use this option if the single system task corresponds to more than one of tasks above, implemented either as separate modules pipelined together, or as one-step generation, other than *deep generation* and *surface realisation*.

□ ***image/video description***: input includes *visual*, and the output describes it in some way.

□ ***post-editing/correction***: system edits and/or corrects the input text (typically itself the textual output from another system) to yield an improved version of the text.

□ ***other (please specify)***: if task is none of the above, choose this option and describe it.

Question 2.4: Input Language(s), or 'N/A'.

This field records the language(s) of the inputs accepted by the system(s) being evaluated.

What to enter in the text box: any language name(s) that apply, mapped to standardised full language names in ISO 639-1[7]. E.g. English, Herero, Hindi. If no language is accepted as (part of) the input, enter 'N/A'.

Question 2.5: Output Language(s), or 'N/A'.

This field records the language(s) of the outputs generated by the system(s) being evaluated.

What to enter in the text box: any language name(s) that apply, mapped to standardised full language names in ISO 639-1 (2019)[7]. E.g. English, Herero, Hindi. If no language is generated, enter 'N/A'.

A.3 Questions about Output Sample, Evaluators, Experimental Design

A.3.1 Sample of system outputs (or human-authored stand-ins) evaluated (Questions 3.1.1–3.1.3)

Questions 3.1.1–3.1.3 record information about the size of the sample of outputs (or human-authored stand-ins) evaluated per system, how the sample was selected, and what its statistical power is.

Question 3.1.1: How many system outputs (or other evaluation items) are evaluated per system in the evaluation experiment? Answer should be an integer.

What to enter in the text box: The number of system outputs (or other evaluation items) that are evaluated per system by at least one evaluator in the experiment, as an integer.

Question 3.1.2: How are system outputs (or other evaluation items) selected for inclusion in the evaluation experiment? If none match, select 'Other' and describe.

Multiple-choice options (select one):

- ***by an automatic random process from a larger set***: outputs were selected for inclusion in the experiment by a script using a pseudo-random number generator; don't use this option if the script selects every nth output (which is not random).
- ***by an automatic random process but using stratified sampling over given properties***: use this option if selection was by a random script as above, but with added constraints ensuring that the sample is representative of the set of outputs it was selected from, in terms of given properties, such as sentence length, positive/negative stance, etc.
- ***by manual, arbitrary selection***: output sample was selected by hand, or automatically from a manually compiled list, without a specific selection criterion.
- ***by manual selection aimed at achieving balance or variety relative to given properties***: selection by hand as above, but with specific selection criteria, e.g. same number of outputs from each time period.
- ***Other (please specify)***: if selection method is none of the above, choose this option and describe it.

Question 3.1.3: What is the statistical power of the sample size?

What to enter in the text box: The results of a statistical power calculation on the output sample: provide numerical results and a link to the script used (or another way of identifying the script). See, e.g., Card et al. (2020); Howcroft and Rieser (2021).

A.3.2 Evaluators (Questions 3.2.1–3.2.5)

Questions 3.2.1–3.2.5 record information about the evaluators participating in the experiment.

Question 3.2.1: How many evaluators are there in this experiment? Answer should be an integer.

What to enter in the text box: the total number of evaluators participating in the experiment, as an integer.

[7] https://en.wikipedia.org/wiki/List_of_ISO_639-1_codes

Question 3.2.2: What kind of evaluators are in this experiment? Select all that apply. If none match, select 'Other' and describe. In all cases, provide details in the text box under 'Other'.

Check-box options (select all that apply):

- □ ***experts***: participants are considered domain experts, e.g. meteorologists evaluating a weather forecast generator, or nurses evaluating an ICU report generator.
- □ ***non-experts***: participants are not domain experts.
- □ ***paid (including non-monetary compensation such as course credits)***: participants were given some form of compensation for their participation, including vouchers, course credits, and reimbursement for travel unless based on receipts.
- □ ***not paid***: participants were not given compensation of any kind.
- □ ***previously known to authors***: (one of the) researchers running the experiment knew some or all of the participants before recruiting them for the experiment.
- □ ***not previously known to authors***: none of the researchers running the experiment knew any of the participants before recruiting them for the experiment.
- □ ***evaluators include one or more of the authors***: one or more researchers running the experiment was among the participants.
- □ ***evaluators do not include any of the authors***: none of the researchers running the experiment were among the participants.
- □ ***Other*** (fewer than 4 of the above apply): we believe you should be able to tick 4 options of the above. If that's not the case, use this box to explain.

Question 3.2.3: How are evaluators recruited?

What to enter in the text box: Please explain how your evaluators are recruited. Do you send emails to a given list? Do you post invitations on social media? Posters on university walls? Were there any gatekeepers involved? What are the exclusion/inclusion criteria?

Question 3.2.4: What training and/or practice are evaluators given before starting on the evaluation itself?

What to enter in the text box: Use this space to describe any training evaluators were given as part of the experiment to prepare them for the evaluation task, including any practice evaluations they did. This includes any introductory explanations they're given, e.g. on the start page of an online evaluation tool.

Question 3.2.5: What other characteristics do the evaluators have, known either because these were qualifying criteria, or from information gathered as part of the evaluation?

What to enter in the text box: Use this space to list any characteristics not covered in previous questions that the evaluators are known to have, either because evaluators were selected on the basis of a characteristic, or because information about a characteristic was collected as part of the evaluation. This might include geographic location of IP address, educational level, or demographic information such as gender, age, etc. Where characteristics differ among evaluators (e.g. gender, age, location etc.), also give numbers for each subgroup.

A.3.3 Experimental Design Questions 3.3.1–3.3.8

Questions 3.3.1–3.3.8 record information about the experimental design of the evaluation experiment.

Question 3.3.1: Has the experimental design been preregistered? If yes, on which registry?

What to enter in the text box: State 'Yes' or 'No'; if 'Yes' also give the name of the registry and a link to the registration page for the experiment.

Question 3.3.2: How are responses collected? E.g. paper forms, online survey tool, etc.

What to enter in the text box: Use this space to describe how you collected responses, e.g. paper forms, Google forms, SurveyMonkey, Mechanical Turk, CrowdFlower, audio/video recording, etc.

Question 3.3.3: What quality assurance methods are used? Select all that apply. If none match, select 'Other' and describe. In all cases, provide details in the text box under 'Other'.

Check-box options (select all that apply):

- □ ***evaluators are required to be native speakers of the language they evaluate***: mechanisms are in place to ensure all participants are native speakers of the language they evaluate.
- □ ***automatic quality checking methods are used during/post evaluation***: evaluations are checked for quality by automatic scripts during or after evaluations, e.g. evaluators are given known bad/good outputs to check they're given bad/good scores on MTurk.
- □ ***manual quality checking methods are used during/post evaluation***: evaluations are checked for quality by a manual process during or after evaluations, e.g. scores assigned by evaluators are monitored by researchers conducting the experiment.
- □ ***evaluators are excluded if they fail quality checks (often or badly enough)***: there are conditions under which evaluations produced by participants are not included in the final results due to quality issues.
- □ ***some evaluations are excluded because of failed quality checks***: there are conditions under which some (but not all) of the evaluations produced by some participants are not included in the final results due to quality issues.
- □ ***none of the above***: tick this box if none of the above apply.
- □ ***Other (please specify)***: use this box to describe any other quality assurance methods used during or after evaluations, and to provide additional details for any of the options selected above.

Question 3.3.4: What do evaluators see when carrying out evaluations? Link to screenshot(s) and/or describe the evaluation interface(s).

What to enter in the text box: Use this space to describe the interface, paper form, etc. that evaluators see when they carry out the evaluation. Link to a screenshot/copy if possible. If there is a separate introductory interface/page, include it under Question 3.2.4.

3.3.5: How free are evaluators regarding when and how quickly to carry out evaluations? Select all that apply. In all cases, provide details in the text box under 'Other'.

Check-box options (select all that apply):

- □ ***evaluators have to complete each individual assessment within a set time***: evaluators are timed while carrying out each assessment and cannot complete the assessment once time has run out.
- □ ***evaluators have to complete the whole evaluation in one sitting***: partial progress cannot be saved and the evaluation returned to on a later occasion.
- □ ***neither of the above***: Choose this option if neither of the above are the case in the experiment.
- □ ***Other (please specify)***: Use this space to describe any other way in which time taken or number of sessions used by evaluators is controlled in the experiment, and to provide additional details for any of the options selected above.

3.3.6: Are evaluators told they can ask questions about the evaluation and/or provide feedback? Select all that apply. In all cases, provide details in the text box under 'Other'.

Check-box options (select all that apply):

- □ ***evaluators are told they can ask any questions during/after receiving initial training/instructions, and before the start of the evaluation***: evaluators are told explicitly that they can ask questions about the evaluation experiment *before* starting on their assessments, either during or after training.
- □ ***evaluators are told they can ask any questions during the evaluation***: evaluators are told explicitly that they can ask questions about the evaluation experiment *during* their assessments.
- □ ***evaluators are asked for feedback and/or comments after the evaluation, e.g. via an exit questionnaire or a comment box***: evaluators are explicitly asked to provide feedback and/or comments about the experiment *after* their assessments, either verbally or in written form.
- □ ***None of the above***: Choose this option if none of the above are the case in the experiment.
- □ ***Other (please specify)***: use this space to describe any other ways you provide for evaluators to ask questions or provide feedback.

3.3.7: What are the experimental conditions in which evaluators carry out the evaluations? If none match, select 'Other' and describe.

Multiple-choice options (select one):

- ○ ***evaluation carried out by evaluators at a place of their own choosing, e.g. online, using a paper form, etc.***: evaluators are given access to the tool or form specified in Question 3.3.2, and subsequently choose where to carry out their evaluations.
- ○ ***evaluation carried out in a lab, and conditions are the same for each evaluator***: evaluations are carried out in a lab, and conditions in which evaluations are carried out *are* controlled to be the same, i.e. the different evaluators all carry out the evaluations in identical conditions of quietness, same type of computer, same room, etc. Note we're not after very fine-grained differences here, such as time of day or temperature, but the line is difficult to draw, so some judgment is involved here.
- ○ ***evaluation carried out in a lab, and conditions vary for different evaluators***: choose this option if evaluations are carried out in a lab, but the preceding option does not apply, i.e. conditions in which evaluations are carried out are *not* controlled to be the same.
- ○ ***evaluation carried out in a real-life situation, and conditions are the same for each evaluator***: evaluations are carried out in a real-life situation, i.e. one that would occur whether or not the evaluation was carried out (e.g. evaluating a dialogue system deployed in a live chat function on a website), and conditions in which evaluations are carried out *are* controlled to be the same.
- ○ ***evaluation carried out in a real-life situation, and conditions vary for different evaluators***: choose this option if evaluations are carried out in a real-life situation, but the preceding option does not apply, i.e. conditions in which evaluations are carried out are *not* controlled to be the same.
- ○ ***evaluation carried out outside of the lab, in a situation designed to resemble a real-life situation, and conditions are the same for each evaluator***: evaluations are carried out outside of the lab, in a situation intentionally similar to a real-life situation (but not actually a real-life situation), e.g. user-testing a navigation system where the destination is part of the evaluation design, rather than chosen by the user. Conditions in which evaluations are carried out *are* controlled to be the same.
- ○ ***evaluation carried out outside of the lab, in a situation designed to resemble a real-life situation, and conditions vary for different evaluators***: choose this option if evaluations are carried out outside of the lab, in a situation intentionally similar to a real-life situation, but the preceding option does not apply, i.e. conditions in which evaluations are carried out are *not* controlled to be the same.
- ○ ***Other (please specify)***: Use this space to provide additional, or alternative, information

about the conditions in which evaluators carry out assessments, not covered by the options above.

3.3.8: Unless the evaluation is carried out at a place of the evaluators' own choosing, briefly describe the (range of different) conditions in which evaluators carry out the evaluations.

What to enter in the text box: use this space to describe the variations in the conditions in which evaluators carry out the evaluation, for both situations where those variations are controlled, and situations where they are not controlled.

A.4 Quality Criterion *n* – Definition and Operationalisation

Questions in this section collect information about the nth quality criterion assessed in the single human evaluation experiment that this sheet is being completed for.

A.4.1 Quality criterion properties (Questions 4.1.1–4.1.3)

Questions 4.1.1–4.1.3 capture the aspect of quality that is assessed by a given quality criterion in terms of three orthogonal properties. They help determine whether or not the same aspect of quality is being evaluated in different evaluation experiments. The three properties characterise quality criteria in terms of (i) what type of quality is being assessed; (ii) what aspect of the system output is being assessed; and (iii) whether system outputs are assessed in their own right or with reference to some system-internal or system-external frame of reference. For full explanations see Belz et al. (2020).

Question 4.1.1: What type of quality is assessed by the quality criterion?

Multiple-choice options (select one):

- ○ ***Correctness***: Select this option if it is possible to state, generally for all outputs, the conditions under which outputs are maximally correct (hence of maximal quality). E.g. for *Grammaticality*,[8] outputs are (maximally) correct if they contain no grammatical errors; for *Semantic Completeness*, outputs are correct if they express all the content in the input.
- ○ ***Goodness***: Select this option if, in contrast to correctness criteria, there is no single, general mechanism for deciding when outputs are maximally good, only for deciding for any two outputs which is better and which is worse. E.g. for *Fluency*, even if outputs contain no disfluencies, there may be other ways in which any given output could be more fluent.
- ○ ***Feature***: Choose this option if, in terms of property X captured by the criterion, outputs are not generally better if they are more X, but instead, depending on evaluation context, more X may be either better or worse. E.g. for *Specificity*, outputs can be more specific or less specific, but it's not the case that outputs are, in the general case, better when they are more specific.

Question 4.1.2: Which aspect of system outputs is assessed by the quality criterion?

Multiple-choice options (select one):

- ○ ***Form of output***: Choose this option if the criterion assesses the form of outputs alone, e.g. *Grammaticality* is only about the form, a sentence can be grammatical yet be wrong or nonsensical in terms of content.
- ○ ***Content of output***: Select this option if the criterion assesses the content/meaning of the output alone, e.g. *Meaning Preservation* only assesses content; two sentences can be considered to have the same meaning, but differ in form.
- ○ ***Both form and content of output***: Choose this option if the criterion assesses outputs as a whole, not just form or just content. E.g. *Coherence* is a property of outputs as a whole, either form or meaning can detract from it. Inherently extrinsic criteria such as *Usefulness* or *Task Completion* also fall in this category.

[8] We take all examples of quality criteria from published reports of evaluations, via the annotated database compiled by Howcroft et al. (2020).

Question 4.1.3: Is each output assessed for quality in its own right, or with reference to a system-internal or external frame of reference?

Multiple-choice options (select one):

- ○ ***Quality of output in its own right***: Select this option if output quality is assessed without referring to anything other than the output itself, i.e. no system-internal or external frame of reference. E.g. *Poeticness* is assessed by considering (just) the output and how poetic it is.
- ○ ***Quality of output relative to the input***: Choose this option if output quality is assessed relative to the input. E.g. *Answerability* is the degree to which the output question can be answered from information in the input.
- ○ ***Quality of output relative to a system-external frame of reference***: Choose this option if output quality is assessed with reference to system-external information, such as a knowledge base, a person's individual writing style, or the performance of an embedding system. E.g. *Factual Accuracy* assesses outputs relative to a source of real-world knowledge.

A.4.2 Evaluation mode properties (Questions 4.2.1–4.2.3)

Questions 4.2.1–4.2.3 record properties that are orthogonal to quality criteria (covered by questions in the preceding section), i.e. any given quality criterion can in principle be combined with any of the modes (although some combinations are more common than others).

Question 4.2.1: Does an individual assessment involve an objective or a subjective judgment?

Multiple-choice options (select one):

- ○ ***Objective***: Choose this option if the evaluation uses objective assessment, e.g. any automatically counted or otherwise quantified measurements such as mouse-clicks, occurrences in text, etc. Repeated assessments of the same output with an objective-mode evaluation method always yield the same score/result.
- ○ ***Subjective***: Choose this option in all other cases. Subjective assessments involve ratings, opinions and preferences by evaluators. Some criteria lend themselves more readily to subjective assessments, e.g. *Friendliness* of a conversational agent, but an objective measure e.g. based on lexical markers is also conceivable.

Question 4.2.2: Are outputs assessed in absolute or relative terms?

Multiple-choice options (select one):

- ○ ***Absolute***: Select this option if evaluators are shown outputs from a single system during each individual assessment.
- ○ ***Relative***: Choose this option if evaluators are shown outputs from multiple systems at the same time during assessments, typically ranking or preference-judging them.

Question 4.2.3: Is the evaluation intrinsic or extrinsic?

Multiple-choice options (select one):

- ○ ***Intrinsic***: Choose this option if quality of outputs is assessed *without* considering their *effect* on something external to the system, e.g. the performance of an embedding system or of a user at a task.
- ○ ***Extrinsic***: Choose this option if quality of outputs is assessed in terms of their *effect* on something external to the system such as the performance of an embedding system or of a user at a task.

A.4.3 Response elicitation (Questions 4.3.1–4.3.11)

The questions in this section concern response elicitation, by which we mean how the ratings or other measurements that represent assessments for the quality criterion in question are obtained, covering what is presented to evaluators, how they select response and via what type of tool, etc. The eleven questions (4.3.1–4.3.11) are based on the information annotated in the large scale survey of human evaluation methods in NLG by Howcroft et al. (2020).

Question 4.3.1: What do you call the quality criterion in explanations/interfaces to evaluators? Enter 'N/A' if criterion not named.

What to enter in the text box: the name you use to refer to the quality criterion in explanations and/or interfaces created for evaluators. Examples of quality criterion names include Fluency, Clarity, Meaning Preservation. If no name is used, state 'N/A'.

Question 4.3.2: What definition do you give for the quality criterion in explanations/interfaces to evaluators? Enter 'N/A' if no definition given.

What to enter in the text box: Copy and past the verbatim definition you give to evaluators to explain the quality criterion they're assessing. If you don't explicitly call it a definition, enter the nearest thing to a definition you give them. If you don't give any definition, state 'N/A'.

Question 4.3.3: Size of scale or other rating instrument (i.e. how many different possible values there are). Answer should be an integer or 'continuous' (if it's not possible to state how many possible responses there are). Enter 'N/A' if there is no rating instrument.

What to enter in the text box: The number of different response values for this quality criterion. E.g. for a 5-point Likert scale, the size to enter is 5. For two-way forced-choice preference judgments, it is 2; if there's also a no-preference option, enter 3. For a slider that is mapped to 100 different values for the purpose of recording assessments, the size to enter is 100. If no rating instrument is used (e.g. when evaluation gathers post-edits or qualitative feedback only), enter 'N/A'.

Question 4.3.4: List or range of possible values of the scale or other rating instrument. Enter 'N/A', if there is no rating instrument.

What to enter in the text box: list, or give the range of, the possible values of the rating instrument. The list or range should be of the size specified in Question 4.3.3. If there are too many to list, use a range. E.g. for two-way forced-choice preference judgments, the list entered might be *A better, B better*; if there's also a no-preference option, the list might be *A better, B better, neither*. For a slider that is mapped to 100 different values for the purpose of recording assessments, the range *1–100* might be entered. If no rating instrument is used (e.g. when evaluation gathers post-edits or qualitative feedback only), enter 'N/A'.

Question 4.3.5: How is the scale or other rating instrument presented to evaluators? If none match, select 'Other' and describe.

Multiple-choice options (select one):

- ○ ***Multiple-choice options***: choose this option if evaluators select exactly one of multiple options.
- ○ ***Check-boxes***: choose this option if evaluators select any number of options from multiple given options.
- ○ ***Slider***: choose this option if evaluators move a pointer on a slider scale to the position corresponding to their assessment.
- ○ ***N/A (there is no rating instrument)***: choose this option if there is no rating instrument.
- ○ ***Other (please specify)***: choose this option if there is a rating instrument, but none of the above adequately describe the way you present it to evaluators. Use the text box to describe the rating instrument and link to a screenshot.

Question 4.3.6: If there is no rating instrument, describe briefly what task the evaluators perform (e.g. ranking multiple outputs, finding information, playing a game, etc.), and what information is recorded. Enter 'N/A' if there is a rating instrument.

What to enter in the text box: If (and only if) there is no rating instrument, i.e. you entered 'N/A' for Questions 4.3.3–4.3.5, describe the task evaluators perform in this space. Otherwise, here enter 'N/A' if there *is* a rating instrument.

Question 4.3.7: What is the verbatim question, prompt or instruction given to evaluators (visible to them during each individual assessment)?

What to enter in the text box: Copy and paste the verbatim text that evaluators see during each assessment, that is intended to convey the evaluation task to them. E.g. *Which of these texts do you prefer?* Or *Make any corrections to this text that you think are necessary in order to improve it to the point where you would be happy to provide it to a client.*

Question 4.3.8: Form of response elicitation. If none match, select 'Other' and describe.

Multiple-choice options (select one):[9]

- ○ ***(dis)agreement with quality statement***: Participants specify the degree to which they agree with a given quality statement by indicating their agreement on a rating instrument. The rating instrument is labelled with degrees of agreement and can additionally have numerical labels. E.g. *This text is fluent — 1=strongly disagree...5=strongly agree.*
- ○ ***direct quality estimation***: Participants are asked to provide a rating using a rating instrument, which typically (but not always) mentions the quality criterion explicitly. E.g. *How fluent is this text? — 1=not at all fluent...5=very fluent.*
- ○ ***relative quality estimation (including ranking)***: Participants evaluate two or more items in terms of which is better. E.g. *Rank these texts in terms of fluency*; *Which of these texts is more fluent?*; *Which of these items do you prefer?*.
- ○ ***counting occurrences in text***: Evaluators are asked to count how many times some type of phenomenon occurs, e.g. the number of facts contained in the output that are inconsistent with the input.
- ○ ***qualitative feedback (e.g. via comments entered in a text box)***: Typically, these are responses to open-ended questions in a survey or interview.
- ○ ***evaluation through post-editing/annotation***: Choose this option if the evaluators' task consists of editing or inserting annotations in text. E.g. evaluators may perform error correction and edits are then automatically measured to yield a numerical score.
- ○ ***output classification or labelling***: Choose this option if evaluators assign outputs to categories. E.g. *What is the overall sentiment of this piece of text? — Positive/neutral/negative.*
- ○ ***user-text interaction measurements***: choose this option if participants in the evaluation experiment interact with a text in some way, and measurements are taken of their interaction. E.g. reading speed, eye movement tracking, comprehension questions, etc. Excludes situations where participants are given a task to solve and their performance is measured which comes under the next option.
- ○ ***task performance measurements***: choose this option if participants in the evaluation experiment are given a task to perform, and measurements are taken of their performance at the task. E.g. task is finding information, and task performance measurement is task completion speed and success rate.
- ○ ***user-system interaction measurements***: choose this option if participants in the evaluation experiment interact with a system in some way, while measurements are taken of their interaction. E.g. duration of interaction, hyperlinks followed, number of likes, or completed sales.
- ○ ***Other (please specify)***: Use the text box to describe the form of response elicitation used in assessing the quality criterion if it doesn't fall in any of the above categories.

Question 4.3.9: How are raw responses from participants aggregated or otherwise processed to obtain reported scores for this quality criterion? State if no scores reported.

What to enter in the text box: normally a set of separate assessments is collected from evaluators

[9] Explanations adapted from Howcroft et al. (2020).

and is converted to the results as reported. Describe here the method(s) used in the conversion(s). E.g. macro-averages or micro-averages are computed from numerical scores to provide summary, per-system results.

Question 4.3.10: Method(s) used for determining effect size and significance of findings for this quality criterion.

What to enter in the text box: A list of methods used for calculating the effect size and significance of any results, both as reported in the paper given in Question 1.1, for this quality criterion. If none calculated, state 'None'.

Question 4.3.11: Has the inter-annotator and intra-annotator agreement between evaluators for this quality criterion been measured? If yes, what method was used, and what are the agreement scores?

What to enter in the text box: the methods used to compute, and results obtained from, any measures of inter-annotator and intra-annotator agreement obtained for the quality criterion.

A.5 Ethics Questions (Questions 5.1-5.4)

The questions in this section relate to ethical aspects of the evaluation. Information can be entered in the text box provided, and/or by linking to a source where complete information can be found.

Question 5.1: Has the evaluation experiment this sheet is being completed for, or the larger study it is part of, been approved by a research ethics committee? If yes, which research ethics committee?

What to enter in the text box: Typically, research organisations, universities and other higher-education institutions require some form ethical approval before experiments involving human participants, however innocuous, are permitted to proceed. Please provide here the name of the body that approved the experiment, or state 'No' if approval has not (yet) been obtained.

Question 5.2: Do any of the system outputs (or human-authored stand-ins) evaluated, or do any of the responses collected, in the experiment contain personal data (as defined in GDPR Art. 4, §1: https://gdpr.eu/article-4-definitions/)? If yes, describe data and state how addressed.

What to enter in the text box: State 'No' if no personal data as defined by GDPR was recorded or collected, otherwise explain how conformity with GDPR requirements such as privacy and security was ensured, e.g. by linking to the (successful) application for ethics approval from Question 5.1.

Question 5.3: Do any of the system outputs (or human-authored stand-ins) evaluated, or do any of the responses collected, in the experiment contain special category information (as defined in GDPR Art. 9, §1: https://gdpr.eu/article-9-processing-special-categories-of-personal-data-prohibited/)? If yes, describe data and state how addressed.

What to enter in the text box: State 'No' if no special-category data as defined by GDPR was recorded or collected, otherwise explain how conformity with GDPR requirements relating to special-category data was ensured, e.g. by linking to the (successful) application for ethics approval from Question 5.1.

Question 5.4: Have any impact assessments been carried out for the evaluation experiment, and/or any data collected/evaluated in connection with it? If yes, summarise approach(es) and outcomes.

What to enter in the text box: Use this box to describe any *ex ante* or *ex post* impact assessments that have been carried out in relation to the evaluation experiment, such that the assessment plan and process, as well as the outcomes, were captured in written form. Link to documents if possible. Types of impact assessment include data protection impact assessments, e.g. under GDPR.[10] Environmental and social impact assessment frameworks are also available.

[10]https://ico.org.uk/for-organisations/guide-to-data-protection/guide-to-the-general-data-protection-regulation-gdpr/accountability-and-governance/data-protection-impact-assessments/

Toward More Effective Human Evaluation for Machine Translation

Belén Saldías[1], **George Foster**[2], **Markus Freitag**[2], **Qijun Tan**[2]
[1]MIT Media Lab
[2]Google Research
belen@mit.edu, {fosterg, freitag, qijuntan}@google.com

Abstract

Improvements in text generation technologies such as machine translation have necessitated more costly and time-consuming human evaluation procedures to ensure an accurate signal. We investigate a simple way to reduce cost by reducing the number of text segments that must be annotated in order to accurately predict a score for a complete test set. Using a sampling approach, we demonstrate that information from document membership and automatic metrics can help improve estimates compared to a pure random sampling baseline. We achieve gains of up to 20% in average absolute error by leveraging stratified sampling and control variates. Our techniques can improve estimates made from a fixed annotation budget, are easy to implement, and can be applied to any problem with structure similar to the one we study.

1 Introduction

As automatic natural language generation systems improve, evaluating them is becoming more challenging for both human and automatic methods (Çelikyilmaz et al., 2020; Gehrmann et al., 2022). In machine translation, this has led to increased adoption of techniques such as MQM (Freitag et al., 2021a,b), an elaborate error-based methodology for scoring output, typically carried out by skilled human annotators. While MQM is more accurate than traditional crowd-based Likert-type scoring, it can also be significantly slower and more expensive, creating a strong incentive to reduce annotation time and cost.

In this paper we investigate a simple solution to this problem, namely reducing the number of text segments that a human annotator must rate. We assume a basic scenario in which a single annotator is given a test set to rate, and the task is to predict the average MQM score they would assign to the whole set by having them rate only a selected subset. This is a natural and versatile way to deploy human annotation effort within a framework like MQM; it differs from the tasks considered by recent work with similar motivation, which focus on system ranking (Mendonça et al., 2021; Thorleiksdóttir et al., 2021) or combining human and metric scores without the express aim of predicting human performance (Hashimoto et al., 2019; Singla et al., 2021). Although our experiments are carried out with MQM-based scores, our methodology is applicable to any setting in which numerical scores are assigned to items for later averaging.

We approach the task of choosing segments as a sampling problem, and investigate classical methods for reducing sample variance and bounding estimation error. To improve accuracy, we employ two sources of supplementary information. First, in keeping with recent practice, we assume segments are grouped into documents. This lets us exploit the tendency of segments within a document to be relatively homogeneous. Second, we make use of modern automatic metrics such as COMET (Rei et al., 2020) and BLEURT (Sellam et al., 2020) which correlate better at the segment level with human judgments than traditional surface-based metrics like BLEU (Papineni et al., 2002). These serve as a rough proxy for human scores.

We show that document and metric information can be used to reduce average estimation error by up to 20% over a pure random sampling baseline. Due to high sample variance, it is difficult to reliably achieve a similar reduction in annotator effort for a given error tolerance. However, we suggest an alternative perspective in which our technique can be used to improve estimates made on the basis of a fixed rating budget. Although there is no guarantee of beating random sampling in any particular case, there is a high probability of improving on average. This improved estimator is easy to implement, and applicable to any human labeling task that produces numerical scores, and for which document membership and automatic metrics are available.

Proceedings of the 2nd Workshop on Human Evaluation of NLP Systems (HumEval), pages 76 - 89
May 27, 2022 ©2022 Association for Computational Linguistics

Our work is most similar to that of Chaganty et al. (2018), which we extend in several ways. We adopt their use of control variates, but consider multiple metrics rather than just one, including learned metric combinations; we also employ modern neural metrics rather than metrics based on surface information. We combine control variates with stratified sampling using either proportional or optimal allocation, and additionally evaluate an incremental scenario in which sampling adapts to observed ratings. Finally, we investigate two analytical methods for bounding the error in our estimate.

2 Methods

We assume a fixed test set consisting of translated segment pairs, and a single human rater who assigns scores to segments. Each segment belongs to a document, and has an associated vector of scores from automatic metrics. Our goal is to select an informative subset of segments to be labeled by the rater, and use the subset to predict the average score that would have resulted if we had asked the rater to label the whole set. By exploiting document and metric information, we hope to reduce the number of segments that must be manually labeled.

Formally, let $x_1, \ldots x_N$ be the segment scores, $\mu = \sum_{i=1}^{N} x_i/N$ be the test-set score to be predicted, and σ^2 be the variance of the scores. The following side information is available for each segment i: an index d_i that indicates its membership in one of D documents, and a vector of automatic-metric scores $\mathbf{y_i} \in \mathbb{R}^M$. Unlike the segment scores, which are only revealed if they are in the selected subset, the side information is always available for the whole test set.

We approach this task as the problem of sampling $n \leq N$ scores $X_1, \ldots, X_n$ without replacement from the test set and deriving an estimate $\hat{\mu}$ for μ from the sample such that $E(\hat{\mu}) = \mu$ (that is, $\hat{\mu}$ is unbiased) and $\text{Var}(\hat{\mu})$ is as small as possible. Low-variance estimators make it more likely that the estimation error $|\mu - \hat{\mu}|$ will be small. A baseline is to draw n segments at random and compute their mean. This gives an estimate that is unbiased, with variance:

$$\text{Var}(\hat{\mu}) = \frac{\sigma^2}{n}\left(\frac{N-n}{N-1}\right)$$

We investigated two classical unbiased strategies for reducing variance relative to this baseline: stratified sampling and control variates (Rice, 2007; Bratley et al., 2012).

2.1 Stratified sampling

Stratified sampling involves partitioning scores into bins that group similar items, then sampling some items from each bin. Intuitively, the idea is that if the variance within each bin is low, drawing too many samples from a particular bin is inefficient because it only serves to improve an already good estimate—therefore the sample should be spread evenly (in some sense) across bins. See Figure 1a for an illustration. As a side benefit, having human scores more evenly distributed across different types of segments is a useful characteristic if the labeled segments are to be the subject of further analysis.

Formally, suppose the test set is divided into L bins, where bin l contains N_l segments of which n_l have been sampled, with sample mean $\hat{\mu}_l$. Then the stratified estimate is:

$$\hat{\mu} = \sum_{l=1}^{L} \hat{\mu}_l \, N_l/N. \tag{1}$$

It is easy to verify that this is unbiased.

Stratified sampling requires a method for partitioning the test set into bins and a way of allocating the n segments in the sample to individual bins. We investigated two methods for partitioning the test set: by documents and by metric-score similarity. The optimal (lowest variance) allocation assigns segments proportional to a bin's size and variance:

$$n_l = n \frac{\sigma_l N_l}{\sum_{l=1}^{L} \sigma_l N_l}. \tag{2}$$

Since the bin variances σ_l are unknown, a conservative strategy is to assume they are all equal, resulting in pure proportional allocation: $n_l = n\, N_l/N$. A potential enhancement is to approximate optimal allocation using estimated variances $\hat{\sigma}_l \approx \sigma_l$ derived from the metric scores in each bin.

Two technical issues arise in stratified sampling. First, the per-bin sizes specified by equation (2) are not necessarily whole numbers. This can be solved using a rounding scheme that minimizes $\sum_{l=1}^{L} |n_l - n'_l|$, where n'_l are whole numbers that sum to n. A second problem is that n_l can be greater than the number of available segments N_l when using optimal allocation in high-variance bins. When this occurs, we choose the bin for which $n_l - N_l$ is largest, set $n_l = N_l$, then recursively reallocate the remaining bins. Note that both these strategies can result in bins for which $n_l = 0$ when n is small.

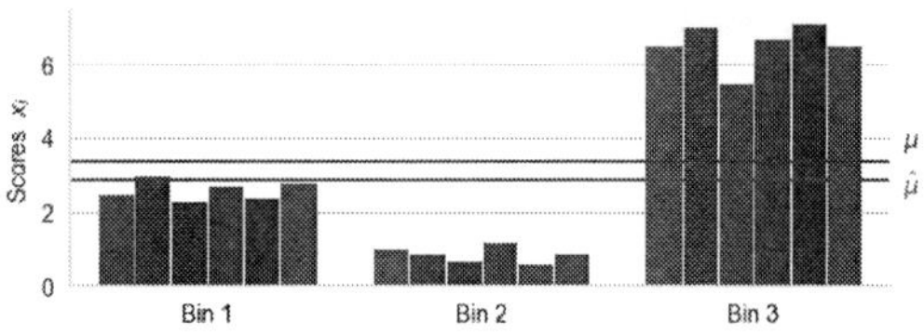

(a) Stratified sampling forces sampled segments (shown in red) to be evenly distributed across bins, resulting in better estimates when the score variance within bins is lower than the variance across bins.

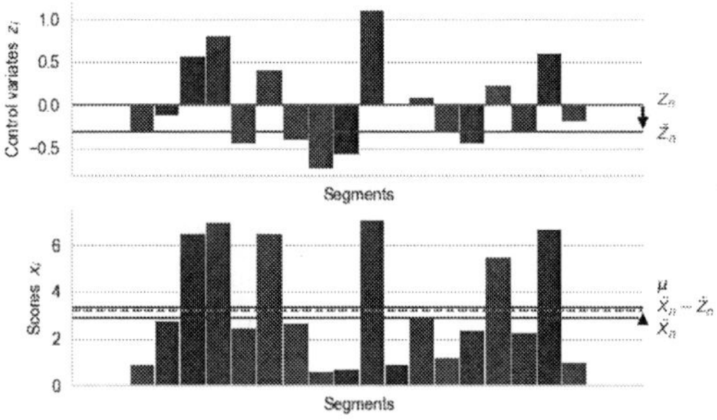

(b) Control variates allow for reversing the shift of the sample mean $\bar{X}_n$ depending on the strength of the correlation between X and Z. In this illustration, where X and Z are highly correlated (~0.9), $\bar{Z}_n < 0$ reflects the negative shift in $\bar{X}_n$.

Figure 1: Complementary strategies for reducing the variance of the estimated average score.

Incremental sampling

Hitherto we have assumed that sampling works by choosing a fixed batch of n segments, then sending them to a rater for scoring. It is also possible to consider an interactive scenario where the rater labels segments sequentially, and the sampling procedure is refined after each new rating is received. A convenient way to incorporate known ratings is to use them for improving the per-bin variance estimates $\hat{\sigma}_l$ in optimal allocation. We tested two ways of accomplishing this: empirically estimate $\hat{\sigma}_l$ from the known ratings in each bin; and learn a general mapping from metrics $\mathbf{y}$ to rating x over *all* known ratings, then use this mapping to estimate the unknown ratings in each bin, and derive $\hat{\sigma}_l$ from those estimates.

2.2 Control variates

The control-variates estimator makes use of an auxiliary random variable Z that is standardized (has zero mean and unit variance) on the test set:

$$\begin{aligned}\hat{\mu} &= \bar{X}_n - \frac{\text{Cov}(X,Z)}{\text{Var}(Z)}\bar{Z}_n \\ &= \bar{X}_n - \text{Cov}(X,Z)\,\bar{Z}_n\end{aligned} \tag{3}$$

where $\bar{X}_n$ and $\bar{Z}_n$ are mean values over the sample, and the covariance is over the whole test set. This is the lowest-variance estimator that uses information from Z. It is unbiased because $\bar{X}_n$ is unbiased, $\text{Cov}(X, Z)$ is independent of the current sample, and $E(\bar{Z}_n) = 0$. The control-variates estimator can be thought of as using $\bar{Z}_n$ to infer the direction that $\bar{X}_n$ has been shifted away from μ and reversing this shift by an amount that depends on the degree of correlation between X and Z—see Figure 1b for an illustration. In general, $\text{Cov}(X, Z)$ is unknown, but it can be estimated from the sample as follows:[1]

$$\text{Cov}(X,Z) \approx \frac{1}{n}\sum_{i=1}^{n} X_i Z_i.$$

The control-variates estimator can be extended to handle multiple auxiliary variables by forming a linear combination (Glynn and Szechtman, 2002):

$$\hat{\mu} = \bar{X}_n - (E(\mathbf{Z}\mathbf{Z}^T)^{-1}E(X\mathbf{Z}))^T\,\bar{\mathbf{Z}}_n \tag{4}$$

where $\mathbf{Z}$ is a vector of standardized variables, $\bar{\mathbf{Z}}_n$ is its mean over the sample, and the expectations of the covariance matrix $\mathbf{Z}\mathbf{Z}^T$ and weighted vectors $X\mathbf{Z}$ are taken over the test set. The latter is unknown, but as in the scalar case it can be estimated from the sample:

$$E(X\mathbf{Z}) \approx \frac{1}{n}\sum_{i=1}^{n} X_i \mathbf{Z}_i.$$

In our setting, control variates are easily derived by standardizing the metric scores $\mathbf{y}_i$, which are available for all segments in the test set. The resulting estimator is convenient because it is applied after sampling is complete, making it independent of the sampling method, including whether the sample is drawn incrementally or in batch mode.

2.3 Error Bounds

For practical applications it is desirable to upper-bound the error $|\mu - \hat{\mu}|$ in the estimated score with some degree of confidence. Given a confidence level γ (e.g., 0.95), we would like to find an error bound t such that:

$$P(|\mu - \hat{\mu}| \leq t) \geq \gamma \tag{5}$$

[1] This equation follows from expanding $\text{Cov}(X, Z)$ over the complete test set, dropping all terms that contain the true mean of Z (0 by construction) and estimating the one term that remains from the sample. Alternatively one can choose to estimate $\text{Cov}(X, Z)$ purely from the sample as $\sum_{i=1}^{n}(X_i - \bar{X})(Z_i - \bar{Z})/n$.

A classical bound can be derived from Hoeffding's inequality, which states that equation (5) holds if:

$$t = R\sqrt{\frac{k_n \log(2/\delta)}{2n}},$$

where R is the difference between the largest and smallest scores in the test set, $\delta = 1 - \gamma$, and $k_n = 1 - (n-1)/N$ is an adjustment for sampling without replacement (Serfling, 1974). A problem with Hoeffding's inequality is that it scales with the range of the scores and does not take variance into account, so its bound will be pessimistic if variance is small relative to the extremes. In such cases, the Bernstein bound (Mnih et al., 2008) will be tighter:

$$t = \hat{\sigma}\sqrt{\frac{2\log(3/\delta)}{n}} + \frac{3R\log(3/\delta)}{n},$$

where $\hat{\sigma}$ is a sample estimate of the variance. Note that the contribution of R diminishes as $1/n$ in this formula, compared with $1/\sqrt{n}$ in the Hoeffding bound. Both these bounds are general in the sense that they make no assumptions about the score distribution.

3 Data

Our development data consists of MQM ratings made available by Freitag et al. (2021a) for 10 English-German and 10 Chinese-English "systems" (including human translations and MT) from the WMT 2020 news test sets (Barrault et al., 2020). Each segment was annotated by three expert raters who assigned scores ranging from 0 (perfect) to 25 (worst). There were six annotators per language pair, each of whom rated all system outputs for a set of documents comprising approximately half the complete test set (about 710 segments / rater for German, and 1000 segments / rater for Chinese).

We created simulations for each rater and system combination, excluding the *Human-A* "system", as it was the reference for the MT metrics we used as features. This resulted in 54 simulations for each language pair. For each simulation, the task is to predict the average score over the complete subset of segments annotated by a single rater for a single system. No knowledge of other segments, system outputs, or rater decisions is permitted to leak across simulations. As features, we used the 10 metrics submitted to the WMT 2020 metrics task (Mathur et al., 2020) that had highest average segment-level Pearson correlation with the MQM scores in our dev data.[2] These correlations are generally poor: from 0.279–0.410 for English-German, and 0.425–0.465 for Chinese-English.[3]

To eliminate the effects of hyper-parameter tuning on the development data, we carried out additional evaluation on a test set consisting of newstest data from the WMT 2021 metrics shared task (Freitag et al., 2021b) for English-German (17 systems), Chinese-English (15 systems), and English-Russian (16 systems). This is similar to the dev data, except that only one MQM rating is available per segment. The number of rated segments was 527 for German and Russian, and 650 for Chinese. English-Russian ratings were annotated using a different MQM methodology (from Unbabel rather than Google), resulting in scores on a 0–100 scale, with 100 being best. As before, we created separate simulations for each system, omitting the human "system" used as a reference for the metrics. To avoid bias, rather than selecting metrics according to correlation, we chose the WMT 2021 primary submissions of two top-performing metrics from the dev data: BLEURT and COMET.[4]

Appendix A contains further details about scores and rater assignments for the dev and test sets.

4 Results

We tested the sampling and estimation strategies described in section 2 by comparing them to the baseline of simple random sampling with a mean estimator. For each simulation we considered sample sizes ranging from 5–50% of the available data, at 5% intervals.[5] For each sample size and technique for establishing $\hat{\mu}$, we drew 100 random samples, computed the average and std deviation of the error $|\mu - \hat{\mu}|$ across the samples, then averaged the results across simulations to summarize performance at that sample size. We also measured the number of "wins"—simulations in which a technique had a lower average error than the baseline. Finally, we aggregated these results across sample sizes to summarize performance in a single number.

[2]We also tried using *all* submitted metrics, with slightly worse results.

[3]For comparison, target sequence length correlations are 0.223 and 0.439 respectively (better than the three lowest-ranked metrics for Chinese).

[4]The primary submissions were *BLEURT-20* and *COMET-MQM_2021*.

[5]Beyond 50%, the variance of the baseline estimator becomes very low and there is limited opportunity for improvement.

4.1 Stratified sampling

	method	abs error	sdev	win %
EnDe	baseline	0.171	0.128	–
	docs-prop	0.158	0.118	75.7
	docs-opt	0.213	0.145	32.6
	metrics-prop	0.157	0.118	77.2
ZhEn	baseline	0.290	0.217	–
	docs-prop	0.250	0.187	92.4
	docs-opt	0.356	0.233	27.2
	metrics-prop	0.246	0.185	91.1

Table 1: Stratified sampling results aggregated over sample sizes from 5%–50%. Segment allocation is referred to as 'prop' for proportional- and as 'opt' for optimal-allocation with either document-based (docs) or metric-based (metrics) bin membership.

We begin by evaluating the stratified sampling methods described in section 2.1, comparing stratification over documents and over bins defined by metric scores. The latter were formed by scoring each segment with an average of the standardized metric scores assigned to it, then sorting and partitioning so each bin contained approximately 80 segments (8x larger than the average document). More elaborate clustering and metric-selection techniques did not improve over this method. Performance was also quite flat as a function of bin size, though it worsened as bin size approached average document size. We tested both stratification methods with proportional and optimal allocation using averaged metric scores as proxies for human scores when estimating the variance in each bin.

Figure 2 shows absolute error for these methods as a function of sample size, and Table 1 summarizes aggregate performance across sizes. The general pattern is similar for both language pairs: proportional allocation with documents (*docs-prop*) outperforms the random-sampling baseline; proportional allocation with metrics (*metrics-prop*) behaves similarly; and optimal allocation with document bins (*docs-opt*) underperforms, as does optimal allocation with metric bins (not shown, as it is much worse). Optimal allocation focuses sharply on bins with high estimated variance—which will be harmful if the estimates are wrong—so we experimented with various smoothing methods, but none improved over pure proportional allocation.

Although stratification clearly reduces the error on average, the usefulness of this result is tempered by the large variances shown in Table 1. For any given random draw, these imply that the stratified estimate is only slightly more likely to be better than the baseline. Even when comparing errors averaged over 100 random draws per simulation, the stratified estimates are only better than the baseline for approximately 75% of simulations for English-German, and 90% for Chinese-English.

Incremental sampling

	method	abs error	sdev	win %
EnDe	baseline	0.171	0.128	–
	docs-incr-metrics	0.183	0.132	44.1
	docs-incr-human	0.231	0.143	26.7
ZhEn	baseline	0.290	0.217	–
	docs-incr-metrics	0.346	0.239	25.4
	docs-incr-human	0.418	0.251	27.4

Table 2: Incremental stratified sampling results aggregated over sample sizes from 5%–50%.

Table 2 shows aggregate results for incremental stratified sampling using documents as bins, with two methods for estimating per-bin variances for optimal allocation.[6] The *docs-incr-metrics* method involves learning a k-nearest-neighbor (k=25) model with standardized metrics as features on all labeled segments, then using its predictions to estimate variances for the unlabeled segments in each bin. In *docs-incr-human*, the variance of the segments remaining in each bin is estimated from the segments that have already been scored. Both these methods underperform the baseline; in particular, the use of a learned mapping in *docs-incr-metrics* provides only modest gains over the raw averages in *docs-opt*.

4.2 Control variates and combined results

	method	abs error	sdev	win %
EnDe	baseline	0.171	0.128	–
	cv-bleurt	0.158	0.118	74.3
	cv-mean	0.159	0.118	74.8
	cv-multi	0.160	0.118	73.3
	cv-knn	0.158	0.119	74.1
ZhEn	baseline	0.290	0.217	–
	cv-bleurt	0.260	0.193	84.1
	cv-mean	0.251	0.188	88.3
	cv-multi	0.254	0.188	88.5
	cv-knn	0.246	0.185	92.2

Table 3: Control variates results aggregated over sample sizes from 5%–50%.

We now turn to experiments with the control-variate estimators described in section 2.2. Figure 3

[6] We omit the corresponding curves for space reasons.

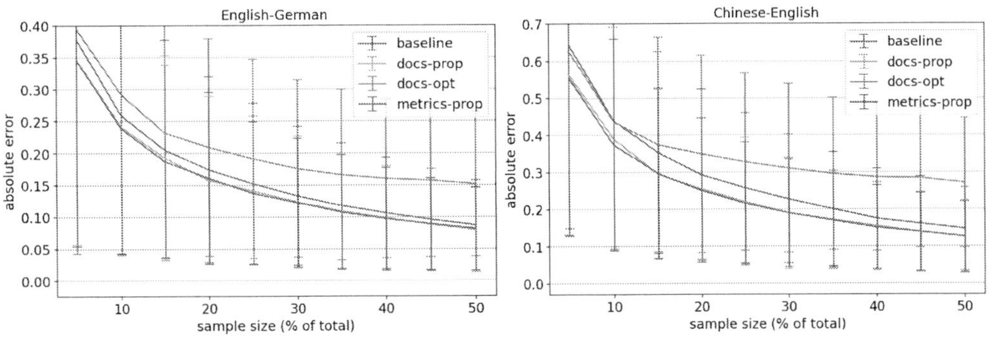

Figure 2: Absolute error and standard deviation for stratified sampling methods.

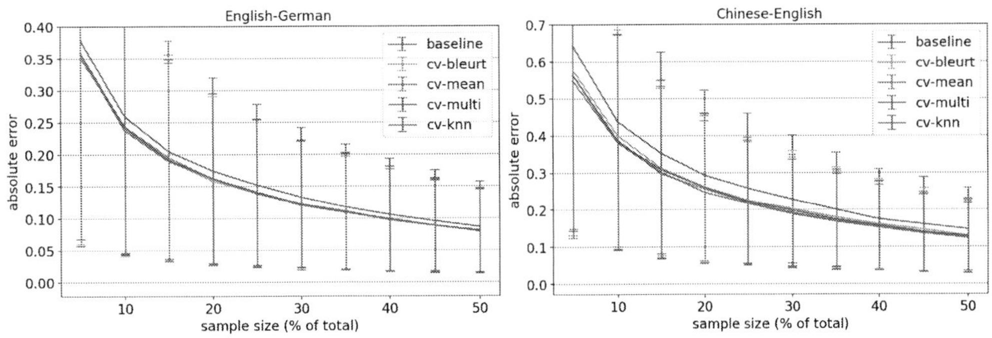

Figure 3: Absolute error and std deviation for different control-variate estimators with random sampling.

	method	abs error	sdev	win %
EnDe	baseline	0.171	0.128	–
	docs-prop	0.158	0.118	75.7
	cv-knn	0.158	0.119	74.1
	docs-prop+cv-knn	0.147	0.110	88.5
	metrics-prop+cv-knn	0.156	0.116	77.8
ZhEn	baseline	0.290	0.217	–
	docs-prop	0.250	0.187	92.4
	cv-knn	0.246	0.185	92.2
	docs-prop+cv-knn	0.224	0.167	98.5
	metrics-prop+cv-knn	0.244	0.182	92.0

Table 4: Combined stratified sampling and control variates aggregated over sample sizes from 5%–50%.

and Table 3 present the results. We derived standardized scalar variates to plug into equation (3) from: a single high-performing metric (BLEURT-extended, *cv-bleurt*); the mean of all metrics (*cv-mean*); and predictions from a knn model learned from all metric values on the labeled segments (*cv-knn*). We also used all standardized metrics directly (*cv-multi*) as input to the vector in equation (4).[7]

All tested variants give reasonable improvements over the baseline, with quite similar error rates, especially for English-German. For Chinese-English, combining all metrics with the knn model improves slightly over BLEURT-extended, reducing the absolute error by 5%. This may reflect somewhat higher metric correlations for this language pair.

As control variate estimation is applied after sampling is complete, it is straightforward to combine it with stratification. Figure 4 and Table 4 show the results of combining proportional stratified sampling using documents with the best control variates estimator (*docs-prop+cv-knn*), along with the component techniques for comparison. As one might hope, the techniques are complementary despite their similar individual performance. Interestingly, this is not the case when metric-based clusters are used for stratification instead of documents (*metrics-prop+cv-knn*, last line in Table 4), because the same information is used for both variance-reduction techniques. The *docs-prop+cv-knn* combination produces our best results, with error reductions of 14% and 23% over the baseline for English-German and English-Chinese, and better average performance in almost 90% and 100% of simulations, respectively. Unfortunately, however, the standard deviation of these estimates remains

[7]Note that the latter combines scores linearly, in contrast to the knn model.

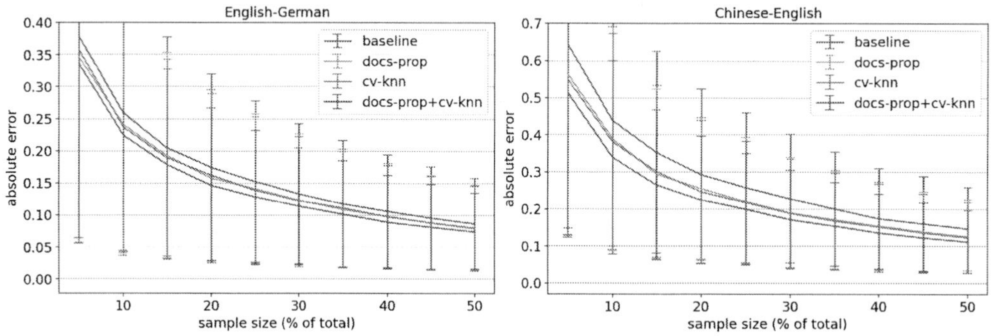

Figure 4: Absolute error and std deviation for control-variate estimators and stratified sampling.

uncomfortably close to the size of the average absolute error.

4.3 Error estimation

size (%)		EnDe Hoeffding (4) cal	slack	t	ZhEn Hoeffding (7) cal	slack	t
10	base	92	0.36	0.61	89	0.56	0.90
	best	96	0.40		97	0.49	
30	base	93	0.19	0.31	90	0.29	0.46
	best	96	0.20		96	0.25	
50	base	92	0.12	0.20	90	0.19	0.30
	best	96	0.13		96	0.16	

Table 5: Performance of error bounds for different sample sizes. Statistics are averaged over simulations: *cal* is % of samples for which the true error was lower than the bound, *slack* is the difference between the bound and the error, and *t* is the bound. *base* is the baseline estimator, and *best* is *docs-prop+cv-knn*.

Despite large variance across individual samples, sampling techniques can be useful in practice if it is possible to reliably bound the error in the estimate derived from a given sample. We computed the bounds from section 2.3 for different sample sizes with *docs-prop+cv-knn*, setting $\gamma = 0.95$. Both the Hoeffding and Bernstein bounds are very loose, overestimating the true error in 100% of samples, by margins that are about an order of magnitude greater than the average error in Figure 4.[8] We hypothesize that this is due to scores having a large range R, and being highly skewed, with $\mu \ll R$.

To test this, we recomputed the Hoeffding bound with empirically-determined R values of 4 and 7 for English-German and Chinese-English. As shown in Table 5, this gives results which are well calibrated (*cal* > 95%) for *doc-prop+cv-knn*, with reasonable error bounds. Performance is somewhat worse for the baseline estimates, although the difference in error between the two techniques is negligible compared to the predicted bound. This oracle experiment suggests that it will be difficult to find non-oracle bounds that are substantially lower for *doc-prop+cv-knn* than for the baseline.

4.4 Results on test data

	method	abs err	sdev	win %
EnDe	baseline	0.203	0.153	–
	docs-prop+cv-knn	0.188	0.140	78.1
ZhEn	baseline	0.359	0.267	–
	docs-prop+cv-knn	0.283	0.212	97.9
EnRu	baseline	1.601	1.197	–
	docs-prop+cv-knn	1.482	1.117	77.3

Table 6: Results on test data for baseline and best combined estimator aggregated over sample sizes from 5%–50%.

Figure 5 and Table 6 show results comparing baseline random sampling with *docs-prop+cv-knn* on our evaluation set. Both the curves and the aggregate results display a similar pattern to the development results, with relatively large gains over the baseline for Chinese-English (21% relative error reduction, wins in 98% of simulations), and smaller ones for English-German and English-Russian[9] (reductions of 7% and win rates of about 77%). As before, standard deviations are very high.

[8]Surprisingly, the Bernstein bound is somewhat worse, likely due to our small sample sizes in conjunction with the large multiplier on R in the Bernstein formula.

[9]Note that the absolute errors are higher for English-Russian due to the 4x scale for ratings.

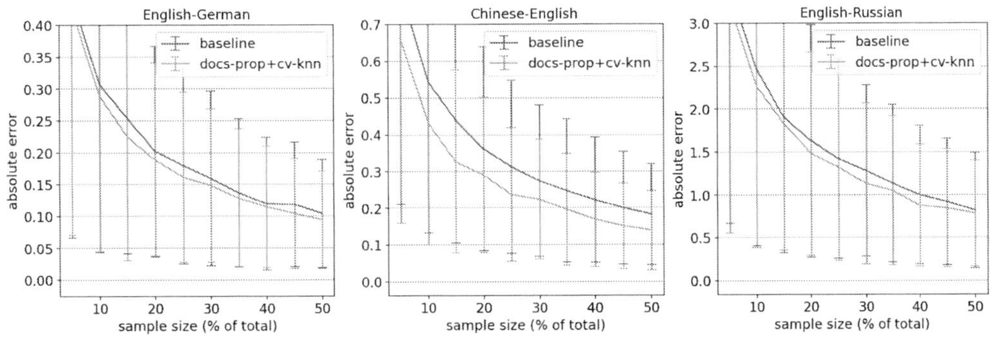

Figure 5: Absolute error for control-variate estimators and stratified sampling on eval data.

5 Discussion

How should we interpret these results? If we had a more reliable way of binning segments with similar human ratings, or metrics that correlated better at the segment level, it would be possible to reduce variance to levels that would permit realistic error bounds. That would enable a scenario in which we could determine the number of segments n that need to be rated in order to estimate the complete test-set score to within a given tolerance. As it is, however, our error bounds are very large—and we do not manage to reduce them significantly with improved sampling and estimation methods. This is unlikely to change soon for complex annotation tasks like MT because because humans are noisy raters; as shown in Table 12, they are difficult to predict even when using other humans as oracles.

In the absence of more reliable signals for reducing variance, a way to make practical use of the techniques we study is to flip the scenario around and aim to improve the quality of an estimate made from a fixed budget of n human ratings. It is common practice to obtain human annotations for only a portion of a larger test set due to time or cost constraints (Barrault et al., 2020; Freitag et al., 2021a). In this setting, our techniques can lead to improved estimates compared to just taking the mean of randomly-selected segments (although there is no guarantee that they will do so for any given sample).

The risks in applying this strategy are low. Stratified sampling with proportional allocation provides an unbiased estimate of the test-set mean, with variance that is $\leq$ random sampling (Rice, 2007), and equality only in the case that the bins have identical statistics. The situation is trickier for control variates. In theory, the control-variate estimator is also unbiased, with lower variance than the sample mean, but this assumes that the test-set covariance $\mathrm{Cov}(X, Z)$ between scores X and the auxiliary variable Z is known. Since we only know the scores in the sample, we must rely on an estimate for $\mathrm{Cov}(X, Z)$, creating the possibility for errors if this is significantly larger than the true covariance. However, as Chaganty et al. (2018) point out, the error in the sample estimate for $\mathrm{Cov}(X, Z)$ diminishes as $1/n$, much faster than the $1/\sqrt{n}$ rate for the error $|\mu - \hat{\mu}|$ in the estimated score. In our data, we found no appreciable degradation of performance on small samples, even ones containing as few as 30 items.

Based on these observations, we can make the following recommendations for improving the estimated mean score of a test set containing N items given a fixed number $n < N$ of items to be manually annotated:

1. Use prior information such as document membership to partition items into bins, then choose items using stratified sampling as described in equation (1), with proportional allocation. Beware of rounding errors when only a few samples are taken from each bin.

2. Use an automatic metric or other feature that correlates with human scores as a control variate in equation (3). This step is carried out after sampling is complete, and is independent of the sampling method used. If multiple metrics are available, combine them into a single variate by averaging or applying a smooth regressor learned on the sample (knn with k=25 worked well for us). Be alert to the possibility of errors in the covariance estimate when n is small (≤ 30).

6 Related Work

Chaganty et al. (2018) pioneered control variates for NLP evaluation, using them to improve estimates for summarization and question answering. Despite some technical differences—they measure variance ratios rather than absolute error, simulate human variance by sampling from a collection of raters, and use bootstrapped confidence intervals—their findings are roughly in line with ours. We extend their work by showing that gains from stratified sampling are complementary to those from control variates, and explore a broader range of scenarios, including using multiple variates and incremental sampling.

Recent work has investigated incremental labeling tasks and/or combining human scores with automatic metrics. Mendonça et al. (2021) apply online learning algorithms to an MT system-ranking task in which different segments are selected for human evaluation on each iteration, using COMET to fill in missing human scores in WMT 2019 data. Their algorithm converges to correct results after several hundred iterations, but this condition is not detected automatically. Thorleiksdóttir et al. (2021) use Hoeffding's inequality to measure confidence in pairwise ranking decisions of varying difficulties for controlled text generation output; they consider human scores only. Singla et al. (2021) sample foreign-language test responses for human grading, with the aim of improving over purely automatic scoring; a reverse problem to ours. Hashimoto et al. (2019) propose a synergistic combination of human and automatic scoring for evaluating text generation.

Finally, there has been considerable work on measuring and rectifying inaccuracies in human annotation (Sun et al., 2020; Wei and Jia, 2021; Gladkoff et al., 2021; Paun et al., 2018). We sidestep this issue by aiming to predict the performance of a single human rater, assuming that if this can be done accurately, conflicts among raters can be resolved in a post-processing step.

7 Conclusion

We investigate two classical variance-reduction techniques for improving the accuracy of sampled human ratings of MT output, measured against the mean of all ratings for a given test set. We find that stratified sampling and control variates are complementary, contributing about equally to gains of up to 20% in average absolute error reduction compared to random sampling. Exploiting this result to dynamically reduce annotator effort given a target error tolerance is not feasible due to the high variance in our data, but we propose that our techniques could instead be used to improve estimates made from a fixed annotation budget. Concrete recommendations for this scenario are provided in section 5. Our method is easy to implement, and can be applied to any setting involving averaged numerical item-wise scores where document (or other prior grouping) and automatic metric side information is available.

In future work we look forward to delving into questions raised by our results: why doesn't optimal allocation work better, particularly in the incremental setting; is there a better way to estimate variance from metrics; why aren't metric combinations more helpful; and can error bounds be improved, perhaps with bootstrapping methods?

References

Loïc Barrault, Magdalena Biesialska, Ondřej Bojar, Marta R. Costa-jussà, Christian Federmann, Yvette Graham, Roman Grundkiewicz, Barry Haddow, Matthias Huck, Eric Joanis, Tom Kocmi, Philipp Koehn, Chi-kiu Lo, Nikola Ljubešić, Christof Monz, Makoto Morishita, Masaaki Nagata, Toshiaki Nakazawa, Santanu Pal, Matt Post, and Marcos Zampieri. 2020. Findings of the 2020 Conference on Machine Translation (WMT20). In *Proceedings of the Fifth Conference on Machine Translation*, pages 1–55, Online. Association for Computational Linguistics.

P. Bratley, B.L. Fox, and L.E. Schrage. 2012. *A Guide to Simulation*. Springer New York.

Arun Chaganty, Stephen Mussmann, and Percy Liang. 2018. The price of debiasing automatic metrics in natural language evalaution. In *Proceedings of the 56th Annual Meeting of the Association for Computational Linguistics (Volume 1: Long Papers)*, pages 643–653, Melbourne, Australia. Association for Computational Linguistics.

Markus Freitag, George Foster, David Grangier, Viresh Ratnakar, Qijun Tan, and Wolfgang Macherey. 2021a. Experts, Errors, and Context: A Large-Scale Study of Human Evaluation for Machine Translation. *Transactions of the Association for Computational Linguistics*, 9:1460–1474.

Markus Freitag, Ricardo Rei, Nitika Mathur, Chi-kiu Lo, Craig Stewart, George Foster, Alon Lavie, and Ondřej Bojar. 2021b. Results of the WMT21 metrics shared task: Evaluating metrics with expert-based human evaluations on TED and news domain. In *Proceedings of the Sixth Conference on Machine*

Translation, pages 733–774, Online. Association for Computational Linguistics.

Sebastian Gehrmann, Elizabeth Clark, and Thibault Sellam. 2022. Repairing the cracked foundation: A survey of obstacles in evaluation practices for generated text. *arXiv preprint arXiv:2202.06935*.

Serge Gladkoff, Irina Sorokina, Lifeng Han, and Alexandra Alekseeva. 2021. Measuring uncertainty in translation quality evaluation (tqe). *arXiv preprint arXiv:2111.07699*.

Peter W Glynn and Roberto Szechtman. 2002. Some new perspectives on the method of control variates. In *Monte Carlo and Quasi-Monte Carlo Methods 2000*, pages 27–49. Springer.

Tatsu Hashimoto, Hugh Zhang, and Percy Liang. 2019. Unifying human and statistical evaluation for natural language generation. In *North American Association for Computational Linguistics (NAACL)*.

Nitika Mathur, Johnny Wei, Markus Freitag, Qingsong Ma, and Ondřej Bojar. 2020. Results of the WMT20 metrics shared task. In *Proceedings of the Fifth Conference on Machine Translation*, pages 688–725, Online. Association for Computational Linguistics.

Vânia Mendonça, Ricardo Rei, Luísa Coheur, Alberto Sardinha, and Ana Lúcia Santos. 2021. Online learning meets machine translation evaluation: Finding the best systems with the least human effort. In *Proceedings of the 59th Annual Meeting of the Association for Computational Linguistics and the 11th International Joint Conference on Natural Language Processing (Volume 1: Long Papers)*, pages 3105–3117.

Volodymyr Mnih, Csaba Szepesvári, and Jean-Yves Audibert. 2008. Empirical bernstein stopping. In *Proceedings of the 25th international conference on Machine learning*, pages 672–679.

Kishore Papineni, Salim Roukos, Todd Ward, and Wei-Jing Zhu. 2002. Bleu: a method for automatic evaluation of machine translation. In *Proceedings of the 40th annual meeting of the Association for Computational Linguistics*, pages 311–318.

Silviu Paun, Bob Carpenter, Jon Chamberlain, Dirk Hovy, Udo Kruschwitz, and Massimo Poesio. 2018. Comparing bayesian models of annotation. *Transactions of the Association for Computational Linguistics*, 6:571–585.

Ricardo Rei, Craig Stewart, Ana C Farinha, and Alon Lavie. 2020. COMET: A neural framework for MT evaluation. In *Proceedings of the 2020 Conference on Empirical Methods in Natural Language Processing (EMNLP)*, pages 2685–2702, Online. Association for Computational Linguistics.

J.A. Rice. 2007. *Mathematical Statistics and Data Analysis*. Advanced series. Cengage Learning.

Thibault Sellam, Dipanjan Das, and Ankur Parikh. 2020. BLEURT: Learning robust metrics for text generation. In *Proceedings of the 58th Annual Meeting of the Association for Computational Linguistics*, pages 7881–7892, Online. Association for Computational Linguistics.

R. J. Serfling. 1974. Probability inequalities for the sum in sampling without replacement. *The Annals of Statistics*, 2(1).

Yaman Kumar Singla, Sriram Krishna, Rajiv Ratn Shah, and Changyou Chen. 2021. Using sampling to estimate and improve performance of automated scoring systems with guarantees.

David Q. Sun, Hadas Kotek, Christopher Klein, Mayank Gupta, William Li, and Jason D. Williams. 2020. Improving human-labeled data through dynamic automatic conflict resolution. In *Proceedings of the 28th International Conference on Computational Linguistics*, pages 3547–3557, Barcelona, Spain (Online). International Committee on Computational Linguistics.

Thórhildur Thorleiksdóttir, Cedric Renggli, Nora Hollenstein, and Ce Zhang. 2021. Dynamic human evaluation for relative model comparisons.

Johnny Wei and Robin Jia. 2021. The statistical advantage of automatic NLG metrics at the system level. In *Proceedings of the 59th Annual Meeting of the Association for Computational Linguistics and the 11th International Joint Conference on Natural Language Processing (Volume 1: Long Papers)*, pages 6840–6854, Online. Association for Computational Linguistics.

Asli Çelikyilmaz, Elizabeth Clark, and Jianfeng Gao. 2020. Evaluation of text generation: A survey. *ArXiv*, abs/2006.14799.

	EnDe		ZhEn	
rater	segs	docs	segs	docs
rater1	713	64	993	76
rater2	683	66	992	76
rater3	705	66	1012	78
rater4	709	65	996	79
rater5	722	64	1021	77
rater6	722	65	986	79
corpus	1418	130	2000	155

Table 7: Numbers of segments and documents annotated by each rater for each system in WMT 2020 newstest.

EnDe		ZhEn	
system	MQM	system	MQM
Human-B	0.75	**Human-A**	3.43
Human-A	0.91	Human-B	3.62
Human-P	1.41	VolcTrans	5.03
Tohoku	2.02	WeChat	5.13
OPPO	2.25	Tencent	5.19
eTranslation	2.33	OPPO	5.20
Tencent	2.35	THUNLP	5.34
VolcTrans	2.45	DeepMind	5.41
Online-B	2.48	DiDi_NLP	5.48
Online-A	2.99	Online-B	5.85

Table 8: MQM scores for WMT 2020 outputs from (Freitag et al., 2021a). Scores range from 0 (perfect) to 25 (worst). The reference used for metrics is shown in bold.

A Data

This section gives details of the development and test data used in our experiments. Table 7 shows the numbers of segments and documents assigned to each rater in our development data. Table 8 contains the scores assigned to all ten evaluated systems; each score is an average of three rater scores per segments, averaged over all segments in the test set. Table 9 lists the selected metrics used for the development-set experiments, along with the segment-level Pearson correlation for each metric. Tables 10 and 11 contain rater assignments and system scores for the three language pairs used in the test data.

EnDe		ZhEn	
metric	r	metric	r
BLEURT-extended	0.410	COMET-QE	0.465
COMET-2R	0.379	BLEURT-extended	0.460
COMET-MQM	0.364	YiSi-2	0.453
COMET-QE	0.358	COMET-2R	0.452
COMET	0.349	BERT-base-L2	0.446
COMET-HTER	0.326	OpenKiwi-XLMR	0.440
OpenKiwi-XLMR	0.314	BERT-large-L2	0.440
mBERT-L2	0.306	BLEURT	0.437
prism	0.293	COMET	0.433
YiSi-1	0.279	mBERT-L2	0.425
target-length	0.223	target-length	0.439

Table 9: Segment-level Pearson correlations between selected automatic metrics and MQM ratings on system outputs from WMT 2020 newstest. The correlations shown are computed separately for each rater and system (excluding human outputs), then averaged.

	EnDe		ZhEn		EnRu	
rater	segs	docs	segs	docs	segs	docs
rater	527	32	650	51	527	32
corpus	1002	68	1948	156	1002	68

Table 10: Numbers of segments and documents annotated by each rater for each system in WMT 2021 newstest.

EnDe		ZhEn		EnRu	
system	MQM	system	MQM	system	MQM
ref-C	0.51	**ref-B**	4.27	**ref-A**	99.65
ref-D	0.52	ref-A	4.35	ref-B	98.40
ref-B	0.80	metricsystem1	4.42	Facebook-AI	92.75
VolcTrans-GLAT	1.04	metricsystem4	4.62	Online-W	91.80
Facebook-AI	1.05	NiuTrans	4.63	metricsystem4	91.25
ref-A	1.22	SMU	4.84	metricsystem5	90.88
Nemo	1.34	MiSS	4.93	metricsystem1	90.79
HuaweiTSC	1.38	Borderline	4.94	metricsystem2	89.86
Online-W	1.46	metricsystem2	5.04	Online-A	87.87
UEdin	1.51	DIDI-NLP	5.09	Nemo	87.50
eTranslation	1.70	IIE-MT	5.14	Online-G	87.22
VolcTrans-AT	1.74	Facebook-AI	5.21	Manifold	86.86
metricsystem4	2.05	metricsystem3	5.39	Online-B	85.66
metricsystem1	2.07	Online-W	5.57	metricsystem3	85.65
metricsystem3	2.27	metricsystem5	6.39	NiuTrans	83.47
metricsystem2	2.58			Online-Y	79.27
metricsystem5	2.61				

Table 11: MQM scores for WMT 2021 outputs from (Freitag et al., 2021b). Scores range from 0 (perfect) to 25 (worst), except for English-Russian, where they range from 0 (worst) to 100 (perfect). The reference used for metrics is shown in bold.

B Variabililty in human scores

A difficulty in predicting human ratings is that humans are noisy annotators (Wei and Jia, 2021). To quantify the noise in our data, we computed the error when predicting each rater's average score over their assigned segments using the average of the other two raters who also rated those segments. Table 12 shows that this varies substantially across raters and languages, with the hardest-to-predict rater's error being over 3x that of the easiest-to-predict rater in both languages, and Chinese-English errors being higher than English-German. (Variance across raters may be due in part to differences in their assigned subsets of segments, as some segments are harder to rate than others. Variances across languages is likely due to Chinese-English system scores being higher (worse) than German-English scores.) Comparing the average errors of 0.3 and 0.8 for English-German and Chinese-English to Figure 4, we observe that only a small number of samples (less than 10%) of a particular annotator's own ratings are sufficient to predict their test-set score with greater precision than knowing the average of other raters' scores over the whole test set (a rough proxy for the "true" test-set score).

A key element of our technique is using automatic MT metrics to predict human scores at the segment level. Figure 6 shows scatter plots for a single high-performing metric (COMET) that illustrate the challenges with this: the relation with MQM scores is noisy and non-linear, and there are extreme outliers due to segments that were assigned the worst possible MQM score. Furthermore, as indicated by the slope of the regression lines, the relation can vary substantially across different settings, even for different systems scored by a single rater, or for the same system scored by different raters. This implies that a strategy of pre-calibrating a particular metric on data that is independent of the current rater and system is likely to be ineffective for our problem.

	EnDe	ZhEn
rater1	0.13	0.37
rater2	0.22	0.60
rater3	0.47	0.38
rater4	0.32	1.55
rater5	0.14	1.40
rater6	0.33	0.69
avgs	0.27	0.83

Table 12: Absolute errors when predicting each rater's score from the average of other raters' scores. Numbers shown are averages over all systems and all segments annotated by the given rater.

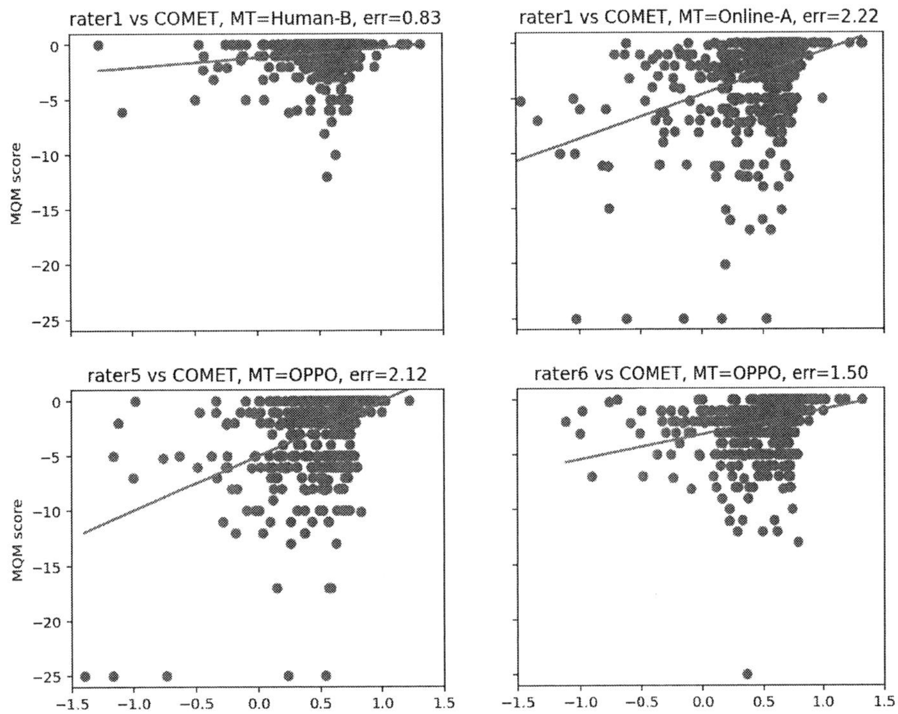

Figure 6: Example WMT20 EnDe human MQM versus COMET scores for the same rater but different MT systems (top panels), and different raters but the same MT system (bottom panels). Each point represents a single segment, and the lines show the best linear fit. Errors are average absolute segment-level differences between the line and the points.

A Study on Manual and Automatic Evaluation for Text Style Transfer: The Case of Detoxification

Varvara Logacheva[1*], **Daryna Dementieva**[1,5*], **Irina Krotova**[2], **Alena Fenogenova**[3], **Irina Nikishina**[1], **Tatiana Shavrina**[3,4], **and Alexander Panchenko**[1]
[1]Skolkovo Institute of Science and Technology (Skoltech), [2]Mobile TeleSystems (MTS), [3]SberDevices (Sber), [4]AI Research Institute (AIRI), [5]Technical University of Munich (TUM)
{v.logacheva, daryna.dementieva, irina.nikishina, a.panchenko}@skoltech.ru, fenogenova.a.s@sberbank.ru, rybolos@gmail.com, i.krotova@mts.ai

Abstract

It is often difficult to reliably evaluate models which generate text. Among them, text style transfer is a particularly difficult to evaluate, because its success depends on a number of parameters. We conduct an evaluation of a large number of models on a detoxification task. We explore the relations between the manual and automatic metrics and find that there is only weak correlation between them, which is dependent on the type of model which generated text. Automatic metrics tend to be less reliable for better-performing models. However, our findings suggest that, ChrF and BertScore metrics can be used as a proxy for human evaluation of text detoxification to some extent.

1 Introduction

There exist many Natural Language Processing (NLP) tasks whose output is a text (dialogue, summarization, etc.). They often adopt the evaluation techniques from Machine Translation (MT). Namely, researchers often compare the output of a model with a pre-defined reference answer and measure the model quality as the similarity to this reference. The similarity can be computed at the level of words and phrases (e.g. BLEU or METEOR) or be more semantically motivated and compare the embeddings (e.g. BertScore or BLEURT).

This approach has a number of drawbacks which make it inapplicable to some generation tasks, e.g. style transfer. This is a task of changing a text such that its meaning stays the same and the *style* changes. Style can refer to any attribute concerning only the form of the text (e.g. degree of formality or politeness) or its content (e.g. sentiment, author features, etc.). When evaluating the output of a style transfer model, we need to pay attention to both the style change and the content preservation. The traditional MT evaluation metrics mainly check the semantic similarity, which makes them unsuitable for style transfer.

There exist evaluation metrics (Krishna et al., 2020) which were devised to consider all important aspects of style transfer quality (style, semantic similarity and sometimes fluency). However, they heavily rely on automatic models (e.g. style classifier) whose performance is not perfect. Many works acknowledge the low reliability of such metrics and arrange manual evaluation to get the objective information on the models performance. Unfortunately, such evaluation is laborious and cannot be conducted often, so during development of models researchers still have to resort to automatic metrics.

Although works on style transfer acknowledge that automatic evaluation metrics are unreliable, there is little work on the analysis of their performance. There exist analysis of content preservation metrics (Yamshchikov et al., 2021) and of all style transfer evaluation metrics (Briakou et al., 2021a). The latter work provides an evaluation where metrics are tested on different systems and different style transfer directions.

We further extend this line of research by testing the evaluation metrics on a new style transfer task (detoxification) and a new language (Russian). For this comparison we create a large parallel corpus for detoxification. We compare the performance of models based on different principles, which allows more robust evaluation. Furthermore, since we compare a large number of models, we can understand to what extent the automatic metrics can *rank* the models correctly. Besides that, due to the large number of tested models we decided to use crowdsourced evaluation instead of experts. We describe our crowdsourcing annotation setup and analyse the performance of crowd workers. Finally, the large-scale evaluation allows us to gain insights on the performance of various style transfer models. The research was based on the data of a competition of detoxification models for the Russian language

[*] Equal contribution

Proceedings of the 2nd Workshop on Human Evaluation of NLP Systems (HumEval), pages 90 - 101
May 27, 2022

organized by the authors of this paper.[1]

2 Evaluation

2.1 Style Transfer Formulation

The style transfer task is formulated as follows. We would like to rewrite a text so that it keeps most of its content, but one particular attribute of this text (denoted as *style*) changes. The "style" can refer to various features of the text such as the level of formality, politeness, simplicity, the presence of bias or the features of the author (e.g. gender or membership in a political party). The task is usually to transfer between two "opposite" styles (polite–impolite, positive–negative), but there can exist models which support multiple exclusive or non-exclusive styles.

Style transfer task can be formally defined as follows. We have a set of styles $S = \{s_{src}, s_{tg}\}$[2] and two corpora $D^{src} = \{d_1^{src}, ..., d_n^{src}\}$ and $D^{tg} = \{d_1^{tg}, ..., d_m^{tg}\}$ in the styles s_{src} and s_{tg}, respectively. Let us also define the following functions. The style of a sentence is measured with $\sigma : D \to S$. A binary function $\delta : D \times D \to \{0, 1\}$ indicates the equivalence of meanings of the two styles. Finally, the function $\theta : D \to \{0, 1\}$ defines if a text belongs to well-formed sentences.

Text style transfer task is thus defined as a function $\alpha : S \times S \times D \to D$. Given a text d^{src} and its source and target styles s_{src} and s_{tg} it transforms the text to a new text d^{tg} such that:

- the style of the text is changed from the source s_{src} to the target s_{tg}: $\sigma(d^{src}) \neq \sigma(d^{tg})$, $\sigma(d^{tg}) = s_{tg}$,
- the contents of the original and the transformed sentences match: $\delta(d^{src}, d^{tg}) = 1$,
- the resulting sentence is well-formed (fluent): $\theta(d^{tg}) = 1$.

Therefore, a style transfer model has to optimize all three functions. Analogously, to evaluate the performance of a style transfer model, we need to check that all three conditions hold: the style is appropriately changed, the content stayed intact, and the text is fluent. However, these three conditions are often inversely correlated (Pang and Gimpel, 2019). This makes style transfer evaluation a notoriously difficult problem. Since the three conditions have to be explicitly checked, we cannot adopt the techniques used for the evaluation of other text generation models. In this work we make all evaluation on a detoxification task for which more broad definition of style transfer is fully applicable.

2.2 Automatic Evaluation of Style Transfer

In earlier works, reference-based evaluation metrics were considered a holistic evaluation technique (Li et al., 2018), by analogy with Machine Translation. Even some recent works (Sudhakar et al., 2019; Zhu et al., 2021) use BLEU or other metrics such as GLEU as the only means of evaluation. Unfortunately, they often cannot control style. Thus, it became obvious that both content and style have to be directly evaluated.

Some works settle for mere evaluation of style and content (Malmi et al., 2020; Zhang et al., 2020b). However, more often these two metrics are combined by computing their geometric or harmonic mean, as first suggested by (Xu et al., 2018). This technique is often used to get the joint quality score (Riley et al., 2021; Huang et al., 2021; Lai et al., 2021a,b). Many (although not all) works also evaluate the fluency of the generated text. This is almost exclusively done via computing perplexity of text in terms of a language model (e.g. GPT-2 (Radford et al., 2019)). The only alternative used in style transfer works is the use of classifier of linguistic acceptability (Krishna et al., 2020) trained on CoLA dataset (Warstadt et al., 2018). Fluency is sometimes also included to the joint score together with the style and content preservation. (Pang and Gimpel, 2019) compute it as a document-level geometric mean, and (Krishna et al., 2020) multiply the sentence-level scores. In our work we use the latter approach.

2.3 Manual Evaluation of Style Transfer

The researchers have come to a conclusion that these automatic metrics cannot provide an objective evaluation. It has become a de-facto standard to enhance the automatic evaluation with the human evaluation experiments.

There are two main human evaluation scenarios. Outputs of two models can be evaluated side by side, in this case the authors report the number of wins of each of the models (i.e. the number of cases where a particular model generated a better text) and the number of ties (Zhu et al., 2021; Li et al., 2019; Cheng et al., 2020). Alternatively, the outputs of different models are evaluated in-

[1] https://www.dialog-21.ru/evaluation/2022/russe

[2] Style transfer task can be generalized for S with more than two styles or for continuous styles. We use the binary case for simplicity.

dependently. In this case the assessors evaluate the outputs along three parameters: style, content preservation, and fluency. The parameters are often evaluated in terms of a 1-to-5 scale (Zhou et al., 2020; Madaan et al., 2020; John et al., 2019; Lee et al., 2021; Ma et al., 2021). Sometimes the style is evaluated in terms of a 7-value scale (from -3 to 3), content preservation takes values from 1 to 6 (Chawla and Yang, 2020; Briakou et al., 2021b). Other scales are also possible. Besides that, the three individual metrics can be evaluated using the side-by-side scenario (Sudhakar et al., 2019; Lin et al., 2020).

3 Detoxification Competition Details

The evaluation was conducted under the scope of a competition of detoxification models for the Russian language (Dementieva et al., 2022).[3] For this competition we created a Russian parallel corpus of toxic sentences and their manually written non-toxic equivalents. We also developed several baselines.

3.1 Parallel Dataset

We collected a parallel Russian dataset for detoxification for this competition. The corpus was collected via the Yandex.Toloka[4] crowdsourcing platform. We used the data collection setup described by (Logacheva et al., 2022) There, the crowd workers were asked to rewrite a sentence so that it preserves its content, but does not sound toxic. Then other crowd workers checked the rewritten sentence for toxicity and semantic similarity with the original one. The platform of Yandex.Toloka has a special mark for cases of inappropriate and toxic content. Thus, all the crowd workers were notified about possible unethical context of the task and we get approvals for the experiment.

As it was noted, we need the toxic and corresponding neutral sentences to be semantically similar. Therefore, during the generation of the dataset we ask crowd workers to rewrite the sentence in a non-offensive way and keep its content. If it is impossible to detoxify a sentence, a worker can choose to not change it. Such sentences are not included to the resulting dataset. All the generated detoxified sentences are then checked for the absence of toxicity and semantic similarity to the original sentence.

[3] https://russe.nlpub.org/2022/tox

[4] https://toloka.yandex.ru/en

We use Russian toxic sentences from the corpora of user utterances taken from Russian social networks Odnoklassniki (Kaggle, 2019) and Pikabu (Kaggle, 2020), and from the Russian segment of Twitter (Rubtsova, 2015). We select only the sentences which were classified as toxic by a pre-trained toxicity classifier. The classifier is a ruBERT model (Kuratov and Arkhipov, 2019) fine-tuned on the same datasets. Overall, our dataset contains 8,622 sentences. We use 6,947 of them as training data, 800 for validation and 875 for testing models.

3.2 Competition Rules

The competition rules allowed the participants to use the collected dataset and any additional corpora and pre-trained models as long as they are free and publicly available. The participants could also use our baseline models in any way.

We evaluated the participating models both manually and automatically on the test set. We used state-of-the-art techniques for both evaluations. Due to the large amount of manual evaluation we resort to crowdsourcing instead of expert annotation.

4 Detoxification Models

4.1 Baselines

We provide four baselines for detoxification task: a trivial Duplicate baseline, a rule-based Delete approach, fine-tuning on the ruT5 model and the continuous prompt tuning approach for ruGPT3 model.

Duplicate This is a trivial baseline which consists in leaving the input text intact. It provides a lower threshold for models.

Delete Delete is an unsupervised method that eliminates toxic words based on a predefined toxic words vocabulary. The idea is often used on television and other media: rude words are bleeped out or hidden with special characters (usually an asterisk). We provide both the vocabulary and the script that applies it to input sentences.

RuT5 Baseline Another approach is the supervised baseline based on the T5 model. We fine-tune the ruT5-base model[5] on the train part of the provided dataset.

[5] https://huggingface.co/sberbank-ai/ruT5-base

RuPrompts The third baseline is based on the library ruPrompts[6] for fast language model tuning via automatic prompt search. The method Continuous Prompt Tuning (Konodyuk and Tikhonova, 2021) is to train with gradient descent embeddings corresponding to the prompts, such approach is less expensive to compare with classic fine-tuning of a big language models. In the baseline we tuned the prompts for the ruGPT3-large model. Pre-trained prompts for the baseline is available in huggingface[7].

4.2 Participants

We briefly describe the models developed by participants. More details about the participating systems can be found in (Dementieva et al., 2022)

Team 1 (ruT5-finetune) Authors approach is based on the ruT5 model[8]. It was fine-tuned on the part of competition train data with a learning rate 1e-5 on 15 epochs. Only the samples with fluency, similarity, and accuracy higher than 0.5 were selected from the train set. The best output is selected from 32 generated samples using beam search. It was decided not to use sampling.

Team 2 (ruGPT3-filter) This team's solution uses a model based on ruGPT3. The authors filtered the dataset released by the organizers with the following heuristics: (i) cosine similarity between the original and transformed sentences ranges from 0.6 to 0.99; (ii) ROUGE-L between the sentences ranges from 0.1 to 0.8; (iii) the transformed sentence length is less or equal to the original sentence length. This dataset was used to fine-tune ruGPT3.

Team 3 (lewis) solution is based on the LEWIS framework (Reid and Zhong, 2021), a coarse-to-fine editor for style transfer that transforms text using Levenshtein edit operation. First, the sequence of coarse-grain Levenshtein edit types (keep, replace, delete or insert) was predicted for each sentence pair. Next, the resulting tags were used to train the conversational RuBERT[9] for the sequence tagging task. The ruT5-base model was trained to fill in the tokens for coarse-grain edit type *replace*.

Team 4 (ruGPT3-XL) trained RuGPT3 XL[10] to generate a non-toxic text on the competition train data. The input is the concatenation of the toxic and non-toxic sentences.

Team 5 (RoBERTa-replace) solution is based on the RoBERTa-large[11]. The logistic regression model on the FastText vectors trained on the competition data was used as a toxic words classifier. Toxic tokens were substituted by RoBERTa-large model, where the best candidates were chosen by the cosine similarity between the candidate and the toxic token. In case it was not possible to find an acceptable candidate, the toxic word was removed from the sentence.

Team 6 (ruT5-clean) used the ruT5-large model[12] improved by data cleaning. The preprocessing stage consitsts of emoticons and smiley filtering and removing duplicate characters. The Levenshtein Transformer (Susanto et al., 2020) was used as an extra step in preprocessing to clean the ruT5-large model output.

Team 7 (ruT5-large) modified the t5 baseline. RuT5-base was replaced by ruT5-large with beam search used as inference algorithm. 20 candidates were generated for each toxic sentence, the best candidate was selected by the largest J-score metric.

Team 8 (ruT5-preproc) This solution is based on ruT5-base model with additional pre- and post-processing of the texts. Team finetuned the ruT5-base model on the provided data and used heuristics for text pre/processing.

Team 9 (adversarial) This team devised an adversarial training setup where the training data was enriched with the artificially generated sentences which attained the highest scores of the automatic metrics.

Team 10 (ruPrompts-plus) This team advanced over the ruPrompts baseline. The solution is based on RuGPT3-XL (Generative Pretrained Transformer-3 for Russian) [13] adapted to the task via prompt tuning. Using RuGPT3-XL as a frozen backbone, team trains only a sequence of continuous embeddings inserted before and after an input text.

[6]https://sberbank-ai.github.io/ru-prompts

[7]https://huggingface.co/konodyuk/prompt_rugpt3large_detox_russe

[8]https://huggingface.co/sberbank-ai/ruT5-base

[9]https://huggingface.co/DeepPavlov/rubert-base-cased-conversational

[10]https://huggingface.co/sberbank-ai/rugpt3xl

[11]https://huggingface.co/sberbank-ai/ruRoberta-large

[12]https://huggingface.co/sberbank-ai/ruT5-large

[13]https://huggingface.co/sberbank-ai/rugpt3xl

5 Automatic Evaluation

In our automatic evaluation we follow the state-of-the-art evaluation strategies. Namely, we replicate the setup of Krishna et al. (2020). We evaluate the three parameters of style transfer quality: style of a text, content preservation, and fluency of a text. The three metrics are then aggregated to a joint score. We use the following techniques.

Style (STA$_a$) is evaluated with a BERT-based classifier for toxicity detection. We use the same ruBERT-based classifier that was used for pre-selection (see Section 3.1).

Content (SIM$_a$) is evaluated as the cosine similarity of embeddings of the source and the transformed sentences. We use embeddings generated by LaBSE model (Feng et al., 2020) because in our preliminary experiments they showed the best performance for Russian. We prefer the embedding distance over BLEU-like metrics, as Yamshchikov et al. (2021) showed that embedding-based metrics are better correlated with human judgments than ngram-based metrics such as BLEU. We do not use references for the evaluation of content to mimic the setup where references are unavailable, which is very common for style transfer tasks.

Fluency (FL$_a$) Although fluency is usually evaluated as perplexity, we follow Krishna et al. (2020) and use an acceptability classifier. In this work this classifier was trained on CoLA dataset (Warstadt et al., 2018). Since there is no such dataset for Russian, we create synthetic examples of corrupted sentences by randomly replacing, deleting or shuffling words in sentences as suggested by Kann et al. (2018). We choose this method over perplexity, because it ranges from 0 to 1 and its greater values mean higher quality, just like metrics we use for evaluating toxicity and content. This makes it easier to combine the three metrics easier.

Joint (J$_a$) Following Krishna et al. (2020), we combine the three metrics at the sentence level by multiplying them. The document-level score is computed as the average of scores for all sentences.

ChrF We provide an additional reference-based metric which follows the Machine Translation evaluation setup. We choose ChrF (Popović, 2015) over BLEU, because it compares character ngrams and is more suitable for languages with rich morphology, such as Russian.

6 Manual Evaluation

The manual evaluation follows setups used in state-of-the-art works. We separately evaluate the three parameters of the transferred sentences, namely, their style, content, and fluency. We conduct the evaluation via crowdsourcing. For the evaluation we also use Yandex.Toloka platform.

6.1 Evaluation Metrics

All three parameters are evaluated at the sentence level in terms of a binary scale, where 0 refers to the bad quality in terms of the parameter and 1 is the good quality. Assessors are given the following guidelines.

Toxicity (STA$_m$) The toxicity level is defined as:

- **non-toxic** (1) — the sentence does not contain any aggression or offence. However, we allow covert aggression and sarcasm. Note also that toxicity should not be mixed with the lack of formality. Even if a sentence is extremely informal, it is non-toxic unless it attacks someone.
- **toxic** (0) — the sentence contains open aggression and/or swear words (this also applies to meaningless sentences).

Content (SIM$_m$) In terms of content, sentences should be classified as:

- **matching** (1) — the output sentence fully preserves the content of the input sentence. Here, we allow some change of sense which is inevitable during detoxification (e.g. replacement with overly general synonyms: *idiot* becomes *person* or *individual*). It should also be noted that content and toxicity dimensions are independent, so if the output sentence is toxic, it can still be good in terms of content.
- **different** (0) — the sense of the transferred sentence is different from the input. Here, the sense should not be confused with the word overlap. The sentence is different from its original version if its main intent has changed, (cf. *I want to go out* and *I want to sleep*). The partial loss or change of sense is also considered a mismatch (cf. *I want to eat and sleep* and *I want to eat*). Finally, when the transferred sentence is senseless, it should also be considered *different*.

Fluency (FL_m) The fluency evaluation is different from the other metrics. We evaluate it along a ternary scale with the following values:

- **fluent** (1) — sentences with no mistakes, except punctuation and capitalisation errors.
- **partially fluent** (0.5) — sentences which have orthographic and grammatical mistakes, non-standard spellings. However, the sentence should be fully intelligible.
- **non-fluent** (0) — sentences which are difficult or impossible to understand.

However, since all the input sentences are user-generated, they are not guaranteed to be fluent in terms of this scale. People often make mistakes, typos and use non-standard spelling variants. We cannot require that a detoxification model fixes them. Therefore, we consider an output of a model fluent if the model did not make less fluent than the original sentence. Thus, we evaluate both the input and the output sentences and define the final fluency score as **fluent** (1) if the fluency score of the output is greater or equal to that of the input, and **non-fluent** (0) otherwise.

Joint Score (J_m) We aggregate the three metrics by multiplying sentence-level scores. Since all scores are binary, the joint score is 1 only if all three metrics are 1. Therefore, it indicates fully acceptable sentences.

6.2 Crowdsourcing Setup

Each of the three parameters is evaluated in a separate crowdsourcing project. For all the projects, the evaluation was made by only native Russian speakers.

6.2.1 Crowdsourcing tasks

In the toxicity detection task (see Figure 1) we show workers the transferred sentence and ask them if it is offensive. Then, in the content similarity task we show both sentences and ask if they mean the same (see Figure 2). Finally, we apply the fluency evaluation task (see Figure 3) to both the source and the target and compute the final fluency score from the source and target scores.

Each sentence in each of the projects is labelled by 10 to 12 workers. We aggregate their result using Dawid-Skene aggregation method (Dawid and Skene, 1979). It takes into account the dynamically defined reliability of workers. For each example with multiple labels Dawid-Skene method returns the label and its confidence. We use only labels whose confidence is above 90%. The other labels (around 3% of all examples) are later filled by experts.

6.2.2 Quality Control

Before admitting users to accomplishing tasks we need make sure they understand them correctly. For that purpose we devise a pipeline of training and exam tasks. First, a user needs to pass training (a set of tasks with a known label and an explanation of the task shown if the user makes a mistake) and exam (same as training, but no explanations are shown). We only admit users whose exam score is above 80%. Similarly, we control their performance with control questions during labelling. We ban users whose performance on these control question is below 70%.

Finally, we use other heuristics to control the user performance:

- **captcha** — prevents workers from using

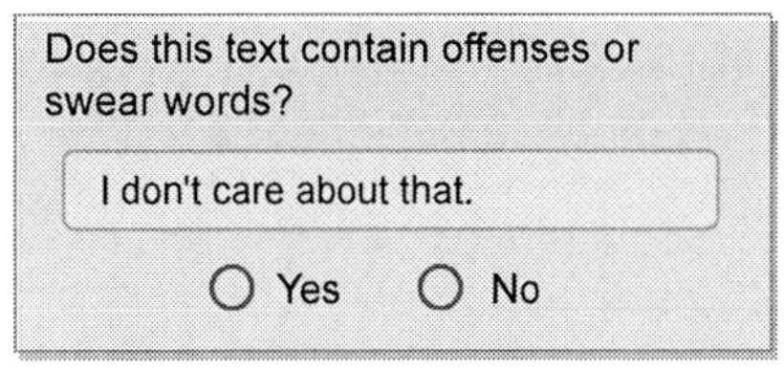

Figure 1: Interface of the toxicity detection task.

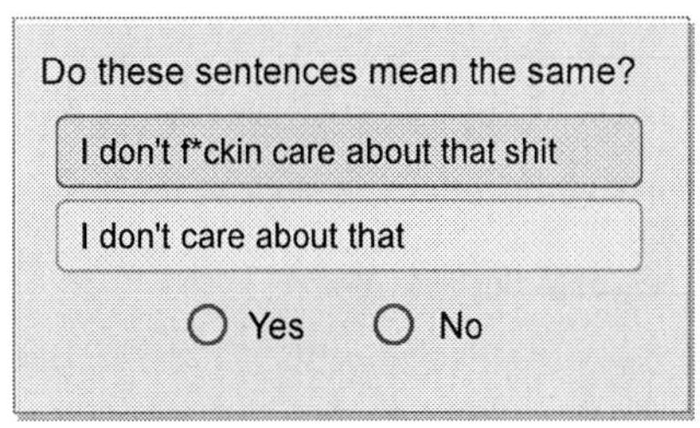

Figure 2: Interface of the content similarity task.

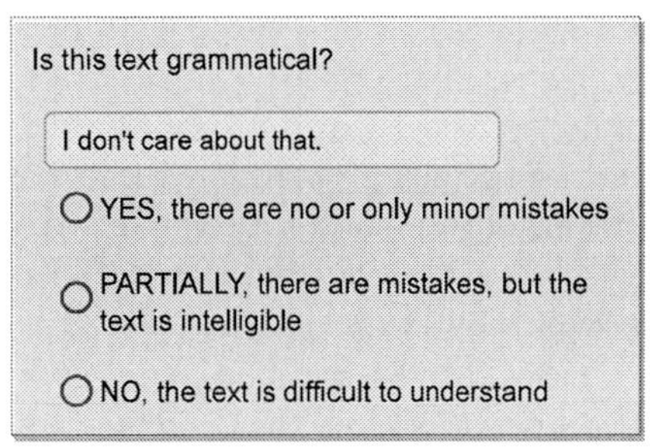

Figure 3: Interface of the fluency evaluation task.

scripts and bots for labelling,

- **fast answers** — we ban users who accomplish a page of tasks in less than 15 seconds (this usually means that the user is not reading the task and is giving random answers),
- **skipped tasks** — we ban users who skip 5 or more task pages (this indicates a user who does not understand the task).

	STA_m	SIM_m	FL_m	J_m
human references	**0.89**	0.82	**0.89**	**0.65**
ruT5-clean	0.79	**0.87**	**0.90**	0.63
RuT5 Baseline	0.79	0.82	**0.92**	0.61
ruT5-large	0.73	**0.87**	**0.92**	0.60
lewis	0.82	0.79	0.85	0.58
ruPrompts-plus	0.78	0.81	**0.90**	0.57
ruT5-finetune	0.80	0.78	0.87	0.56
ruT5-preproc	0.79	0.72	0.78	0.51
ruGPT3-XL	0.81	0.70	0.90	0.50
ruPrompts	0.80	0.70	**0.87**	0.49
ruGPT3-filter	0.77	0.72	0.83	0.45
RoBERTa-replace	0.43	0.62	0.79	0.17
Delete	0.39	0.71	0.73	0.16
Duplicate	0.11	1.00	1.00	0.11
adversarial	0.25	0.13	0.24	0.02

Table 2: Manual evaluation of the participating models, the models are sorted by the J_m metric. The figures **in bold** show the highest value of the metric with the significance level of $\alpha = 0.05$.

	STA_a	SIM_a	FL_a	J_a	ChrF
adversarial	0.97	**0.94**	0.96	**0.87**	0.53
ruT5-finetune	**0.98**	0.86	**0.97**	0.82	0.55
ruT5-large	0.95	0.86	**0.97**	0.78	0.57
ruT5-clean	0.95	0.82	0.91	0.71	0.57
lewis	0.93	0.80	0.88	0.66	0.56
ruGPT3-XL	0.94	0.73	0.89	0.61	0.50
RuT5 Baseline	0.80	0.83	0.84	0.56	0.57
ruPrompts-plus	0.80	0.80	0.83	0.54	0.56
ruPrompts	0.81	0.79	0.80	0.53	0.55
ruT5-preproc	0.85	0.76	0.78	0.52	0.53
human references	0.85	0.72	0.78	0.49	**0.77**
ruGPT3-filter	0.83	0.76	0.76	0.48	0.51
RoBERTa-replace	0.57	0.89	0.91	0.44	0.54
Delete	0.56	0.89	0.85	0.41	0.53
Duplicate	0.24	1.00	1.00	0.24	0.56

Table 1: The performance of the participating models in terms of automatic metrics, sorted by J_a metric.

Metric	STA_a	SIM_a	FL_a	J_a	ChrF
STA_m	0.376	**-0.776**	-0.398	0.278	0.223
SIM_m	-0.046	0.031	0.190	0.000	**0.789**
FL_m	-0.083	-0.032	0.288	0.070	**0.619**
J_m	0.326	-0.495	-0.211	0.350	**0.735**

Table 3: Spearman's correlation coefficient between automatic VS manual metrics on system level. Bold numbers denote the statistically significant correlation (p-value ≤ 0.05).

Metric	STA_a	SIM_a	FL_a	J_a	ChrF
STA_m	**0.695**	**-0.888**	-0.398	0.305	0.264
SIM_m	-0.305	-0.153	-0.042	-0.431	0.276
FL_m	-0.237	-0.291	-0.116	-0.425	0.218
J_m	**0.595**	**-0.746**	-0.380	0.278	0.367

Table 4: Pearson's correlation coefficient between automatic VS manual metrics on system level. Bold numbers denote the statistically significant correlation (p-value ≤ 0.05).

7 Results

In this section, first we present the data, namely the outcome of the shared task on detoxification evaluation. Second, we perform anlysis of correspondance of human and automatic metics. Finally, we conclude with a discussion of assessors's performance and overall difficulty of the task.

7.1 Models Performance

Table 1 shows the performance of the participating models and our baselines in terms of the automatic metrics. The adversarial example generation turns out to be very effective — it attains the highest scores of all metrics, thus yielding the highest J_a score. The next three places in the leaderboard are taken by the models based on our baseline ruT5 system. Notice that the human references are below the majority of models in terms of all metrics except ChrF whose score for the human references is the highest by a large margin.

The manual scores (see Table 2) provide a completely different result. There, the human references are significantly better than other models, but closely followed by one of ruT5-based systems. However, ruT5-clean (the best-performing participant) is not significantly better than the ruT5 baseline. Interestingly, the **adversarial** model whose automatic scores are the highest, in fact produces sentences of an very low quality.

7.2 Automatic vs Manual Metrics

The automatic and manual metrics (Tables 1 and 2) provide very diverse results in terms of participants rankings. This suggests that they are weakly correlated.

We check this assumption by computing the Spearman ρ correlations at three different levels: sentence level, system level and system ranking

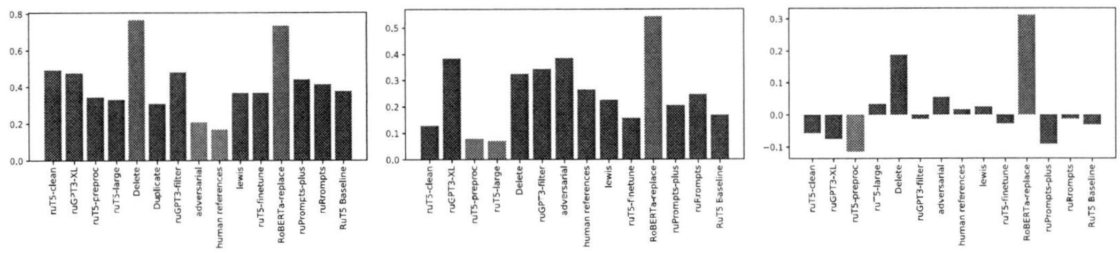

Figure 4: Correlations between automatic and manual metrics at the sentence level for different models. (Right: **STA** metric; Center: **SIM** metric; Left: **FL** metric.)

Metric	STA_a	SIM_a	FL_a	J_a
STA_m	-0.437	**0.679**	0.226	0.345
SIM_m	0.187	-0.126	0.099	0.022
FL_m	0.165	-0.314	0.037	-0.046
J_m	-0.041	0.020	0.275	0.178

Table 5: Spearman's correlation coefficient between automatic VS manual metrics based on system ranking. Bold numbers denote the statistically significant correlation (p-value ≤ 0.05).

Metric	BertScore	ROUGE-L	BLEU	ChrF
STA_m	**-0.710**	**-0.550**	**-0.600**	-0.296
SIM_m	**0.819**	**0.802**	**0.863**	0.495
Fl_m	**0.796**	**0.675**	**0.700**	0.464
J_m	**0.661**	**0.657**	**0.546**	0.325

Table 6: Spearman's correlation coefficient between automatic style transfer VS manual metrics based on system ranking. Bold numbers denote the statistically significant correlation (p-value ≤ 0.05).

level. At sentence level, we compare automatic metrics for each sentence and then compare them across their manual analogies. For the system level we first compute average scores for each participant and each metric and them uses such vectors of scores to calculate correlations. As for the system ranking level, we use the rank of the system in the ranked system list instead of the scores, which allows to not take the difference of score distributions into account. The last metric is trying to assess the capability of a metric to predict the outcome of a competition.

7.2.1 System Level Correlations

At the system level we compute correlation scores of all metrics. We highlight all high correlations (the absolute value above 0.6) in Table 4. We clearly see that none of automatic metrics correlate with their manually measured counterparts. On the other hand, there is strong negative correlation between the manual style and automatic content preservation score.

Moreover, manual content and fluency metrics are correlated with ChrF score. This suggests that ChrF can be used as an automatic evaluation score. On the other hand, ChrF is not sensitive to sentence style, which means that it can be deceived (for example, the trivial Duplicate baseline performs on par with strong T5-based models in terms of ChrF). However, the power of ChrF was also claimed by (Briakou et al., 2021a).

7.2.2 System Ranking Level Correlations

We also compute the correlation of rankings of models produced by different metrics using Spearman's ρ correlation. According to Table 5, we mostly see weak or no correlation. The rankings by automatic metrics of style, content preservation, and fluency do not correlate with their counterparts produced by manual metrics, apart from the correlation of manual metric of style evaluation (STA_m) and automatic metric of content preservation (SIM_a).

Despite that ChrF metric counted as more suitable text generation metric for the Russian Language, additionally we computed correlations for other text generation metrics as BLEU (Papineni et al., 2002), ROUGE-L (Sutherlin et al., 2011), and BertScore (Zhang et al., 2020a). The results are presented in the Table 6. Unexpectedly, ChrF does not correlated at all with the manually computed manual metrics, according to the ranking evaluation. BertScore, ROUGE-L, BLEU demonstrated quite strong correlations with the manual metrics, which are statistically significant in comparison to the ChrF scores. At the same time, from the Table 6 we can conclude that even the highest correlation numbers (0.661) in our case cannot guarantee high-quality prediction of manual metrics, which still requires further manual evaluation steps.

7.2.3 Sentence-level Correlations

The sentence-level correlations show a slightly different picture. The highest correlation is seen for the style metric, the Spearman ρ score of automatic and manual judgments is 0.418 (moderate correlation). The manual and automatic sentence-level similarity, fluency, and joint scores show very weak or no correlation: 0.251, 0.015, and 0.141, respectively.

However, sentence-level correlations between corresponding manual and automatic metrics differ significantly across models (see Figure 4). We see that automatic and manual toxicity scores are much better correlated for the **Delete** and **RoBERTa-replace** models, which are the only models to explicitly remove or replace toxic words identified by a classifier or via a manually compiled list of toxic words. These models apparently produce texts which are easy to classify correctly. Conversely, **adversarial** model and **human references** are the most difficult to classify. The former deliberately "fools" the classifier with artificial examples, while the latter contains non-trivial phrases whose level of toxicity is difficult to grasp automatically.

Analogously, the similarity scores are also better correlated for **RoBERTa-replace** model which leaves the majority of words intact, so for it similarity boils down to word matching. Instead, T5-based models produce non-trivial paraphrases. These T5 outputs are also difficult to correctly classify for fluency, unlike the models based on word replacements (**RoBERTa-replace** and **Delete**). Overall, we see that it is more difficult to correctly classify *better-performing models* and *models based on large pre-trained language models*. This suggests that the automatic evaluation might fail exactly where we need it most, i.e. in discriminating between the good models.

7.3 Assessors Performance

While in many works the human evaluation is considered as undoubtedly reliable, we notice that this is not always true. Human evaluation can suffer from: (i) the low reliability of crowd workers and (ii) the difficulty and subjectivity of the tasks.

In crowdsourcing experiments, it is common to give each example for labelling to 3–5 people and aggregate the labels. It our case 3 annotations per sample were not enough. They yielded a labelling with around 10% mistakes. Thus, we collected 10 annotations per sample. Such labelling was more reliable: the error rate did not exceed 3% for style and content and 6% for fluency.

To measure the difficulty of the task, we compute inter-annotator agreement coefficient Krippendorff's alpha (Krippendorff, 2011). It turns out that the agreement is moderate: content: 0.522, 0.448, and 0.394 for style, content, and fluency, respectively. The expert Krippendorff's alpha scores are close: 0.584, 0.458, and 0.463. This confirms that in the experiment with 10 annotations per example the crowd workers are reliable enough, but the task itself is subjective.

Interestingly, the style evaluation gains the highest inter-annotator agreement, just as it had the highest correlation between the manual and the automatic labelling. This suggests that that toxicity is more stable and better interpreted by both humans and models.

8 Conclusion

We conducted an evaluation of detoxification models for Russian using both automatic and manual metrics. This allowed us to analyse the relationship between the metrics and assess the suitability of automatic metrics for evaluation.

Our analysis shows that the metrics are overall weakly correlated with the human judgements both at the system and the sentence level. We found that ChrF score has a strong correlation with the joint score of style, content, and fluency. Thus, ChrF could be used as a proxy for manual evaluation, but its lack of correlation with the style score makes this metric vulnerable to attacks. At the system ranking level BertScore metric yielded the best correlation with human judgements.

We also discovered that the correlation of manual and automatic scores varies for different models. This shows the necessity to consider diverse style transfer models for metrics analysis.

Overall, although the state-of-the-art evaluation setup for detoxification task (three parameters and the joint score combined from them) is conceptually correct, the current performance of automatic metrics is insufficient to use it as a replacement for manual evaluation. A worse thing is that the automatic metrics produce less reliable for better-performing models, thus blocking the advance of style transfer models.

Acknowledgements

This work was supported by MTS-Skoltech laboratory on AI.

References

Eleftheria Briakou, Sweta Agrawal, Joel Tetreault, and Marine Carpuat. 2021a. Evaluating the evaluation metrics for style transfer: A case study in multilingual formality transfer. In *Proceedings of the 2021 Conference on Empirical Methods in Natural Language Processing*, pages 1321–1336, Online and Punta Cana, Dominican Republic. Association for Computational Linguistics.

Eleftheria Briakou, Di Lu, Ke Zhang, and Joel Tetreault. 2021b. Olá, bonjour, salve! XFORMAL: A benchmark for multilingual formality style transfer. In *Proceedings of the 2021 Conference of the North American Chapter of the Association for Computational Linguistics: Human Language Technologies*, pages 3199–3216, Online. Association for Computational Linguistics.

Kunal Chawla and Diyi Yang. 2020. Semi-supervised formality style transfer using language model discriminator and mutual information maximization. In *Findings of the Association for Computational Linguistics: EMNLP 2020*, pages 2340–2354, Online. Association for Computational Linguistics.

Yu Cheng, Zhe Gan, Yizhe Zhang, Oussama Elachqar, Dianqi Li, and Jingjing Liu. 2020. Contextual text style transfer. In *Findings of the Association for Computational Linguistics: EMNLP 2020*, pages 2915–2924, Online. Association for Computational Linguistics.

Alexander Philip Dawid and Allan M Skene. 1979. Maximum likelihood estimation of observer errorrates using the em algorithm. *Journal of the Royal Statistical Society: Series C (Applied Statistics)*, 28(1):20–28.

Daryna Dementieva, Irina Nikishina, Varvara Logacheva, Alena Fenogenova, David Dale, Irina Krotova, Nikita Semenov, Tatiana Shavrina, and Alexander Panchenko. 2022. RUSSE-2022: Findings of the First Russian Detoxification Task Based on Parallel Corpora. In *Computational Linguistics and Intellectual Technologies: papers from the Annual conference "Dialogue"*.

Fangxiaoyu Feng, Yinfei Yang, Daniel Cer, Naveen Arivazhagan, and Wei Wang. 2020. Language-agnostic BERT sentence embedding. *CoRR*, abs/2007.01852.

Fei Huang, Zikai Chen, Chen Henry Wu, Qihan Guo, Xiaoyan Zhu, and Minlie Huang. 2021. NAST: A non-autoregressive generator with word alignment for unsupervised text style transfer. In *Findings of the Association for Computational Linguistics: ACL-IJCNLP 2021*, pages 1577–1590, Online. Association for Computational Linguistics.

Vineet John, Lili Mou, Hareesh Bahuleyan, and Olga Vechtomova. 2019. Disentangled representation learning for non-parallel text style transfer. In *Proceedings of the 57th Annual Meeting of the Association for Computational Linguistics*, pages 424–434, Florence, Italy. Association for Computational Linguistics.

Kaggle. 2019. Russian language toxic comments. `https://www.kaggle.com/blackmoon/russian-language-toxic-comments`. Accessed: 2021-03-01.

Kaggle. 2020. Toxic russian comments. `https://www.kaggle.com/alexandersemiletov/toxic-russian-comments`. Accessed: 2021-03-01.

Katharina Kann, Sascha Rothe, and Katja Filippova. 2018. Sentence-level fluency evaluation: References help, but can be spared! In *Proceedings of the 22nd Conference on Computational Natural Language Learning*, pages 313–323, Brussels, Belgium. Association for Computational Linguistics.

Nikita Konodyuk and Maria Tikhonova. 2021. Continuous prompt tuning for russian: how to learn prompts efficiently with rugpt3? In *Proceedings of the International Conference on Analysis of Images, Social Networks and Texts*.

Klaus Krippendorff. 2011. Computing krippendorff's alpha-reliability.

Kalpesh Krishna, John Wieting, and Mohit Iyyer. 2020. Reformulating unsupervised style transfer as paraphrase generation. In *Proceedings of the 2020 Conference on Empirical Methods in Natural Language Processing (EMNLP)*, pages 737–762, Online. Association for Computational Linguistics.

Yuri Kuratov and Mikhail Arkhipov. 2019. Adaptation of deep bidirectional multilingual transformers for russian language.

Huiyuan Lai, Antonio Toral, and Malvina Nissim. 2021a. Generic resources are what you need: Style transfer tasks without task-specific parallel training data. In *Proceedings of the 2021 Conference on Empirical Methods in Natural Language Processing*, pages 4241–4254, Online and Punta Cana, Dominican Republic. Association for Computational Linguistics.

Huiyuan Lai, Antonio Toral, and Malvina Nissim. 2021b. Thank you BART! rewarding pre-trained models improves formality style transfer. In *Proceedings of the 59th Annual Meeting of the Association for Computational Linguistics and the 11th International Joint Conference on Natural Language Processing (Volume 2: Short Papers)*, pages 484–494, Online. Association for Computational Linguistics.

Dongkyu Lee, Zhiliang Tian, Lanqing Xue, and Nevin L. Zhang. 2021. Enhancing content preservation in text style transfer using reverse attention and conditional layer normalization. In *Proceedings of the 59th Annual Meeting of the Association for Computational Linguistics and the 11th International Joint Conference on Natural Language Processing (Volume 1: Long Papers)*, pages 93–102, Online. Association for Computational Linguistics.

Dianqi Li, Yizhe Zhang, Zhe Gan, Yu Cheng, Chris Brockett, Bill Dolan, and Ming-Ting Sun. 2019. Domain adaptive text style transfer. In *Proceedings of the 2019 Conference on Empirical Methods in Natural Language Processing and the 9th International Joint Conference on Natural Language Processing (EMNLP-IJCNLP)*, pages 3304–3313, Hong Kong, China. Association for Computational Linguistics.

Juncen Li, Robin Jia, He He, and Percy Liang. 2018. Delete, retrieve, generate: a simple approach to sentiment and style transfer. In *Proceedings of the 2018 Conference of the North American Chapter of the Association for Computational Linguistics: Human Language Technologies, Volume 1 (Long Papers)*, pages 1865–1874, New Orleans, Louisiana. Association for Computational Linguistics.

Kevin Lin, Ming-Yu Liu, Ming-Ting Sun, and Jan Kautz. 2020. Learning to generate multiple style transfer outputs for an input sentence. In *Proceedings of the Fourth Workshop on Neural Generation and Translation*, pages 10–23, Online. Association for Computational Linguistics.

Varvara Logacheva, Daryna Dementieva, Sergey Ustyantsev, Daniil Moskovskiy, David Dale, Irina Krotova, Nikita Semenov, and Alexander Panchenko. 2022. ParaDetox: Detoxification with Parallel Data. In *Proceedings of the 60th Annual Meeting of the Association for Computational Linguistics (Volume 1: Long Papers)*, Dublin, Ireland. Association for Computational Linguistics.

Yun Ma, Yangbin Chen, Xudong Mao, and Qing Li. 2021. Collaborative learning of bidirectional decoders for unsupervised text style transfer. In *Proceedings of the 2021 Conference on Empirical Methods in Natural Language Processing*, pages 9250–9266, Online and Punta Cana, Dominican Republic. Association for Computational Linguistics.

Aman Madaan, Amrith Setlur, Tanmay Parekh, Barnabas Poczos, Graham Neubig, Yiming Yang, Ruslan Salakhutdinov, Alan W Black, and Shrimai Prabhumoye. 2020. Politeness transfer: A tag and generate approach. In *Proceedings of the 58th Annual Meeting of the Association for Computational Linguistics*, pages 1869–1881, Online. Association for Computational Linguistics.

Eric Malmi, Aliaksei Severyn, and Sascha Rothe. 2020. Unsupervised text style transfer with padded masked language models. In *Proceedings of the 2020 Conference on Empirical Methods in Natural Language Processing (EMNLP)*, pages 8671–8680, Online. Association for Computational Linguistics.

Richard Yuanzhe Pang and Kevin Gimpel. 2019. Unsupervised evaluation metrics and learning criteria for non-parallel textual transfer. In *Proceedings of the 3rd Workshop on Neural Generation and Translation*, pages 138–147, Hong Kong. Association for Computational Linguistics.

Kishore Papineni, Salim Roukos, Todd Ward, and Wei-Jing Zhu. 2002. Bleu: a method for automatic evaluation of machine translation. In *Proceedings of the 40th Annual Meeting of the Association for Computational Linguistics, July 6-12, 2002, Philadelphia, PA, USA*, pages 311–318. ACL.

Maja Popović. 2015. chrF: character n-gram F-score for automatic MT evaluation. In *Proceedings of the Tenth Workshop on Statistical Machine Translation*, pages 392–395, Lisbon, Portugal. Association for Computational Linguistics.

Alec Radford, Jeffrey Wu, Rewon Child, David Luan, Dario Amodei, Ilya Sutskever, et al. 2019. Language models are unsupervised multitask learners. *OpenAI blog*, 1(8):9.

Machel Reid and Victor Zhong. 2021. LEWIS: Levenshtein editing for unsupervised text style transfer. In *Findings of the Association for Computational Linguistics: ACL-IJCNLP 2021*, pages 3932–3944, Online. Association for Computational Linguistics.

Parker Riley, Noah Constant, Mandy Guo, Girish Kumar, David Uthus, and Zarana Parekh. 2021. TextSETTR: Few-shot text style extraction and tunable targeted restyling. In *Proceedings of the 59th Annual Meeting of the Association for Computational Linguistics and the 11th International Joint Conference on Natural Language Processing (Volume 1: Long Papers)*, pages 3786–3800, Online. Association for Computational Linguistics.

Yu. Rubtsova. 2015. Rutweetcorp. `https://study.mokoron.com/`. Accessed: 2022-03-01.

Akhilesh Sudhakar, Bhargav Upadhyay, and Arjun Maheswaran. 2019. "transforming" delete, retrieve, generate approach for controlled text style transfer. In *Proceedings of the 2019 Conference on Empirical Methods in Natural Language Processing and the 9th International Joint Conference on Natural Language Processing (EMNLP-IJCNLP)*, pages 3269–3279, Hong Kong, China. Association for Computational Linguistics.

Raymond Hendy Susanto, Shamil Chollampatt, and Liling Tan. 2020. Lexically constrained neural machine translation with Levenshtein transformer. In *Proceedings of the 58th Annual Meeting of the Association for Computational Linguistics*, pages 3536–3543, Online. Association for Computational Linguistics.

Daniel P Sutherlin, Linda Bao, Megan Berry, Georgette Castanedo, Irina Chuckowree, Jenna Dotson, Adrian Folks, Lori Friedman, Richard Goldsmith, Janet Gunzner, et al. 2011. Discovery of a potent, selective, and orally available class i phosphatidylinositol 3-kinase (pi3k)/mammalian target of rapamycin (mtor) kinase inhibitor (gdc-0980) for the treatment of cancer. *Journal of medicinal chemistry*, 54(21):7579–7587.

Alex Warstadt, Amanpreet Singh, and Samuel R Bowman. 2018. Neural network acceptability judgments. *arXiv preprint arXiv:1805.12471*.

Jingjing Xu, Xu Sun, Qi Zeng, Xiaodong Zhang, Xuancheng Ren, Houfeng Wang, and Wenjie Li. 2018. Unpaired sentiment-to-sentiment translation: A cycled reinforcement learning approach. In *Proceedings of the 56th Annual Meeting of the Association for Computational Linguistics (Volume 1: Long Papers)*, pages 979–988, Melbourne, Australia. Association for Computational Linguistics.

Ivan P. Yamshchikov, Viacheslav Shibaev, Nikolay Khlebnikov, and Alexey Tikhonov. 2021. Style-transfer and paraphrase: Looking for a sensible semantic similarity metric. *Proceedings of the AAAI Conference on Artificial Intelligence*, 35(16):14213–14220.

Tianyi Zhang, Varsha Kishore, Felix Wu, Kilian Q. Weinberger, and Yoav Artzi. 2020a. Bertscore: Evaluating text generation with BERT. In *8th International Conference on Learning Representations, ICLR 2020, Addis Ababa, Ethiopia, April 26-30, 2020*. OpenReview.net.

Yi Zhang, Tao Ge, and Xu Sun. 2020b. Parallel data augmentation for formality style transfer. In *Proceedings of the 58th Annual Meeting of the Association for Computational Linguistics*, pages 3221–3228, Online. Association for Computational Linguistics.

Chulun Zhou, Liangyu Chen, Jiachen Liu, Xinyan Xiao, Jinsong Su, Sheng Guo, and Hua Wu. 2020. Exploring contextual word-level style relevance for unsupervised style transfer. In *Proceedings of the 58th Annual Meeting of the Association for Computational Linguistics*, pages 7135–7144, Online. Association for Computational Linguistics.

Wanrong Zhu, Xin Wang, Tsu-Jui Fu, An Yan, Pradyumna Narayana, Kazoo Sone, Sugato Basu, and William Yang Wang. 2021. Multimodal text style transfer for outdoor vision-and-language navigation. In *Proceedings of the 16th Conference of the European Chapter of the Association for Computational Linguistics: Main Volume*, pages 1207–1221, Online. Association for Computational Linguistics.

Human Judgement as a Compass to Navigate Automatic Metrics for Formality Transfer

Huiyuan Lai, Jiali Mao, Antonio Toral, Malvina Nissim
CLCG, University of Groningen / The Netherlands
{h.lai, jiali.mao, a.toral.ruiz, m.nissim}@rug.nl

Abstract

Although text style transfer has witnessed rapid development in recent years, there is as yet no established standard for evaluation, which is performed using several automatic metrics, lacking the possibility of always resorting to human judgement. We focus on the task of formality transfer, and on the three aspects that are usually evaluated: style strength, content preservation, and fluency. To cast light on how such aspects are assessed by common and new metrics, we run a human-based evaluation and perform a rich correlation analysis. We are then able to offer some recommendations on the use of such metrics in formality transfer, also with an eye to their generalisability (or not) to related tasks.[1]

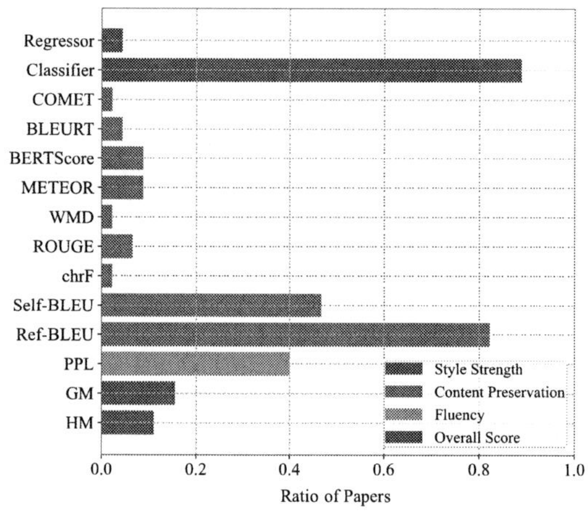

Figure 1: Automatic evaluation metrics in 45 ACL Anthology papers focusing on style transfer and its evaluation in terms of (i) style strength: regressor and classifier; (ii) content preservation: COMET, BLEURT, BERTScore, METEOR, WMD, ROUGE, chrF, Self-BLEU (source-based BLEU) and Ref-BLEU (reference-based BLEU); (iii) fluency: PPL (perplexity); and (iv) overall score: HM (harmonic mean) and GM (geometric mean).

1 Introduction

Text style transfer (TST) is the task of automatically changing the style of a given text while preserving its style-independent content, or theme. Quite different tasks, and thus quite different types of transformations, traditionally fall under the TST label. For example, given the sentence "*i like this screen, it's just the right size...*", we may produce its negative counterpart "*i hate this screen, it is not the right size*" for the task defined as *polarity swap* (Shen et al., 2017; Li et al., 2018a), or turn it into the formal "*I like this screen, it is just the right size.*" for the task called *formality transfer* (Rao and Tetreault, 2018).

For the transfer to be considered successful, the output must be written (i) in the appropriate target style; (ii) in a way such that the original content, or theme, is preserved; and (iii) in proper language, hence fluent and grammatical (relative to the desired style). These aspects to be evaluated are usually defined as (i) *style strength*, (ii) *content preservation*, and (iii) *fluency*, and automatic evaluation metrics are used accordingly, lacking the possibility of using human judgement for any given experiment. Figure 1 shows a survey of such metrics (organised by aspect) as used in 45 papers published over the last three years in the ACL Anthology, which focus on TST in general. A classifier or a regressor is used to assess style strength, a variety of content-based metrics target content preservation, perplexity is used to measure fluency, and some overall metrics combining content and style are often reported.

In spite of the attempts to perform careful automatic evaluation, and of some works studying specific aspects of it, such as traditional metrics for polarity swap (Tikhonov et al., 2019; Mir et al., 2019), content preservation for formality transfer (Yamshchikov et al., 2021), and a recent attempt

[1] Our analysis code, literature list for Figure 1, and all data are available at https://github.com/laihuiyuan/eval-formality-transfer.

Proceedings of the 2nd Workshop on Human Evaluation of NLP Systems (HumEval), pages 102 - 115
May 27, 2022 ©2022 Association for Computational Linguistics

at correlating automatic metrics and human judgment for some aspects of multilingual formality transfer (Briakou et al., 2021a), the community has not yet reached fully shared standards in evaluation practices. We believe this is due to a concurrence of factors.

First, different tasks are conflated under the TST label while they are not exactly the same, and evaluation is a serious issue. Lai et al. (2021a) have shown that polarity swap and formality transfer cannot be considered alike especially in terms of content preservation, as in the former the meaning of the output is expected to be the opposite of the input rather than approximately the same. Hence, it is difficult to imagine that the same metric would capture well the content aspect in both tasks.

Second, the evaluation setting is not necessarily straightforward: if the content of the input has to be preserved in the output, the quality of the generated text can be assessed either against the input itself or against a human-produced reference, specifically crafted for evaluation. However, not all metrics are equally suitable for both assessments. For instance, BLEU (Papineni et al., 2002) is the metric most commonly used for evaluating content preservation (Fig. 1). Intuitively, this n-gram based metric should be appropriate for comparing the output and the human reference, but is much less suitable for comparing the model output and the source sentence, since the whole task is indeed concerned with changing the surface realisation towards a more appropriate target style. On the contrary, neural network-based metrics should also work between the model output and the source sentence. This leads to asking what the best way is to use and possibly combine these metrics under which settings. Closely related to this point, it is not fully clear what the used metrics actually measure and what desirable scores are. For example, comparing source and reference for metrics that measure content similarity should yield high scores, but we will see in our experiments that this is not the case. Recent research has only compared using the reference and the source sentence for one metric: BLEU (Briakou et al., 2021a), and introduced some embeddings-based metrics only to compare the output to the source. A comprehensive picture of a large set of metrics in the two different evaluation conditions (output to source and output to reference) is still missing and provided in this contribution.

Lastly, and related to the previous point, it is yet unclear whether and how the used metrics correlate to human judgements under different conditions (e.g. not only the given source/reference used for evaluation but also different transfer directions, as previous work has assessed human judgement over the informal to formal direction (Briakou et al., 2021a) only), and how they differ from one another. This does not only affect content preservation, as discussed above, but also style strength and fluency.

Focusing on formality transfer, where the aspect of content preservation is clear, we specifically pose the following research questions:

- **RQ1** What is the difference in using a classifier or a regressor to assess style strength and how do they correlate with human judgement?
- **RQ2** How do different content preservation metrics fare in comparison to human judgement, and how do they behave when used to compare TST outputs to source or reference sentences?
- **RQ3** Is fluency well captured by perplexity, and what if the target style is informal?

To address these questions we conduct a human evaluation for a set of system outputs, collecting judgments over the three evaluation aspects, and unpack each of them by means a thorough correlation analysis with automatic metrics.

Contributions Focusing on formality transfer, we offer a comprehensive analysis of this task and the nature of each aspect of its evaluation. Thanks to the analysis of correlations with human judgements, we uncover which automatic metrics are more reliable for evaluating TST systems and which metrics might not be suitable for this task under specific conditions. Since it is not feasible to always have access to human evaluation, having a clearer picture of which metrics better correlate with human evaluation is an important step towards a better systematisation of the task's evaluation.

2 Related Work

Text Style Transfer In the recent tradition of TST, many related tasks have been proposed by researchers. Xu et al. (2012) employ machine translation techniques to transform modern English into Shakespearean English. Sennrich et al. (2016) propose a task that aims to control the level of politeness via side constraints at test time. Polarity swap (Shen et al., 2017; Li et al., 2018b) is a task of transforming sentences, swapping their polarity while preserving their theme. Political slant is the task that preserves the intent of the commenter but modifies their observable political affiliation (Prabhumoye et al., 2018). Formality transfer is the task of reformulating an informal sentence into formal (or viceversa) (Rao and Tetreault, 2018; Briakou et al., 2021b). Cao et al. (2020) propose an expertise style transfer that aims to simplify the professional language in medicine to the level of laypeople descriptions using simple words. Jin et al. (2021) provide an overview for different TST tasks.

Automatic Evaluation In Figure 1 we see that more than 80% of papers employ a style classifier to assess the attributes of transferred text for the aspect of style strength. For content preservation, BLEU is by far the most popular automatic metric, but recent work has also employed other metrics, including string-based (e.g. METEOR (Mir et al., 2019; Lyu et al., 2021; Briakou et al., 2021a)) and neural-based (e.g. BERTScore (Reid and Zhong, 2021; Lee et al., 2021; Briakou et al., 2021a)). In order to further increase the capturing of semantic information beyond the lexical level, Lai et al. (2021b,a) recently also employed BLEURT (Sellam et al., 2020) and COMET (Rei et al., 2020) to evaluate their systems. These *learnable metrics* attempt to directly optimize the correlation with human judgments, and have shown promising results in machine translation evaluation. For fluency, a language model (LM) trained on the training data is used to calculate the perplexity of the transferred text (John et al., 2019; Sudhakar et al., 2019; Huang et al., 2020). Geometric mean and harmonic mean of style accuracy and BLEU are often used for overall performance (Xu et al., 2018; Luo et al., 2019; Krishna et al., 2020; Lai et al., 2021a,b).

Evaluation Practices Although some previous work has run correlations of human judgements and automatic metrics (Rao and Tetreault, 2018; Luo et al., 2019), this was not the focus of the contribution and no deeper analysis or comparison was run. On the other hand, Yamshchikov et al. (2021) examined 13 content-related metrics in the context of formality transfer and paraphrasing, and show that none of the metrics is close enough to the human judgment. Briakou et al. (2021a) have recently evaluated automatic metrics on the task of multilingual formality transfer against human judgement. We also examine automatic metrics in terms of correlation with human judgement, but there are some core differences between our contribution and their work. First, for style strength, they focus on comparing two different architectures in a cross-lingual setting using the correlation on human judgement for regression, and they do not provide this analysis for style classification, rather an evaluation against the gold label. In contrast, we adopt an architecture that provides regression and classification comparisons in fitting human judgments. Second, regarding content, Briakou et al. (2021a) focus on similarity (and therefore metrics) to the source sentence, while we stress the importance of triangulation also with the reference[2]. Also, we introduce two learnable metrics in the evaluation setup, which correlation with human judgement shows to be the most informative. Third, they compare perplexity, likelihood, and pseudo-likelihood scores for fluency evaluation, while we provide a deeper evaluation of just perplexity considering though the two directions (Briakou et al. (2021a) evaluate only the informal-to-formal direction) and highlight differences that point to a potential benefit in using different approaches or evaluation strategies for the two directions.

In addition, we (i) use a continuous scale setting for human judgement which, unlike a discrete Likert scale, allows to normalize judgments (Graham et al., 2013), hence increasing homogeneity of the assessments; (ii) evaluate eight existing, published systems of different sorts (including state-of-the-art models) for both transfer directions, thereby potentially enabling a reconsideration of results as reported in previous work; (iii) study the nature of each evaluation aspect and the corresponding automatic metrics, analyzing the differences in the correlation between metric and human judgements that might arise under different conditions (e.g. looking at high-quality systems).

3 Data

We use GYAFC (Rao and Tetreault, 2018), a formality transfer dataset for English that contains aligned formal and informal sentences from two domains: Entertainment & Music and Family & Relationships. Figure 2 shows an example for alignment, transformation, and evaluation relations be-

[2]Although the reference is not always available, using it in studying evaluation metrics in comparison with how they behave when the source is used provides insights into the overall behaviour of such metrics and how they should best be employed even in the absence of a reference.

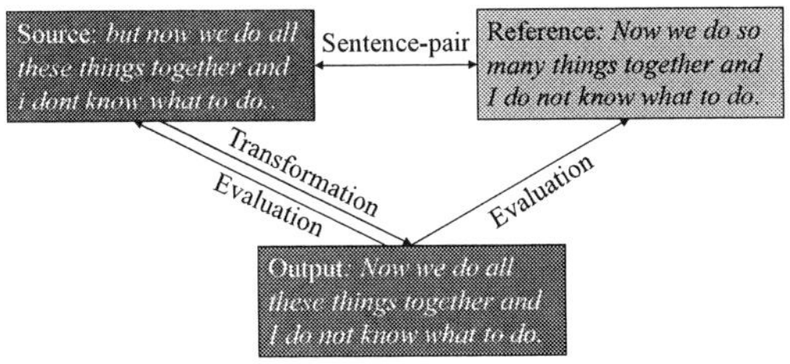

Figure 2: Alignment, transformation, evaluation pairs.

tween input, output, and reference. We run a human evaluation and a battery of automatic metrics on a selection of human- and machine-produced texts.

Source and Reference Texts The source and reference texts we use are from the Family & Relationships domain. The test set contains 1,332 and 1,019 sentences in "informal to formal" and "formal to informal" directions, respectively. There are four human references for each test sentence. We randomly select 80 source sentences (40 for each transfer direction) from the test set, as well as their corresponding human references. For each source sentence, we obtain the corresponding transformations as produced by eight different systems.

System Outputs The evaluation results are often affected by the system's outputs, since if the evaluated systems are of different types, they may exhibit different error patterns so that various automatic evaluation metrics can be differently sensitive to these patterns (Ma et al., 2019; Mathur et al., 2020). To fully examine the evaluation methods, the systems we use are all from previous work, both supervised and unsupervised approaches.[3] Overall, the eight systems yield a total of 640 output sentences (80 per system, 40 in each direction).

4 Methodologies

4.1 Human Evaluation

To facilitate the annotation and obtain a manageable size for each annotator, we split the 80 source sentences (Section 3) into four different surveys with 20 sentences each (10 for each transfer direction), and their corresponding system outputs plus one reference.

We recruited eight highly proficient English speakers for this task, i.e. two per survey, so that two annotations for each target sentence can be collected; from these we can use the average score assigned, and also calculate inter-annotator agreement. The task is to rate the transferred sentence on a continuous scale (0-100), inspired by Direct Assessment (Graham et al., 2013, 2015), in terms of three evaluation aspects: (i) style strength (does the transformed sentence fit the target style?); (ii) content preservation (is the content of the transformed sentence the same as the original sentence?), and (iii) fluency (considering the target style, could the transformed sentence have been written by a native speaker?).

Before starting the rating task, we provided annotators with detailed guidelines and examples of transformed sentences along with plausible assessments for each aspect.[4] We also reminded the annotators that such examples are only indicative of what we believe to be plausible judgements but there are many possible correct answers, of course.

4.2 Automatic Evaluation

We test a wide range of commonly used as well as new automatic metrics on the three aspects.

Style Strength The most commonly used method for assessing style strength is a style classifier, with the problem cast as a binary classification task (formal vs informal in formality transfer). Briakou et al. (2021a) have recently shown that a style regressor fine-tuned with English rating data correlates better with human judgments in other languages (Italian, French, and Portuguese). To run a proper comparison, we use BERT (Devlin et al., 2019) as our base model, and fine-tune it with style labelled data (GYAFC) and the rating data of PT16 (Pavlick and Tetreault, 2016) to obtain a style classifier (C-GYAFC) and a regressor (R-P16), respectively. Following Rao and Tetreault (2018), we collect sentences from PT16 with human rating from -3 to +1 as informal and the rest as formal, and train a style classifier on them (C-PT16). C-GYAFC and C-PT16 achieve an accuracy of 94.4% and 58.6% on the test sets, respectively.

Content Preservation We consider the following metrics, including both surface-based and embedding-based approaches: [5]

- BLEU (Papineni et al., 2002) It compares a given text to others (reference) by using a precision-oriented approach based on n-gram overlap;

[3]Details of the systems are in Appendix A.1.

[4]Screenshots of our annotation guidelines and interface are in Appendix A.3.

[5]The implementation details for automatic metrics are in Appendix A.2.

- chrF (Popović, 2015) It measures the similarity of sentences using the character n-gram F-score;
- ROUGE (Lin, 2004) It compares a given text to others (human reference) by using n-gram/the longest co-occurring in sequence overlap and a recall-oriented approach;
- WMD (Kusner et al., 2015) It measures the dissimilarity between two texts as an optimal transport problem which is based on word embedding.
- METEOR (Banerjee and Lavie, 2005) It computes the similarity score of two texts by using a combination of unigram-precision, unigram-recall, and some additional measures like stemming and synonymy matching.
- BERTScore (Zhang* et al., 2020) It computes a similarity score for each token in the candidate sentence with each token in the reference sentence. Instead of exact matches, it computes token similarity using contextual embeddings.
- BLEURT (Sellam et al., 2020) It is a learned evaluation metric based on BERT (Devlin et al., 2019), trained on human judgements. It is trained with a pre-training scheme that uses millions of synthetic examples to help the model generalize.
- COMET (Rei et al., 2020) It is a learnable metric which leverages cross-lingual pretrained language modeling resulting in multilingual machine translation evaluation models that exploit both source and reference sentences.

For assessing content preservation in the output, we can exploit both the source and the reference (see Fig. 2). When comparing our output to the source, we want to answer the following question: (a) how close in content is the generated text to the original text?, which addresses naturally the content preservation aspect of the task. When comparing our output to the human-produced reference, we want to answer a different question: (b) how similar is the automatically generated text to the human written one? Both are valid strategies, but by answering different questions they are likely to react differently to, and require, different metrics.

The advantages of the (a) approach are that evaluation is possible even without a human reference, it is the most natural way of assessing the task, and it does not incur reference bias (Fomicheva and Specia, 2016). The core problem lies in the use and interpretation of metrics: surface-based metrics (like BLEU) would score highest if nothing has changed from input to output (if the model doesn't perform the task, basically), so aiming for a high score is pointless. A very low score is undesirable, too, however. For more sophisticated metrics, the problem is similar in the sense the highest score would be achieved if the two texts are identical, but since it is not fully clear what they measure exactly in terms of similarity, what to aim for isn't straightforward (an indication is provided by using metrics to compare source and reference).

The main advantage of the (b) approach is that metrics can be used in a more standard way: tending to the highest possible score is good for any of them, since getting close to the human solution is desirable. However, the gold reference is only one of many possible realisations, and while high scores are good, low scores can be somewhat meaningless, as proper meaning-preserving outputs may be very different from the human-produced ones, especially at surface level.

While we have as yet no specific solution to this, this study contributes substantially to a better understanding of automatic metrics, especially for content preservation, possibly leading to a combined metric which considers mainly the source, and possibly the reference(s) in a learning phase.

Fluency In formality transfer, both informal and formal outputs must be evaluated. Intuitively, the latter should be more fluent and grammatical than the former so that evaluating the fluency of informal sentences might be more challenging, both for humans and automatic metrics. We use the perplexity of the language model GPT-2 (Radford et al., 2019) fine-tuned with style labelled texts. Specifically, we fine-tune two GPT-2 models on informal sentences and formal sentences respectively, and then we use the target-style model to calculate the perplexity of the generated sentence. Finally, we provide a separate correlation analysis between automatic metrics and human judgements for the two transfer directions.

4.3 Correlation Methods

Pearson Correlation We employ Pearson correlation (r) as our main evaluation measure for system-/segment-level metrics:

$$r = \frac{\sum_{i=1}^{n}(H_i - \bar{H})(M - \bar{M})}{\sqrt{\sum_{i=1}^{n}(H_i - \bar{H})^2 \sum_{i=1}^{n}(M_i - \bar{M})^2}} \quad (1)$$

where H_i is the human assessment score, M_i is the corresponding score as predicted by a given metric.

Survey	N	Content	Style	Fluency	Overall
Survey 1	160	0.90	0.45	0.71	0.70
Survey 2	160	0.84	0.48	0.63	0.66
Survey 3	160	0.83	0.68	0.70	0.72
Survey 4	160	0.81	0.62	0.63	0.68
Overall	640	0.86	0.52	0.66	0.70

Table 1: Inter-Annotator Agreement.

$\bar{H}$ and $\bar{M}$ are the their means, respectively.

Kendall's Tau-like formulation We follow the WMT17 Metrics Shared Task (Bojar et al., 2017) and take the official Kendall's Tau-like formulation, τ, as the our main evaluation measure for segment-level metrics. A true pairwise comparison is likely to lead to more stable results for segment-level evaluation (Vazquez-Alvarez and Huckvale, 2002). The Kendall's Tau-like formulation τ is as follows:

$$\tau = \frac{Concordant - Discordant}{Concordant + Discordant} \quad (2)$$

Where $Concordant$ is the number of times for which a given metric suggests a higher score to the "better" hypothesis judged by human and $Discordant$ is the number of times for which a given metric suggests a higher score to the "worse" hypothesis judged by human.

Most automatic metrics, like BLEU, aim to achieve a strong positive correlation with human assessment, with the exception of WMD and perplexity, where the smaller is better. We thereby employ absolute correlation value for WMD and perplexity in the following analysis.

5 Results and Analysis

In this section, we first measure the inter-annotator agreement of the human evaluation, then discuss both system-level and sentence-level evaluation results on the three aforementioned evaluation aspects, so as to provide a different perspective on the correlation between automatic metrics and human judgements under different conditions.

5.1 Inter-Annotator Agreement

There are two human judgements for each sentence and we measure their inter-annotator agreement (IAA) by computing the Pearson Correlation coefficient, instead of the commonly used Cohen's K, since judgements are given on a continuous scale.

Table 1 presents the results of IAA for each aspect in each single survey and overall. Across the four surveys annotators have the highest agreement on the content aspect, followed by fluency, with style yielding the lowest scores, suggesting that annotators have more varied perceptions of sentence style than content. Overall, we achieve reasonable agreement for all surveys and evaluation aspects.

	N	R-PT16	C-PT16	C-GYAFC
System-level (r)	8	<u>0.93</u>	<u>0.93</u>	<u>0.97</u>
Segment-level (τ)	640	0.33	0.39	0.42

Table 2: Correlation of automatic metrics in style strength with human judgements. The underlined scores indicate $p < 0.01$.

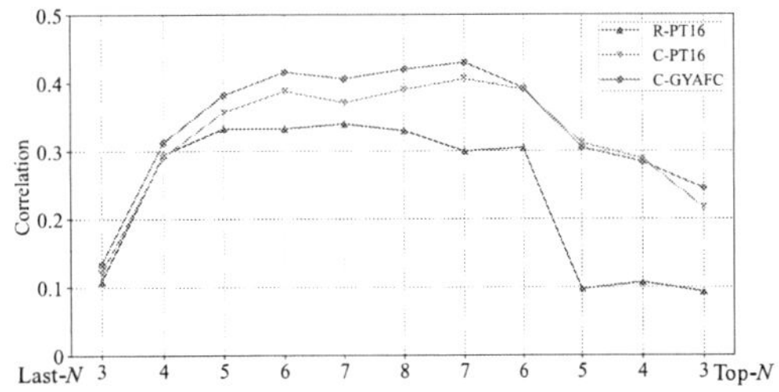

Figure 3: Kendall's Tau-like correlation in style strength computed over the top-/last-N systems which are sorted by human judgements.

5.2 Style Strength

Table 2 shows the correlation of automatic metrics in style strength with human judgements. We see that C-GYAFC achieves the highest correlation at both system- and segment-level, R-PT16 and C-PT16 have the same system-level correlation score while the former has a slightly lower score at segment-level. Given that C-PT16 and C-GYAFC have close correlation scores while their performances on the test set are quite different, we also employ Pearson correlation to compute the segment-level result, and see rather different correlation scores (C-PT16 with 0.33 and C-GYAFC with 0.67). We think that evaluating the system outputs for a given source using C-PT16 and C-GYAFC results in similar scores ranking, so their Kendall's Tau-like correlations are very close.

In general, it is easier to evaluate systems which have large differences in quality, while it is more difficult when systems have similar quality. To assess the reliability of automatic metrics for close-quality systems, we first sort the systems based on human judgements, and plot the correlation of the top-/last-N systems, with N ranging from all systems to the best/worst three systems (Fig. 3). We see that the correlation between automatic metrics

Systems	AVE. z	Source Sentence								Human Reference							
		BLEU	chrF	ROUGE-L	WMD ↓	METEOR	BERTScore	BLEURT	COMET-w	BLEU	chrF	ROUGE-L	WMD ↓	METEOR	BERTScore	BLEURT	COMET-w
Reference	0.009	0.291	0.492	0.501	1.334	0.487	0.605	0.235	0.314	-	-	-	-	-	-		
HIGH	**0.542**	0.608	0.775	0.758	0.672	0.808	**0.880**	**0.851**	0.895	0.366	0.547	0.582	1.086	0.554	0.643	0.347	0.400
NIU	0.491	0.637	0.772	0.769	0.652	0.808	0.873	0.818	**0.899**	0.376	**0.560**	**0.605**	**1.036**	0.567	**0.649**	0.373	0.418
BART	0.370	0.514	0.688	0.692	0.840	0.724	0.798	0.687	0.752	**0.382**	0.555	0.596	1.053	0.573	0.646	**0.388**	**0.425**
IBT	0.337	0.543	0.711	0.717	0.782	0.749	0.838	0.744	0.813	0.373	0.550	0.582	1.094	**0.574**	0.635	0.350	0.391
RAO	0.328	**0.649**	**0.778**	**0.791**	**0.608**	**0.815**	0.833	0.751	0.822	0.336	0.525	0.561	1.145	0.533	0.601	0.234	0.305
ZHOU	-0.659	0.610	0.717	0.765	0.758	0.770	0.739	0.189	0.318	0.253	0.461	0.494	1.351	0.469	0.508	-0.200	-0.125
YI	-0.669	0.547	0.684	0.731	0.823	0.728	0.716	0.148	0.320	0.288	0.483	0.517	1.307	0.491	0.524	-0.154	-0.059
LUO	-0.749	0.472	0.638	0.660	1.034	0.681	0.646	0.020	0.034	0.222	0.416	0.445	1.514	0.434	0.453	-0.289	-0.278

Table 3: Human evaluation (z-score) and automatic metrics in content preservation. Notes: (i) ↓ indicates the lower the score the better; (ii) COMET-w indicates that the input setting is not used.

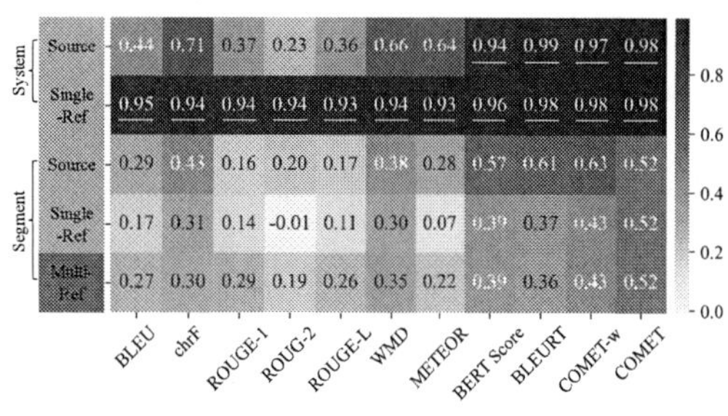

Figure 4: Correlations of automatic metrics computed against source/reference in content preservation with human judgments. Underlining indicates $p < 0.01$.

	BLEU	chrF	ROUGE-1	ROUGE-2	ROUGE-L	WMD	METEOR	BERTScore	BLEURT	COMET-w
Reference 2	0.28	0.37	0.33	0.10	0.36	0.46	0.21	0.59	0.61	0.61
Reference 3	0.25	0.41	0.37	0.12	0.35	0.47	0.34	0.60	0.60	0.55
Reference 4	0.37	0.41	0.46	0.24	0.46	0.49	0.31	0.60	0.56	0.62

Table 4: Kendall's Tau-like correlation between using the first human reference and other references for evaluation content preservation at segment-level.

and human judgements decreases as we decrease N for both top-N and last-N systems, especially R-PT16 in the top-N systems. Again we observe that C-GYAFC and C-PT16 have similar scores over the top-/last-N systems. Overall, C-GYAFC appears to be the most stable model.

5.3 Content Preservation

As mentioned in the Introduction, since a style-transformed output should not alter the meaning of the input, content preservation can be measured against the input itself, or against a human reference in the expected target style. However, metrics cannot be used interchangeably (Section 4.2), as, for instance, the output is expected to have a higher n-gram overlap with the reference, while this is not desirable with respect to the input.

Table 3 presents the results of human and automatic evaluation: all systems have a higher n-gram overlap (BLEU, chrF) with the source sentence than the human reference, indicating that existing models tend to copy from the input and lack diverse rewriting abilities. We also report the results for the reference against the source. Bearing in mind that the reference can be conceived as an optimal output, it is interesting to see that it does not score high in any metric, not even the learnable ones. This leaves some crucial open questions: how can these metrics be best used to assess content preservation in generated outputs? What are desirable scores? We also observe that RAO's system has the highest scores of surface-based metrics (e.g. BLEU) with the source sentence while its scores with learnable metrics (e.g. BLEURT) are lower than some other systems (e.g. HIGH). In the evaluation against the human reference, the system BART and NIU achieve better results on most metrics.

Figure 4 shows the correlations of content preservation metrics with human judgments. For the system-level results, there is a big gap in correlation between source sentence and human reference for surface-based metrics (e.g. BLEU), but not for neural network based ones (e.g. COMET). Using the latter therefore seems to open up the possibility of automatically evaluating content without a human reference. It is interesting to see that the correlations of using source sentences at segment-level are all higher than using the human reference, and surface-based metrics of the latter correlate particularly poorly with human scores. We suggest two main reasons: (i) existing systems lack diverse rewriting ability given the source sentences, and

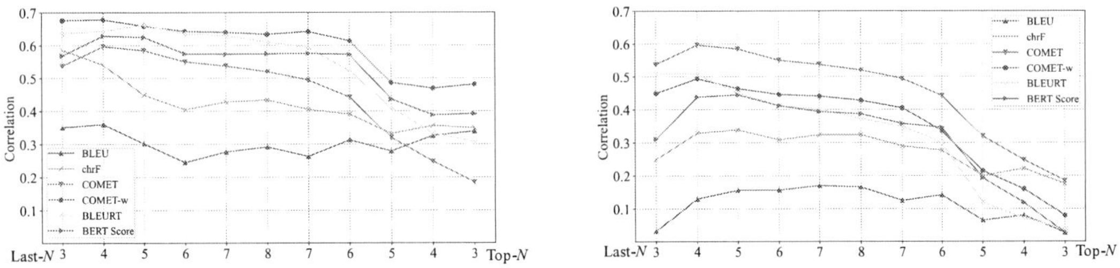

(a) Automatic metrics results against source sentence.

(b) Automatic metrics results against human reference.

Figure 5: Kendall's Tau-like correlation in content preservation computed over the top-/last-N systems which are sorted by human judgements.

the annotators rate the generated sentences comparing them to the source sentence, not to a reference; (ii) human references are linguistically more diverse (e.g. word choice and order). The first one is not within the scope of this work. For the second aspect, we exploit the fact that we have multiple references available, and run the evaluation in a multi-reference setting; we observe that correlations for surface-based metrics improve as more variety is included, but not for neural ones. In Table 4, we see that learnable metrics using the first reference have higher correlation with other references than surface-based metrics. Overall, learnable metrics always have the highest correlation scores in evaluating content preservation using source sentences or human references, while surface-based metrics generally require a multi-reference setting.

Similar to style strength, we plot the correlation of the top-/last-N systems sorted by human judgements for the content aspect (Fig. 5). The correlation score between automatic metrics and human scores decreases as we decrease N for the top-N systems while this shows stability for the last-N systems. This suggests that evaluating high-quality TST systems is more challenging than evaluating low-quality systems. Again, we see that the correlation when using the source sentence has better stability than when using human references. Although BLEU and charF show stable performances, their correlations are lower than those by other metrics in most cases. Regardless of whether we use human references or source sentences, COMET(-w) generally has the highest correlation scores with human judgements under different conditions.

5.4 Fluency

Table 5 shows the absolute correlation of fluency metrics with human judgements. Unsurprisingly,

	N	Informal-to-Formal	Formal-to-Informal
System-level (r)	8	<u>0.96</u>	0.65
Segment-level (τ)	320	0.52	0.35

Table 5: Absolute correlation of automatic metrics in fluency with human judgements. The underlined scores indicate $p < 0.01$.

	Informal-to-Formal			Formal-to-Informal		
	GPT2-Inf	GPT2-For	r	GPT2-Inf	GPT2-For	r
Source	76	143	-	87	68	-
Reference	60	37	0.21	115	270	0.13
BART	34	**26**	0.33	**24**	**28**	0.02
IBT	**32**	**26**	0.32	33	40	0.17
NIU	43	37	0.30	71	75	0.03
HIGH	41	35	**0.62**	80	75	0.00
RAO	54	57	0.33	54	55	0.02
ZHOU	189	218	0.36	103	111	**0.42**
YI	160	182	0.31	205	436	0.27
LUO	128	152	0.43	6962	8191	0.17

Table 6: Results of GPT-2 based perplexity scores and their absolute Pearson correlation with human judgements at segment-level. Notes: (i) GPT2-Inf and GPT2-For are fine-tuned with informal sentences and formal sentences, respectively; (ii) the correlation is calculated using the perplexity of GPT-2 in the target style with human judgment.

we see that GPT-2 based perplexity correlates better with human scores in the direction informal-to-formal than in the opposite one, at both system- and segment-level. In general, a "good" formal sentence should be fluent, while an informal sentence might as well not be, and there can be varied perceptions by people. Indeed, we see higher IAA scores in the informal-to-formal direction (informal-to-formal: 0.70 vs informal-to-formal: 0.63). Table 6 presents the results of correlations and perplexity scores of GPT-2 in the two transfer directions for each system. The perplexity scores for most sentences are in the *correct* place, i.e. the scores from GPT2-Inf are higher than those from GPT2-For for the informal sentences, and viceversa. However,

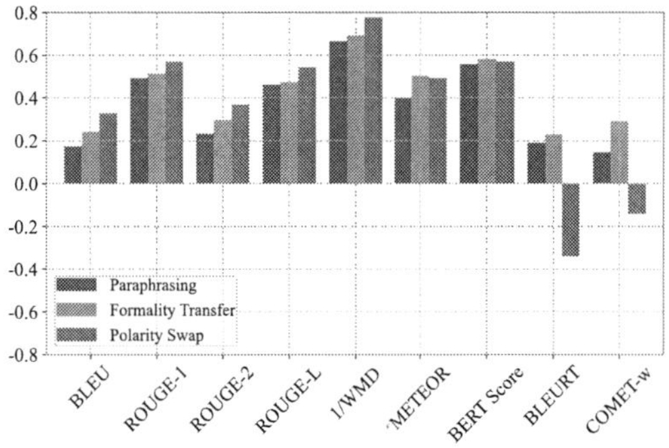

Figure 6: The distance between the source and target sentences as measured by content-related metrics.

we also observe that the correlations of informal-to-formal for each system (except ZHOU) are higher than those for the formal-to-informal direction. This confirms our hypothesis that assessing the fluency of informal sentences is not that obvious even for humans.

5.5 Broader Implications for Style Transfer

We have focused here on formality transfer, but polarity swap is also commonly defined as a style transfer task. In previous work, we have suggested that these tasks are intrinsically different, especially in terms of content preservation, since while formality transfer is somewhat akin to paraphrasing, in polarity swap the meaning is substantially altered (Lai et al., 2021a). This would imply that content-measuring metrics could not be used in the same way in the two tasks.

We further peek here into this issue, in view of future work that should evaluate metrics for the assessment of polarity swap, too, and show in Figure 6 the use of different metrics to measure the distance between the source and target sentences for paraphrasing, formality transfer, and polarity swap. Using n-gram based metrics, we see that the distance between source and target sentences in polarity swap is closer than in the other two tasks. With learnable metrics, instead, we see that source and target sentences for polarity swap are quite distant. Formality transfer shows overall the same trend as paraphrasing in all metrics, suggesting that it's much more of a content-preserving paraphrase-like task than polarity swap, and metrics should be selected accordingly. Future work will explore how to best use them in polarity swap under different settings (using source vs reference, for example).

6 Conclusion

We have considered a wide range of automatic metrics on the three evaluation aspects of formality transfer, and assessed them against human judgements that we have elicited.

For **style strength**, we have compared the style classifiers and regressor in the setting of using the same raw data for training (with a binary label for classification and continuous scores for regression), as well as classifiers with different performances. We have observed that there is little difference among them when evaluating multiple TST systems. However, the style regressor performs worse when evaluating high-quality TST systems. For classifiers with different performances, we recommend the one with the highest performance since it results in the highest overall Pearson correlation with human judgements.

To assess **content preservation**, we have explored different kinds of automatic metrics using the source or reference(s), and have observed the follwoing: (i) if using the source sentence, we strongly recommend employing learnable metrics since their correlation in that condition is much higher than those of traditional surface-based metrics (which are not indicative, since high scores correspond to not changing the input, hence not performing the task); still, the question of how scores should be interpreted and what score ranges are desirable remains open; (ii) most metrics are reliable to be used to measure and compare the performances at system-level when a human reference is available; (iii) however, we do not recommend to use surface-base metrics to measure sentence-level comparisons, especially with only one reference. Overall, learnable metrics seem to provide a more reliable measurement.

For **fluency**, perplexity can be used for evaluating the informal-to-formal direction, either at system- or segment-level, while it is clearly less reliable for the opposite direction, and it remains to be investigated how to best perform evaluation in this transfer direction, considering the wide variability of acceptable outputs.

This study focuses on formality transfer, and offers a better understanding of automatic evaluation thanks to the comprehensive correlations with human judgments herein conducted. However, the findings may not generalise to other tasks usually considered similar, such as polarity swap. To this end, future dedicated work will be required.

Acknowledgments

This work was partly funded by the China Scholarship Council (CSC). We are very grateful to the anonymous reviewers for their useful comments, especially in connection to closely related work, which contributed to strengthening this paper. We would also like to thank the Center for Information Technology of the University of Groningen for their support and for providing access to the Peregrine high performance computing cluster. We thank the annotators as well as Ana Guerberof Arenas and Amy Isard for testing, and helping us to improve, a preliminary version of the survey.

References

Satanjeev Banerjee and Alon Lavie. 2005. METEOR: An automatic metric for MT evaluation with improved correlation with human judgments. In *Proceedings of the ACL Workshop on Intrinsic and Extrinsic Evaluation Measures for Machine Translation and/or Summarization*, pages 65–72, Ann Arbor, Michigan. Association for Computational Linguistics.

Ondřej Bojar, Yvette Graham, and Amir Kamran. 2017. Results of the WMT17 metrics shared task. In *Proceedings of the Second Conference on Machine Translation*, pages 489–513, Copenhagen, Denmark. Association for Computational Linguistics.

Eleftheria Briakou, Sweta Agrawal, Joel Tetreault, and Marine Carpuat. 2021a. Evaluating the evaluation metrics for style transfer: A case study in multilingual formality transfer. In *Proceedings of the 2021 Conference on Empirical Methods in Natural Language Processing*, pages 1321–1336, Online and Punta Cana, Dominican Republic. Association for Computational Linguistics.

Eleftheria Briakou, Di Lu, Ke Zhang, and Joel Tetreault. 2021b. Olá, bonjour, salve! XFORMAL: A benchmark for multilingual formality style transfer. In *Proceedings of the 2021 Conference of the North American Chapter of the Association for Computational Linguistics: Human Language Technologies*, pages 3199–3216, Online. Association for Computational Linguistics.

Yixin Cao, Ruihao Shui, Liangming Pan, Min-Yen Kan, Zhiyuan Liu, and Tat-Seng Chua. 2020. Expertise style transfer: A new task towards better communication between experts and laymen. In *Proceedings of the 58th Annual Meeting of the Association for Computational Linguistics*, pages 1061–1071, Online. Association for Computational Linguistics.

Jacob Devlin, Ming-Wei Chang, Kenton Lee, and Kristina Toutanova. 2019. BERT: Pre-training of deep bidirectional transformers for language understanding. In *Proceedings of the 2019 Conference of the North American Chapter of the Association for Computational Linguistics: Human Language Technologies, Volume 1 (Long and Short Papers)*, pages 4171–4186, Minneapolis, Minnesota. Association for Computational Linguistics.

Marina Fomicheva and Lucia Specia. 2016. Reference bias in monolingual machine translation evaluation. In *Proceedings of the 54th Annual Meeting of the Association for Computational Linguistics (Volume 2: Short Papers)*, pages 77–82, Berlin, Germany. Association for Computational Linguistics.

Yvette Graham, Timothy Baldwin, Alistair Moffat, and Justin Zobel. 2013. Continuous measurement scales in human evaluation of machine translation. In *Proceedings of the 7th Linguistic Annotation Workshop and Interoperability with Discourse*, pages 33–41, Sofia, Bulgaria. Association for Computational Linguistics.

Yvette Graham, Timothy Baldwin, Alistair Moffat, and Justin Zobel. 2015. Can machine translation systems be evaluated by the crowd alone. *Natural Language Engineering*, 23:3 – 30.

Yufang Huang, Wentao Zhu, Deyi Xiong, Yiye Zhang, Changjian Hu, and Feiyu Xu. 2020. Cycle-consistent adversarial autoencoders for unsupervised text style transfer. In *Proceedings of the 28th International Conference on Computational Linguistics*, pages 2213–2223, Barcelona, Spain (Online). International Committee on Computational Linguistics.

Di Jin, Zhijing Jin, Zhiting Hu, Olga Vechtomova, and Rada Mihalcea. 2021. Deep learning for text style transfer: A survey. *arXiv preprint, arXiv: 2011.00416.*

Vineet John, Lili Mou, Hareesh Bahuleyan, and Olga Vechtomova. 2019. Disentangled representation learning for non-parallel text style transfer. In *Proceedings of the 57th Annual Meeting of the Association for Computational Linguistics*, pages 424–434, Florence, Italy. Association for Computational Linguistics.

Diederik P. Kingma and Jimmy Ba. 2015. Adam: A method for stochastic optimization. In *Proceedings of the International Conference on Learning Representations.*

Kalpesh Krishna, John Wieting, and Mohit Iyyer. 2020. Reformulating unsupervised style transfer as paraphrase generation. In *Proceedings of the 2020 Conference on Empirical Methods in Natural Language Processing (EMNLP)*, pages 737–762, Online. Association for Computational Linguistics.

Matt Kusner, Yu Sun, Nicholas Kolkin, and Kilian Weinberger. 2015. From word embeddings to document distances. In *Proceedings of the 32nd In-*

ternational Conference on Machine Learning*, volume 37 of *Proceedings of Machine Learning Research*, pages 957–966, Lille, France.

Huiyuan Lai, Antonio Toral, and Malvina Nissim. 2021a. Generic resources are what you need: Style transfer tasks without task-specific parallel training data. In *Proceedings of the 2021 Conference on Empirical Methods in Natural Language Processing*, pages 4241–4254, Online and Punta Cana, Dominican Republic. Association for Computational Linguistics.

Huiyuan Lai, Antonio Toral, and Malvina Nissim. 2021b. Thank you BART! rewarding pre-trained models improves formality style transfer. In *Proceedings of the 59th Annual Meeting of the Association for Computational Linguistics and the 11th International Joint Conference on Natural Language Processing (Volume 2: Short Papers)*, pages 484–494, Online. Association for Computational Linguistics.

Dongkyu Lee, Zhiliang Tian, Lanqing Xue, and Nevin L. Zhang. 2021. Enhancing content preservation in text style transfer using reverse attention and conditional layer normalization. In *Proceedings of the 59th Annual Meeting of the Association for Computational Linguistics and the 11th International Joint Conference on Natural Language Processing (Volume 1: Long Papers)*, pages 93–102, Online. Association for Computational Linguistics.

Juncen Li, Robin Jia, He He, and Percy Liang. 2018a. Delete, retrieve, generate: a simple approach to sentiment and style transfer. In *Proceedings of the 2018 Conference of the North American Chapter of the Association for Computational Linguistics: Human Language Technologies, Volume 1 (Long Papers)*, pages 1865–1874, New Orleans, Louisiana. Association for Computational Linguistics.

Juncen Li, Robin Jia, He He, and Percy Liang. 2018b. Delete, retrieve, generate: a simple approach to sentiment and style transfer. In *Proceedings of the 2018 Conference of the North American Chapter of the Association for Computational Linguistics: Human Language Technologies, Volume 1 (Long Papers)*, pages 1865–1874, New Orleans, Louisiana. Association for Computational Linguistics.

Chin-Yew Lin. 2004. ROUGE: A package for automatic evaluation of summaries. In *Text Summarization Branches Out*, pages 74–81, Barcelona, Spain. Association for Computational Linguistics.

Fuli Luo, Peng Li, Jie Zhou, Pengcheng Yang, Baobao Chang, Zhifang Sui, and Xu Sun. 2019. A dual reinforcement learning framework for unsupervised text style transfer. In *Proceedings of the 28th International Joint Conference on Artificial Intelligence*, pages 5116–5122.

Yiwei Lyu, Paul Pu Liang, Hai Pham, Eduard Hovy, Barnabás Póczos, Ruslan Salakhutdinov, and Louis-Philippe Morency. 2021. StylePTB: A compositional benchmark for fine-grained controllable text style transfer. In *Proceedings of the 2021 Conference of the North American Chapter of the Association for Computational Linguistics: Human Language Technologies*, pages 2116–2138, Online. Association for Computational Linguistics.

Qingsong Ma, Johnny Wei, Ondřej Bojar, and Yvette Graham. 2019. Results of the WMT19 metrics shared task: Segment-level and strong MT systems pose big challenges. In *Proceedings of the Fourth Conference on Machine Translation (Volume 2: Shared Task Papers, Day 1)*, pages 62–90, Florence, Italy. Association for Computational Linguistics.

Nitika Mathur, Johnny Wei, Markus Freitag, Qingsong Ma, and Ondřej Bojar. 2020. Results of the WMT20 metrics shared task. In *Proceedings of the Fifth Conference on Machine Translation*, pages 688–725, Online. Association for Computational Linguistics.

Remi Mir, Bjarke Felbo, Nick Obradovich, and Iyad Rahwan. 2019. Evaluating style transfer for text. In *Proceedings of the 2019 Conference of the North American Chapter of the Association for Computational Linguistics: Human Language Technologies, Volume 1 (Long and Short Papers)*, pages 495–504, Minneapolis, Minnesota. Association for Computational Linguistics.

Xing Niu, Sudha Rao, and Marine Carpuat. 2018. Multi-task neural models for translating between styles within and across languages. In *Proceedings of the 27th International Conference on Computational Linguistics*, pages 1008–1021, Santa Fe, New Mexico, USA. Association for Computational Linguistics.

Kishore Papineni, Salim Roukos, Todd Ward, and Wei-Jing Zhu. 2002. Bleu: a method for automatic evaluation of machine translation. In *Proceedings of the 40th Annual Meeting of the Association for Computational Linguistics*, pages 311–318, Philadelphia, Pennsylvania, USA. Association for Computational Linguistics.

Ellie Pavlick and Joel Tetreault. 2016. An empirical analysis of formality in online communication. *Transactions of the Association for Computational Linguistics*, 4:61–74.

Maja Popović. 2015. chrF: character n-gram F-score for automatic MT evaluation. In *Proceedings of the Tenth Workshop on Statistical Machine Translation*, pages 392–395, Lisbon, Portugal. Association for Computational Linguistics.

Shrimai Prabhumoye, Yulia Tsvetkov, Ruslan Salakhutdinov, and Alan W Black. 2018. Style transfer through back-translation. In *Proceedings of the 56th Annual Meeting of the Association for Computational Linguistics (Volume 1: Long Papers)*, pages 866–876, Melbourne, Australia. Association for Computational Linguistics.

Alec Radford, Jeff Wu, Rewon Child, David Luan, Dario Amodei, and Ilya Sutskever. 2019. Language models are unsupervised multitask learners.

Sudha Rao and Joel Tetreault. 2018. Dear sir or madam, may I introduce the GYAFC dataset: Corpus, benchmarks and metrics for formality style transfer. In *Proceedings of the 2018 Conference of the North American Chapter of the Association for Computational Linguistics: Human Language Technologies, Volume 1 (Long Papers)*, pages 129–140, New Orleans, Louisiana. Association for Computational Linguistics.

Ricardo Rei, Craig Stewart, Ana C Farinha, and Alon Lavie. 2020. COMET: A neural framework for MT evaluation. In *Proceedings of the 2020 Conference on Empirical Methods in Natural Language Processing (EMNLP)*, pages 2685–2702, Online. Association for Computational Linguistics.

Machel Reid and Victor Zhong. 2021. LEWIS: Levenshtein editing for unsupervised text style transfer. In *Findings of the Association for Computational Linguistics: ACL-IJCNLP 2021*, pages 3932–3944, Online. Association for Computational Linguistics.

Thibault Sellam, Dipanjan Das, and Ankur Parikh. 2020. BLEURT: Learning robust metrics for text generation. In *Proceedings of the 58th Annual Meeting of the Association for Computational Linguistics*, pages 7881–7892, Online. Association for Computational Linguistics.

Rico Sennrich, Barry Haddow, and Alexandra Birch. 2016. Controlling politeness in neural machine translation via side constraints. In *Proceedings of the 2016 Conference of the North American Chapter of the Association for Computational Linguistics: Human Language Technologies*, pages 35–40, San Diego, California. Association for Computational Linguistics.

Tianxiao Shen, Tao Lei, Regina Barzilay, and Tommi Jaakkola. 2017. Style transfer from non-parallel text by cross-alignment. In *Proceedings of the 31st International Conference on Neural Information Processing Systems*, NIPS'17, page 6833–6844, Red Hook, NY, USA. Curran Associates Inc.

Akhilesh Sudhakar, Bhargav Upadhyay, and Arjun Maheswaran. 2019. "transforming" delete, retrieve, generate approach for controlled text style transfer. In *Proceedings of the 2019 Conference on Empirical Methods in Natural Language Processing and the 9th International Joint Conference on Natural Language Processing (EMNLP-IJCNLP)*, pages 3269–3279, Hong Kong, China. Association for Computational Linguistics.

Alexey Tikhonov, Viacheslav Shibaev, Aleksander Nagaev, Aigul Nugmanova, and Ivan P. Yamshchikov. 2019. Style transfer for texts: Retrain, report errors, compare with rewrites. In *Proceedings of the 2019 Conference on Empirical Methods in Natural Language Processing and the 9th International Joint Conference on Natural Language Processing (EMNLP-IJCNLP)*, pages 3936–3945, Hong Kong, China. Association for Computational Linguistics.

Yolanda Vazquez-Alvarez and Mark Huckvale. 2002. The reliability of the itu-t p.85 standard for the evaluation of text-to-speech systems.

Thomas Wolf, Lysandre Debut, Victor Sanh, Julien Chaumond, Clement Delangue, Anthony Moi, Pierric Cistac, Tim Rault, Remi Louf, Morgan Funtowicz, Joe Davison, Sam Shleifer, Patrick von Platen, Clara Ma, Yacine Jernite, Julien Plu, Canwen Xu, Teven Le Scao, Sylvain Gugger, Mariama Drame, Quentin Lhoest, and Alexander Rush. 2020. Transformers: State-of-the-art natural language processing. In *Proceedings of the 2020 Conference on Empirical Methods in Natural Language Processing: System Demonstrations*, pages 38–45, Online. Association for Computational Linguistics.

Jingjing Xu, Xu Sun, Qi Zeng, Xiaodong Zhang, Xuancheng Ren, Houfeng Wang, and Wenjie Li. 2018. Unpaired sentiment-to-sentiment translation: A cycled reinforcement learning approach. In *Proceedings of the 56th Annual Meeting of the Association for Computational Linguistics (Volume 1: Long Papers)*, pages 979–988, Melbourne, Australia. Association for Computational Linguistics.

Wei Xu, Alan Ritter, Bill Dolan, Ralph Grishman, and Colin Cherry. 2012. Paraphrasing for style. In *Proceedings of COLING 2012*, pages 2899–2914, Mumbai, India. The COLING 2012 Organizing Committee.

Ivan P. Yamshchikov, Viacheslav Shibaev, Nikolay Khlebnikov, and Alexey Tikhonov. 2021. Style-transfer and paraphrase: Looking for a sensible semantic similarity metric. In *Proceedings of the AAAI Conference on Artificial Intelligence*, pages 14213–14220.

Xiaoyuan Yi, Zhenghao Liu, Wenhao Li, and Maosong Sun. 2020. Text style transfer via learning style instance supported latent space. In *Proceedings of the Twenty-Ninth International Joint Conference on Artificial Intelligence, IJCAI-20*, pages 3801–3807.

Tianyi Zhang*, Varsha Kishore*, Felix Wu*, Kilian Q. Weinberger, and Yoav Artzi. 2020. Bertscore: Evaluating text generation with bert. In *International Conference on Learning Representations*.

Chulun Zhou, Liangyu Chen, Jiachen Liu, Xinyan Xiao, Jinsong Su, Sheng Guo, and Hua Wu. 2020. Exploring contextual word-level style relevance for unsupervised style transfer. In *Proceedings of the 58th Annual Meeting of the Association for Computational Linguistics*, pages 7135–7144, Online. Association for Computational Linguistics.

A Appendices:

These Appendices include: (i) evaluated systems (A.1); (ii) implementation details for automatic metrics (A.2); and (iii) annotation guidelines and interface (A.3).

A.1 Evaluated Systems

Table A.1 presents the systems' ranking based on the human judgements. We use eight published systems of different sorts (including state-of-the-art models). For **supervised approaches**, we include the following systems:

- RAO (Rao and Tetreault, 2018): A copy-enriched NMT model trained on the rule-processed data and the additional forward and backward translations produced by the PBMT model;
- NIU (Niu et al., 2018): A bi-directional model trained on formality-tagged bilingual data using multi-task learning;
- BART (Lai et al., 2021b): Fine-tuning a pre-trained model BART with gold parallel data and reward strategies;
- HIGH (Lai et al., 2021a): Fine-tuning BART with high-quality synthetic parallel data and reward strategies.

For **unsupervised approaches**, we include the following systems:

- LUO (Luo et al., 2019): A dual reinforcement learning framework that directly transforms the style of the text via a one-step mapping model without parallel data;
- YI (Yi et al., 2020): A style instance supported method that learns a more discriminative and expressive latent space to enhance style signals and make a better balance between style and content;
- Zhou (Zhou et al., 2020): An attentional seq2seq model that pre-trains the model to reconstruct the source sentence and re-predict its word-level style relevance;
- IBT (Lai et al., 2021a): An iterative back-translation framework based on the pre-trained seq2seq model BART.

Table A.2 presents automatic evaluation results in content preservation.

A.2 Implementation Details for Automatic Metrics

- BLEU: We adopt `sentence_bleu` of the NLTK library with a smoothing function to compute the segment-level score, and `multi-bleu.perl` with default settings for system-level.[6]
- chrF: Following Briakou et al. (2021a), we use use `sentence_chrf` of the open-sourced implementation sacreBLEU.[7]
- ROUGE: We use the open-sourced implementations Rouge.[8]
- WMD: We employ the `gensim` library and word embedding `googlenews-vectors-negative300.bin`.[9]
- METEOR: We adopt the NLTK library.
- BERTScore: We use the official implementation with a rescaling function.[10]
- BLEURT: We use the official checkpoint of `bleurt-large-512`.[11]
- COMET: We adopt the official checkpoint of `wmt-large-da-estimator-1719`.[12] COMET-QE is a referenceless metric that uses source and output only. But we found that it yielded lower correlations with human judgements than COMET in our evaluations. This may be because the input and output are different languages in COMET-QE training.
- Style and Fluency: All experiments are implemented atop Transformers (Wolf et al., 2020) using BERT base model (cased) for style and GPT-2 base model for fluency. We fine-tune models using the Adam optimiser (Kingma and Ba, 2015) with learning rate of 1e-5 for BERT and 3e-5 for GPT-2, with a batch size of 32 for all experiments.

A.3 Annotation Guidelines and Interface

Figure A.1 show the screenshots of task guidelines and annotation interface.

[6] https://www.nltk.org/
[7] https://github.com/mjpost/sacrebleu
[8] https://github.com/pltrdy/rouge
[9] https://radimrehurek.com/gensim/index.html
[10] https://github.com/Tiiiger/bert_score
[11] https://github.com/google-research/bleurt
[12] https://github.com/Unbabel/COMET

Style				Content				Fluency			
System	Rank	AVE. s	AVE. z	System	Rank	AVE. s	AVE. z	System	Rank	AVE. s	AVE. z
BART	1	82.7	0.494	HIGH	1	92.4	0.542	BART	1	87.8	0.540
REF	2	82.3	0.469	NIU	2	90.7	0.491	IBT	2	86.0	0.491
IBT	3	80.1	0.407	BART	3	86.5	0.370	NIU	3	84.9	0.463
NIU	4	76.9	0.297	IBT	4	85.1	0.337	HIGH	4	83.3	0.420
HIGH	5	76.3	0.293	RAO	5	84.7	0.328	REF	5	82.4	0.385
RAO	6	70.2	0.085	REF	6	73.6	0.009	RAO	6	77.3	0.247
YI	7	51.1	-0.588	ZHOU	7	50.9	-0.659	ZHOU	7	45.1	-0.717
ZHOU	8	47.2	-0.726	YI	8	50.5	-0.669	YI	8	38.6	-0.903
LUO	9	46.7	-0.731	LUO	9	47.6	-0.749	LUO	9	37.9	-0.926

Table A.1: Results based on original human evaluation and z-score.

	BLEU	chrF	ROUGE-1	ROUGE-2	ROUGE-L	WMD ↓	METEOR	BERTScore	BLEURT	COMET-w	BLEU	chrF	ROUGE-1	ROUGE-2	ROUGE-L	WMD ↓	METEOR	BERTScore	BLEURT	COMET-w
Systems	**Reference 1**										**Reference 2**									
Reference	0.291	0.492	0.533	0.307	0.501	1.334	0.487	0.605	0.235	0.314	0.231	0.459	0.494	0.259	0.449	1.469	0.444	0.565	0.155	0.202
HIGH	0.366	0.547	0.624	0.401	0.582	1.086	0.554	0.643	0.347	0.400	0.300	0.515	0.564	0.342	0.512	1.260	0.521	0.605	0.317	0.289
NIU	0.376	0.560	0.646	0.434	0.605	1.036	0.567	0.649	0.373	0.418	0.333	0.525	0.578	0.369	0.526	1.202	0.538	0.617	0.329	0.286
BART	0.382	0.555	0.632	0.412	0.596	1.053	0.573	0.646	0.388	0.425	0.305	0.511	0.561	0.349	0.513	1.278	0.526	0.605	0.353	0.279
IBT	0.373	0.550	0.620	0.404	0.582	1.094	0.574	0.635	0.350	0.391	0.291	0.503	0.553	0.335	0.503	1.289	0.512	0.595	0.305	0.271
RAO	0.336	0.525	0.602	0.367	0.561	1.145	0.533	0.601	0.234	0.305	0.297	0.505	0.556	0.344	0.512	1.281	0.512	0.568	0.200	0.196
ZHOU	0.253	0.461	0.536	0.300	0.494	1.351	0.469	0.508	-0.200	-0.125	0.245	0.451	0.495	0.271	0.444	1.488	0.476	0.478	-0.206	-0.212
YI	0.288	0.483	0.551	0.324	0.517	1.307	0.491	0.524	-0.154	-0.059	0.225	0.443	0.497	0.263	0.454	1.475	0.457	0.488	-0.203	-0.167
LUO	0.222	0.416	0.483	0.272	0.445	1.514	0.434	0.453	-0.289	-0.278	0.189	0.381	0.419	0.209	0.378	1.694	0.389	0.425	-0.266	-0.368
Systems	**Reference 3**										**Reference 4**									
Reference	0.213	0.442	0.472	0.231	0.434	1.537	0.433	0.567	0.102	0.190	0.231	0.459	0.505	0.261	0.461	1.438	0.466	0.595	0.224	0.293
HIGH	0.316	0.513	0.566	0.340	0.528	1.229	0.506	0.617	0.236	0.326	0.295	0.511	0.585	0.343	0.535	1.227	0.526	0.634	0.327	0.412
NIU	0.325	0.509	0.574	0.351	0.534	1.232	0.505	0.612	0.257	0.309	0.310	0.518	0.607	0.365	0.552	1.173	0.548	0.637	0.349	0.413
BART	0.341	0.517	0.577	0.361	0.539	1.208	0.526	0.617	0.274	0.354	0.327	0.532	0.621	0.384	0.574	1.128	0.565	0.655	0.405	0.447
IBT	0.307	0.514	0.570	0.344	0.531	1.220	0.522	0.614	0.267	0.328	0.316	0.520	0.592	0.363	0.543	1.217	0.534	0.632	0.332	0.388
RAO	0.293	0.499	0.556	0.329	0.511	1.288	0.493	0.574	0.140	0.252	0.293	0.505	0.577	0.336	0.526	1.234	0.541	0.600	0.250	0.315
ZHOU	0.227	0.419	0.478	0.245	0.438	1.496	0.421	0.489	-0.257	-0.186	0.210	0.425	0.507	0.248	0.453	1.451	0.448	0.507	-0.212	-0.162
YI	0.220	0.436	0.487	0.255	0.449	1.477	0.416	0.488	-0.263	-0.149	0.204	0.432	0.501	0.250	0.458	1.466	0.430	0.509	-0.182	-0.086
LUO	0.189	0.380	0.422	0.244	0.390	1.671	0.371	0.431	-0.346	-0.356	0.197	0.393	0.458	0.243	0.410	1.591	0.420	0.451	-0.282	-0.317

Table A.2: Automatic evaluation results in content preservation. Notes: (i) the results of Reference is the distance between source and reference sentence measuring by metrics; (ii) ↓ indicates the lower score is better.

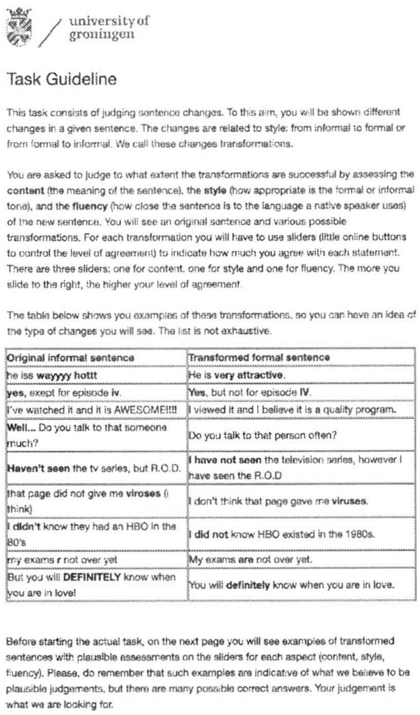

(a) A screenshot of task guidelines.

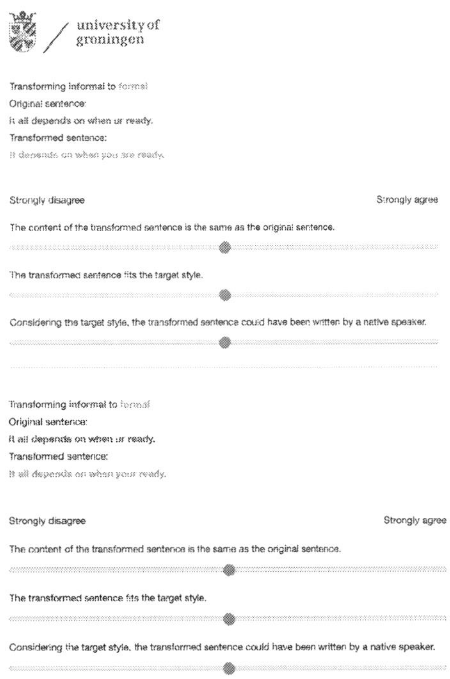

(b) A screenshot of annotation interface.

Figure A.1: Screenshots of our interface.

Towards Human Evaluation of Mutual Understanding in Human–Computer Spontaneous Conversation: An Empirical Study of Word Sense Disambiguation for Naturalistic Social Dialogs in American English

Alex Lưu
Brandeis University
alexluu@brandeis.edu

Abstract

Current evaluation practices for social dialog systems, dedicated to human–computer spontaneous conversation, exclusively focus on the quality of system-generated surface text, but not human-verifiable aspects of mutual understanding between the systems and their interlocutors. This work proposes Word Sense Disambiguation (WSD) as an essential component of a valid and reliable human evaluation framework, whose long-term goal is to radically improve the usability of dialog systems in real-life human–computer collaboration. The practicality of this proposal is proved via experimentally investigating (1) the WordNet 3.0 sense inventory coverage of lexical meanings in spontaneous conversation between humans in American English, assumed as an upper bound of lexical diversity of human–computer communication, and (2) the effectiveness of state-of-the-art WSD models and pretrained transformer-based contextual embeddings on this type of data.[1]

1 Introduction

As surveyed in Finch and Choi (2020), current evaluation practices for human–computer spontaneous conversation, including open domain dialog systems and chatbots, exclusively focus on the quality of system responses, e.g. how well the responses match ground truth human responses (based on certain automated metrics) or whether they are on-topic with the immediate dialog history (judged by a human). These evaluation practices potentially drive researchers into the race of generating better surface text while undermining or ignoring the ultimate goal of capturing mutual understanding between the systems and humans throughout the conversation (cf. the Great Misalignment Problem raised by Hämäläinen and Alnajjar, 2021). Consequently, current systems are unable to effectively function in real-life human–computer collaboration tasks. For example, the lack of genuine conceptual alignment with users leads to language learning chatbots being used only as reactive systems, even though theoretically they could provide the learners with the opportunity for free and flexible meaningful conversation (Bibauw et al., 2019), and consequently play a key role in supporting autonomous language learning beyond the classroom. To improve the usability of dialog systems for human–computer spontaneous conversation, their evaluation should include human-verifiable aspects of language competence which facilitate mutual understanding (instead of treating them as black box functions). Moreover, breaking down the evaluation into such concrete components would allow users' participation in system evaluation from early development stages (Heuer and Buschek, 2021).

Currently, talking to social chatbots without knowing which sense of a semantically ambiguous word[2] the chatbots have in their internal interpretation, human evaluators cannot identify the root cause of a problematic conversational move performed by the chatbots to provide more useful feeback. For example, examining the dialog shown in Figure 1, we can agree that the last utterance produced by the chatbot is not appropriate. However, we cannot know for sure if that is due to the chatbot's inadequate interpretation of "bank"[3] in the preceding question "What do you do at a river bank?", or its complete ignorance of the meaning of this word by just generating the most probable utterance according to the dataset it is trained on.

Arguably, one of the most natural ways for social chatbots to enhance the quality of their interaction with humans is explicitly assigning semantically ambiguous words specific senses, aka Word Sense Disambiguation (WSD), and using these senses

[1] The live version of this publication is located at https://osf.io/8u3gf/.

[2] Either polysemous or homonymous.

[3] As a financial institution instead of the land alongside a river, which is more felicitous in this particular context.

Proceedings of the 2nd Workshop on Human Evaluation of NLP Systems (HumEval), pages 116 - 125
May 27, 2022 ©2022 Association for Computational Linguistics

```
Enter Your Message: I just had a walk along the Charles river. The bank is gorgeous.
[TransformerGenerator]: i ' ll have to check it out , thanks !
Enter Your Message: What do you do at a river bank?
[TransformerGenerator]: i ' m a teller at the river bank .
```

Figure 1: A dialog between me and a state-of-the-art (SOTA) chatbot developed by Meta Research (Roller).

for further reasoning[4] to demonstrate the chatbots' understanding capability with human-readable aspects of grounding (Clark, 1996) in the course of spontaneous conversation. This would improve human–computer communication in collaborative tasks by allowing the human partners to directly access the interpretable form of computers' model of conversation anytime they need to so that they can make adequate on-the-fly conversational adjustments. In addition, being able to access the computer's human-readable representation of conversational context in the evaluation regime, a human evaluator does not need to construct different interpretation alternatives and therefore can be confident that they are on the same page with other evaluators (cf. Appendix A – a small experiment that shows a wide divergence in human interpretation of a word token in spontaneous conversation). This transparency definitely reduces the subjectivity of the evaluation task, and therefore improves its reliability and reproducibility (Specia, 2021).

This work proposes and evaluates WSD as an essential component of a novel human evaluation framework intended for human–computer mutual understanding in spontaneous conversation in English, but also sensible for any tasks involving natural language interpretation. Specifically, based on the state of the art in WSD (Bevilacqua et al., 2021), it addresses the following research questions:

1. Can WordNet 3.0 (Fellbaum, 2010), the most popular English sense inventory, approximate word meaning in spontaneous dialog[5] well?
2. Are state-of-the-art (SOTA) WSD models, using transfer learning with both pretrained transformers and non-conversational sense-annotated data, ready for conversational text?
3. How effective is it to directly use contextual embeddings of pretrained transformers, e.g. BERT (Devlin et al., 2019) or its variants, to address WSD in spontaneous conversation?

The rationale behind (3) is to test the hypothesis that contextual embeddings of word tokens in spontaneous conversation are well correlated with definitions of their context-sensitive senses (versus task-oriented scenarios where the word senses are constrained by the task). When deploying a dialog system, the transparent integration of these embeddings with other components in the NLP pipeline is preferable over the "black box" nature of off-the-shelf end-to-end WSD models, which poses the challenges of how to (a) align these models' output with the system's NLP pipeline's, and (b) improve their real-time performance using knowledge about a specific instance of conversation.

To address (1–3), I first automatically annotated WordNet senses of ambiguous words in NEWT-SBCSAE, a publicly accessible corpus of naturally occurring spontaneous dialogs in American English (Lưu and Malamud, 2020; Riou, 2015; Du Bois et al., 2000), using both a SOTA WSD model and a simple baseline model directly based on contextual embeddings of pretrained transformers (Section 2.2). Next, I collected human judgements on the outputs of these models as well as the appropriate senses of the target words (Section 2.3). These judgments were then used to assess the coverage of the WordNet sense inventory (Section 3) and the efficacy of WSD models, including both models used in automatic sense annotation (Section 4.1) and variants of the baseline model based on various pretrained transformers (Section 4.2).

2 Experimental Setup

The experiment reflects the proposed WSD-based evaluation protocol: ambiguous words in spontaneous dialog are first disambiguated by dialog systems and then evaluated by humans (or, less interactively, against predefined gold standard data).

2.1 Selected Corpus

NEWT-SBCSAE, released by Lưu and Malamud (2020), includes seven *15*-minute extracts of face-to-face casual dialogs from the Santa Barbara Corpus of Spoken American English (SBCSAE) (Du Bois et al., 2000), segmented into *3253* turn-constructional units (TCUs) by Riou (2015) and accompanied by audio files publicly browsable at TalkBank.org. This corpus possesses a rare combination[6] of valuable features:

[4] Including the use of sense relation knowledge encoded in thesauri such as WordNet.

[5] Given that language is continuously changing.

[6] The only existing corpus of its kind I am aware of.

- freely and publicly accessible (in a well-developed XML-based data format)
- carefully curated to include only naturally occurring casual dialogs by a wide variety of people, differing in gender, occupation, social background, and regional origin in comparison with its compact size

The selection of this corpus rests upon the assumption that the corpus can serve as an approximate upper bound of lexical diversity of human–computer spontaneous conversation in the same dialect of English within the evaluation scale of this empirical study. The preference for this corpus over a currently available corpus of human-computer spontaneous conversations is also supported by the fact that the latter may not actually be as representative as claimed (Doğruöz and Skantze, 2021). It is worth noting that the results achieved in this study may not generalize to varieties of American English not present in the corpus, to other regional varieties of English, or to other languages.

2.2 Automatic WSD

Automatic Transcript Preprocessing After every prosodic token are replaced with "...", each turn-constructional unit (TCU) is tokenized, lemmatized, and part-of speech (POS) tagged by spaCy[7] (v2.3.5)'s small core model for English. Then each ambiguous word is identified as follows:

- its universal POS is in WordNet, i.e. adjective, adverb, noun, proper noun, or verb
- it has more than one WordNet synset (information about the synsets, i.e. sense names and corresponding definitions, is also retrieved)

SOTA I use Conia and Navigli (2021) as a SOTA WSD model because it is the back end of AMuSE-WSD[8] (AW), the first end-to-end system that provides a web-based API for downstream tasks to obtain high-quality sense information in 40 languages, including English (Orlando et al., 2021). This model is composed of BERT (large-cased, frozen), a non-linear layer and a linear classifier, and trained on the SemCor corpus (Miller et al., 1994) as well as WordNet glosses and examples with a multi-label classification objective. It achieves 80%-accuracy on the concatenation of all Unified Evaluation Framework datasets for English all-words WSD (Raganato et al., 2017).

[7]Under the MIT License.

[8]Under the CC BY-NC-SA 4.0 License.

The AW API takes as input the text string of each TCU and yields a list of tokens automatically annotated with lemma, POS, and WordNet sense if available. Next, this output sequence is aligned with the spaCy preprocessing output.

Baseline The baseline WSD model (cf. Oele and van Noord, 2018) picks the best sense of each ambiguous word (identified in preprocessing) by ranking similarity scores between the contextual embeddings of the word and of the definitions of its WordNet senses, accessed via spacy-wordnet[7]. The contextual embeddings are from DistilBERT (Sanh et al., 2019), accessed via spacy-transformers[7].

2.3 Human WSD Judgment

Task The models' output was evaluated by two annotators, both Linguistics majors (incl. Formal Semantics) and native speakers of English[9].

For each target word, the annotators saw:

- the WordNet senses assigned to the word by AW and the baseline model[10]
- the list of possible WordNet senses for the word, taking into account its POS

The annotators were asked to decide if:

- AW sense is appropriate (and different from the baseline) – label ***'1'***
- the baseline sense is appropriate (and different from AW) – label ***'2'***
- Both are the same & appropriate – label ***'both'***
- No sense is appropriate and at least one of them has a correct POS – label ***'0'***
- Both senses have incorrect POS and their actual POS are still covered by WordNet – label ***'c'*** (i.e. *'content word but wrong POS'*)
- Both senses have incorrect POS and their actual POS are not covered by WordNet – label ***'f'*** (i.e. *'function word'*)

For ***'0'*** and ***'c'***, the annotators provided the appropriate senses, sometimes from WordNet senses.

The annotation was run in two rounds. In the first round (R.1), both annotators worked on the same dialog so that their inter-annotation agreement (IAA) could be assessed as shown in Table 1(a). The agreement level was substantial (Lan-

[9]From North-Eastern US. They were paid $15–16/hour.

[10]The listing order of these senses are the same for all target words. Consequently, the annotators could recognize that one system is better and treat its prediction as the default for borderline cases, which might slightly inflate the better system's results. On the other hand, this setting reflects real evaluation scenarios in which evaluators are aware of the performance of a specific dialog system throughout their evaluation sessions.

dis and Koch, 1977) and the inter-annotator consistency likely improved after the review of this annotation round and the corresponding revision of annotation guidelines for the final round (R.2), in which the annotators worked on different dialogs.

	(a) IAA		(b) Count		
Tokens	**Ratio**	**Kappa**	**R.1**	**R.2**	**Total**
all	0.750	0.660	669	5681	6350
AW	0.741	0.641	632	5366	5998

Table 1: Statistics of the annotation task.

In Table 1, **all** tokens are the ambiguous words identified in preprocessing; **AW** tokens exclude:

- proper nouns for which AW does not provide WordNet senses
- tokens that AW doesn't tag as adjectives, adverbs, nouns, proper nouns or verbs
- tokens that cannot be aligned with AW outputs

Table 1(b) shows the counts of these types of tokens for each annotation round and in total. The existence of non-AW tokens (5.5% of all tokens in total) demonstrates the challenge of aligning the output of off-the-shelf end-to-end WSD models with the output of the NLP pipeline inherent in a dialog system in real-life situations.

Further annotation details (e.g. data format, platform and examples) can be found in Appendix B.

Outcome[11] To facilitate fair comparisons between AW and the baseline WSD model, only AW tokens are considered in the following statistics. In addition, the counts of the first round only cover instances that get the same judgments from both annotators on the aspects the counts concern.

Table 2 shows the various sense judgments, corresponding to the labels listed in Section 2.3.

	'1'	*'2'*	*'both'*	*'0'*	*'c'*	*'f'*	$\sum$
R. 1	200	40	123	94	2	9	468
R. 2	2225	440	1255	1007	55	384	5366
Total	2425	480	1378	1101	57	393	5834

Table 2: Counts of the human WSD judgment.

Table 3 shows key statistics as the prerequisite for answering the research questions in Section 1. Table 3(a) shows two groups of sense annotations, based on whether the annotated appropriate sense (unavailable for *'f'* cases) is covered by WordNet or not (Section 3). Table 3(b) shows main POS-based groups of sense annotations that are used as gold standard to evaluate automatic WSD effectiveness (Section 4). This data only include cases in which both AW and the baseline senses have correct POS and the appropriate WordNet sense is available.

3 WordNet Sense Coverage

WordNet senses cover 96.3% of ambiguous words as shown in Table 3(a). POS-wise, they cover 95.6% adjectives, 98.2% adverbs, 95.7% nouns, 96.6% verbs. Among 200 non-WordNet tokens:

- 1 token is sub-word ("toes" in "Of the different cantos or cantos or whatever toes.")
- 4 tokens are named entities
- 64 tokens are components of multiword expressions or used idiomatically. Handling multiword expressions by feeding phrases instead of tokens into the WordNet search engine would improve the WordNet coverage to 96.7% as more 19 tokens are covered.

So, WordNet coverage for conversations is good.

4 Automatic WSD Effectiveness

The gold standard data presented in Table 3(b) covers 1046 lemmas, including 191 adjectives, 80 adverbs, 501 nouns and 274 verbs.

4.1 Initial WSD Models

Table 4 shows the performances of AW and the baseline models across POS and in total. The values in ***'both'*** columns illustrate the portion of correct disambiguated senses shared by both models.

AW model performs well on conversational text with the accuracy of 73.7%, though it does not achieve 80% as it did on non-conversational data. In addition, it performs consistently across all POS.

The 36%-level accuracy of the DistilBERT-based baseline model is encouraging, given that the average number of WordNet senses per word token (sense average) is 9.9. Its low performance on verbs can be explained by the high sense average of this POS: 15.5 (versus adjectives – 7.5, adverbs – 4.7, and nouns – 6.3). To improve this model's performance, we can experiment with different ways of manipulating the text containing target words before feeding it into a pretrained transformer.

4.2 Experiments with Pretrained Transformers

Table 5 shows the performances of the baseline model, using BERT, XLNet (Yang et al., 2019) and RoBERTa (Liu et al., 2019), accessed via spacy-transformers. Comparing to the DistilBERT-based

[11]The annotated data is publicly accessible at https://alexluu.flowlu.com/hc/6/271-wsd.

	(a) WordNet sense coverage			(b) Gold standard data				
	yes	*no*	$\sum$	ADJ	ADV	NOUN	VERB	$\sum$
R.1	439 (98.7)	6 (1.3)	445 (100)	68 (16.8)	61 (15.1)	149 (36.8)	127 (31.3)	445 (100)
R.2	4788 (96.1)	194 (3.9)	4982 (100)	538 (11.4)	755 (16.1)	1507 (32.1)	1899 (40.4)	4699 (100)
Total	5227 (96.3)	200 (3.7)	5427 (100)	606 (11.9)	816 (16.0)	1656 (32.4)	2026 (39.7)	5104 (100)

Table 3: Statistics (counts and percentages) of the human WSD judgment.

	ADJ			ADV			NOUN			VERB			All		
	AW	DB	*'both'*	AW	DB	*'both'*	AW	DB	*'both'*	AW	DB	*'both'*	AW	DB	*'both'*
R.1	66.2	50.0	36.8	83.6	37.7	31.1	77.9	41.6	32.2	85.8	33.1	23.6	79.3	39.8	30.1
R.2	74.5	42.9	32.9	76.2	37.1	30.6	76.0	45.0	33.8	69.5	25.6	17.6	73.2	35.7	26.6
Total	73.6	43.7	33.3	76.7	37.1	30.6	76.2	44.7	33.7	70.7	26.1	18.0	73.7	36.0	26.9

Table 4: Accuracy (%) of initial WSD models (**DB**: DistilBERT).

	ADJ			ADV			NOUN			VERB			All		
	B	X	R	B	X	R	B	X	R	B	X	R	B	X	R
R.1	44.1	36.8	33.8	50.8	16.4	42.6	44.3	22.8	34.9	33.9	20.5	27.6	42.0	23.5	33.6
R.2	42.2	21.7	34.2	34.6	17.9	38.1	43.5	24.0	34.6	22.7	12.5	21.7	33.5	18.1	29.9
Total	42.4	23.4	34.2	35.8	17.8	38.5	43.6	23.9	34.7	23.4	13.0	22.1	34.2	18.5	30.2

Table 5: Accuracy (%) of variants of the baseline WSD models (**B**: BERT, **X**: XLNet, **R**: RoBERTa).

model, the performances decrease in the order of [BERT > RoBERTa > XLNet] across POS and in total, except for the case of adverbs in which RoBERTa performs best. XLNet's performance is noticeably low in comparison with the others.

The empirical results show that DistilBERT is the best option for disambiguating WordNet senses of words by ranking similarity scores between contextual embeddings of the words and of the definitions of their senses. DistilBERT is not only effective but also efficient as it is the only simplified version of BERT among the tested transformers.

5 Discussion

Future Work Next, I will perform a detailed data analysis to gain insights into (1) what the annotators disagreed about, (2) what kinds of errors the WSD models made, and (3) how good incorrect senses are, taking into account the distinction between polysemous and homonymous senses, which is not available in WordNet (Freihat et al., 2016; Habibi et al., 2021; Janz and Maziarz, 2021). These insights will help improve the design of the annotation task and the performance of the WSD models.

I will also study the effect of manipulation of input utterances, by taking into account the linguistic and discourse information about the target words, on the performance of the pretrained transformers. This can shed light on how to create optimal contextual embeddings of ambiguous words for WSD.

Limitations and Challenges Exclusively relying on pre-existing sense inventories such as WordNet, the proposed evaluation method would not only miss semantically ambiguous words that do not have multiple senses in these sense inventories, but also inherit their limitations, due to the fact that their senses have different degrees of granularity and cannot keep up with the continuously involving character of natual languages (Mennes and van der Waart van Gulik, 2020; Bevilacqua et al., 2021).

The proposed evaluation method may not easily be adopted by the developers of end-to-end dialog models, the most popular approach to open-domain dialog systems (Huang et al., 2020), as the "black box" nature of these systems does not facilitate human-readable word-level interpretations.

6 Conclusion

This work proposes WSD, an established NLP task, as a required component of a valid and reliable human evaluation framework for mutual understanding in human–computer spontaneous conversation. The conducted experiments demonstrate the practicality of this proposal for English. To sufficiently evaluate human–computer mutual understanding, I envision that the WSD component will be necessarily coupled with a reasoning judgment component in which human evaluators assess the appropriateness of conversation moves made by a dialog system, including clarifying and adjusting their interpretations, based on the disambiguated word senses in those moves. This setting will help human evaluation become more grounded and therefore more objective than the current common practices, in which human evaluators are asked to rate system responses using vaguely defined criteria and inconsistent numeric scales (Finch and Choi, 2020).

Acknowledgements

The annotation work of this study was funded by a PhD Research Award from the Graduate School of Arts and Sciences, Brandeis University. I am extremely grateful to my annotators, Josh Broderick Phillips and Tali Tukachinsky, for their diligence and professionalism. My deepest gratitude goes to Sophia A. Malamud, who exhaustively discussed every aspect of this study with me. Finally, I would like to thank Nianwen Xue, the anonymous ARR reviewers of the January 2022 deadline and the organizers of HumEval at ACL 2022 for their detailed, constructive and actionable feedback.

References

Michele Bevilacqua, Tommaso Pasini, Alessandro Raganato, and Roberto Navigli. 2021. Recent trends in word sense disambiguation: A survey. In *Proceedings of the Thirtieth International Joint Conference on Artificial Intelligence, IJCAI-21*, pages 4330–4338. International Joint Conferences on Artificial Intelligence Organization. Survey Track.

Serge Bibauw, Thomas François, and Piet Desmet. 2019. Discussing with a computer to practice a foreign language: research synthesis and conceptual framework of dialogue-based CALL. *Computer Assisted Language Learning*, 32(8):827–877. Publisher: Routledge _eprint: https://doi.org/10.1080/09588221.2018.1535508.

Herbert H. Clark. 1996. *Using Language*. 'Using' Linguistic Books. Cambridge University Press, Cambridge.

Simone Conia and Roberto Navigli. 2021. Framing word sense disambiguation as a multi-label problem for model-agnostic knowledge integration. In *Proceedings of the 16th Conference of the European Chapter of the Association for Computational Linguistics: Main Volume*, pages 3269–3275, Online. Association for Computational Linguistics.

Jacob Devlin, Ming-Wei Chang, Kenton Lee, and Kristina Toutanova. 2019. BERT: Pre-training of deep bidirectional transformers for language understanding. In *Proceedings of the 2019 Conference of the North American Chapter of the Association for Computational Linguistics: Human Language Technologies, Volume 1 (Long and Short Papers)*, pages 4171–4186, Minneapolis, Minnesota. Association for Computational Linguistics.

A. Seza Doğruöz and Gabriel Skantze. 2021. How "open" are the conversations with open-domain chatbots? a proposal for speech event based evaluation. In *Proceedings of the 22nd Annual Meeting of the Special Interest Group on Discourse and Dialogue*, pages 392–402, Singapore and Online. Association for Computational Linguistics.

John W Du Bois, Wallace L Chafe, Charles Meyer, Sandra A Thompson, and Nii Martey. 2000. Santa Barbara corpus of spoken American English. *CD-ROM. Philadelphia: Linguistic Data Consortium.*

Christiane Fellbaum. 2010. WordNet. In Roberto Poli, Michael Healy, and Achilles Kameas, editors, *Theory and Applications of Ontology: Computer Applications*, pages 231–243. Springer Netherlands, Dordrecht.

Sarah E. Finch and Jinho D. Choi. 2020. Towards unified dialogue system evaluation: A comprehensive analysis of current evaluation protocols. In *Proceedings of the 21th Annual Meeting of the Special Interest Group on Discourse and Dialogue*, pages 236–245, 1st virtual meeting. Association for Computational Linguistics.

Abed Alhakim Freihat, Fausto Giunchiglia, and Biswanath Dutta. 2016. A taxonomic classification of WordNet polysemy types. In *Proceedings of the 8th Global WordNet Conference (GWC)*, pages 106–114, Bucharest, Romania. Global Wordnet Association.

Amir Ahmad Habibi, Bradley Hauer, and Grzegorz Kondrak. 2021. Homonymy and polysemy detection with multilingual information. In *Proceedings of the 11th Global Wordnet Conference*, pages 26–35, University of South Africa (UNISA). Global Wordnet Association.

Mika Hämäläinen and Khalid Alnajjar. 2021. The great misalignment problem in human evaluation of NLP methods. In *Proceedings of the Workshop on Human Evaluation of NLP Systems (HumEval)*, pages 69–74, Online. Association for Computational Linguistics.

Hendrik Heuer and Daniel Buschek. 2021. Methods for the design and evaluation of HCI+NLP systems. In *Proceedings of the First Workshop on Bridging Human–Computer Interaction and Natural Language Processing*, pages 28–33, Online. Association for Computational Linguistics.

Minlie Huang, Xiaoyan Zhu, and Jianfeng Gao. 2020. Challenges in Building Intelligent Open-domain Dialog Systems. *ACM Transactions on Information Systems*, 38(3):21:1–21:32.

Arkadiusz Janz and Marek Maziarz. 2021. Discriminating homonymy from polysemy in wordnets: English, Spanish and Polish nouns. In *Proceedings of the 11th Global Wordnet Conference*, pages 53–62, University of South Africa (UNISA). Global Wordnet Association.

J. Richard Landis and Gary G. Koch. 1977. The Measurement of Observer Agreement for Categorical Data. *Biometrics*, 33(1):159.

Yinhan Liu, Myle Ott, Naman Goyal, Jingfei Du, Mandar Joshi, Danqi Chen, Omer Levy, Mike Lewis, Luke Zettlemoyer, and Veselin Stoyanov. 2019.

RoBERTa: A Robustly Optimized BERT Pretraining Approach. *arXiv:1907.11692 [cs]*. ArXiv: 1907.11692.

Alex Lưu and Sophia A. Malamud. 2020. Annotating coherence relations for studying topic transitions in social talk. In *Proceedings of the 14th Linguistic Annotation Workshop*, pages 174–179, Barcelona, Spain. Association for Computational Linguistics.

Julie Mennes and Stephan van der Waart van Gulik. 2020. A critical analysis and explication of word sense disambiguation as approached by natural language processing. *Lingua*, 243:102896.

George A. Miller, Martin Chodorow, Shari Landes, Claudia Leacock, and Robert G. Thomas. 1994. Using a semantic concordance for sense identification. In *Human Language Technology: Proceedings of a Workshop held at Plainsboro, New Jersey, March 8-11, 1994*.

Dieke Oele and Gertjan van Noord. 2018. Simple embedding-based word sense disambiguation. In *Proceedings of the 9th Global Wordnet Conference*, pages 259–265, Nanyang Technological University (NTU), Singapore. Global Wordnet Association.

Riccardo Orlando, Simone Conia, Fabrizio Brignone, Francesco Cecconi, and Roberto Navigli. 2021. AMuSE-WSD: An all-in-one multilingual system for easy Word Sense Disambiguation. In *Proceedings of the 2021 Conference on Empirical Methods in Natural Language Processing: System Demonstrations*, pages 298–307, Online and Punta Cana, Dominican Republic. Association for Computational Linguistics.

Alessandro Raganato, Jose Camacho-Collados, and Roberto Navigli. 2017. Word sense disambiguation: A unified evaluation framework and empirical comparison. In *Proceedings of the 15th Conference of the European Chapter of the Association for Computational Linguistics: Volume 1, Long Papers*, pages 99–110, Valencia, Spain. Association for Computational Linguistics.

Marine Riou. 2015. *The Grammar of Topic Transition in American English Conversation. Topic Transition Design and Management in Typical and Atypical Conversations (Schizophrenia)*. Ph.D. thesis, Université Sorbonne Paris Cité.

Stephen Roller. ParlAI tutorial (accessed on 12/12/2021).

Victor Sanh, Lysandre Debut, Julien Chaumond, and Thomas Wolf. 2019. DistilBERT, a distilled version of BERT: smaller, faster, cheaper and lighter. In *The 5th Workshop on Energy Efficient Machine Learning and Cognitive Computing*, Vancouver, Canada.

Lucia Specia. 2021. Disagreement in human evaluation: Blame the task not the annotators. Invited talk at the Workshop on Human Evaluation of NLP systems (HumEval).

Maarten van Gompel, Ko van der Sloot, Martin Reynaert, and Antal van den Bosch. 2017. *FoLiA in Practice: The Infrastructure of a Linguistic Annotation Format*, pages 71–82. Ubiquity Press.

Zhilin Yang, Zihang Dai, Yiming Yang, Jaime Carbonell, Russ R Salakhutdinov, and Quoc V Le. 2019. XLNet: Generalized Autoregressive Pretraining for Language Understanding. In *Advances in Neural Information Processing Systems*, volume 32. Curran Associates, Inc.

A An Example of Divergence in Human Interpretation

12 native speakers of American English (2 PhD, 9 master's, 1 senior undergraduate) in a linguistic course are asked to give their interpretation of entities available in the following excerpt of dialogue between Jim and Michael, adapted from this publicly accessible recording (10'32"–11'04"):

> **Jim**: *So much of today's technology is soulless and has nothing to do with peace. It has to do with chewing up the human experience and turning it into some kind of consumer need.*
>
> **Michael**: *Did you ever get into Tesla?*
>
> **Jim**: *Just ever so peripherally.*
>
> **Michael**: *He had a lot of real wacky ideas on big levels. He wanted a world power system, that you could tap into the air basically, and get power anywhere on earth.*

The interpretation results for the token "Tesla" and the corresponding pronouns "he" is presented in Table 6.

"Tesla"	"he"	Count
Nicola Tesla	Nicola Tesla	6
Nicola Tesla's body of work	Nicola Tesla	4
Tesla, Inc.	Nicola Tesla	1
Tesla, Inc.	Elon Musk, CEO of Tesla, Inc.	1

Table 6: Divergence in human interpretation.

B Annotation in Practice

B.1 Annotation Data Format and Platform

The annotation files are stored in the XML-based FoLiA format[12], which accommodates multiple

[12]An open file format, whose specification and documentation are generated by open source code under GNU General Public License version 3.0.

linguistic annotation types with arbitrary tagsets, and annotated with FLAT[13], FoLiA's web-based annotation tool whose user-interface can show different linguistic annotation layers at the same time (van Gompel et al., 2017).

B.2 Annotation Examples

Figures 2–4 display an annotation file opened on FLAT. The ambiguous words are highlighted in different colors, corresponding to the annotation labels mentioned in Section 2.3, so that the annotators can navigate them quickly.

Figure 3 shows that when a word token such as "guilty" is hovered over, it is highlighted in black while its text turns yellow, and all of its annotation information are displayed in a pop-up box.

Figure 4 shows that when "guilty" is clicked, it is highlighted in yellow, and its annotation layers become editable in the **Annotation Editor**.

[13]Under GNU General Public License version 3.0.

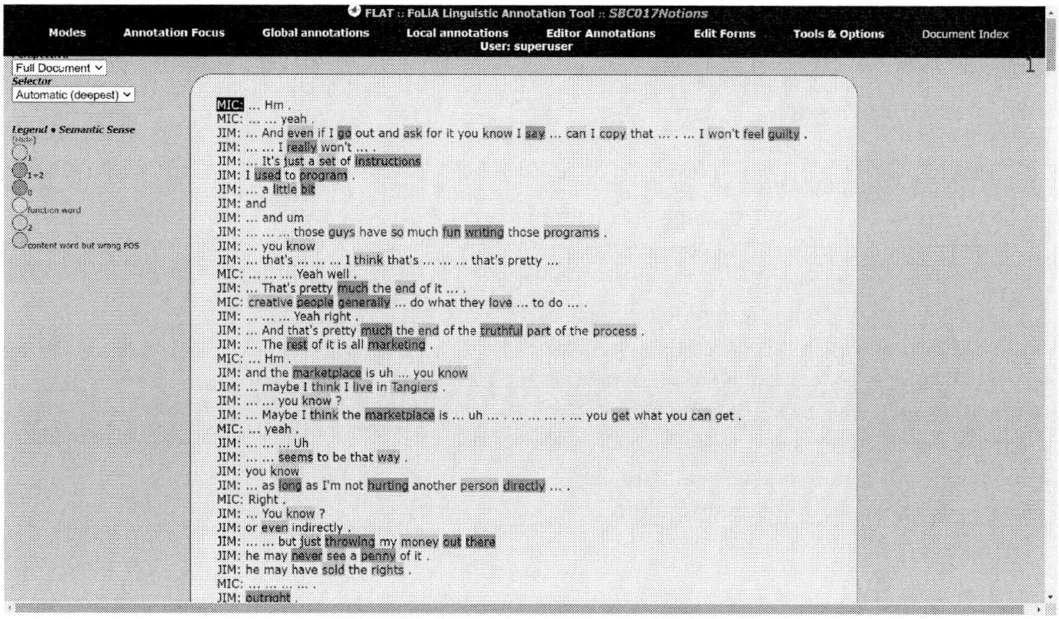

Figure 2: Annotation interface on FLAT.

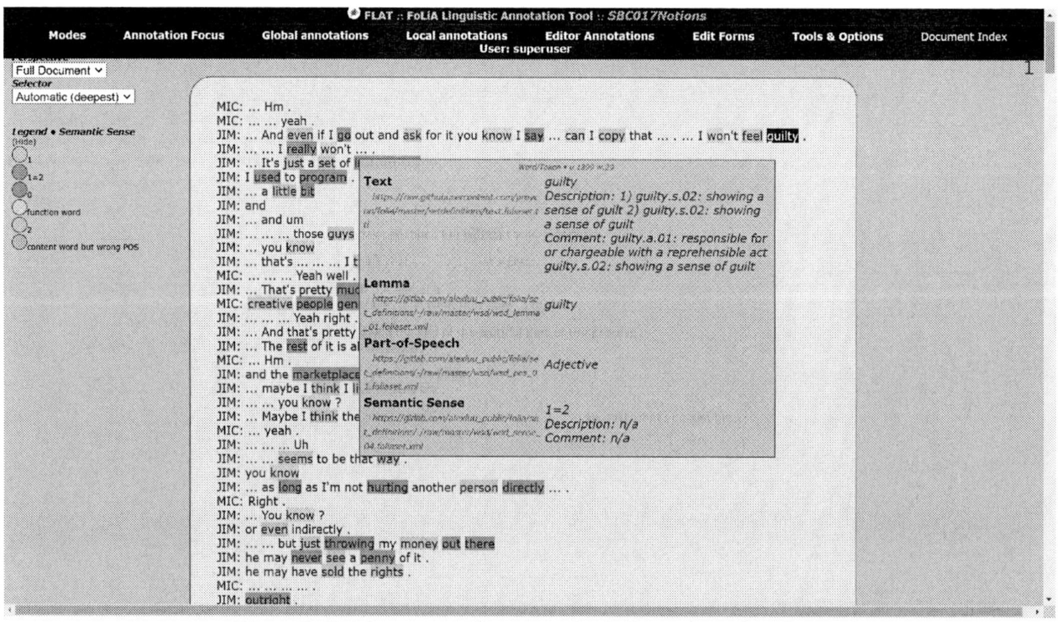

Figure 3: Quick access to the annotation information of a token.

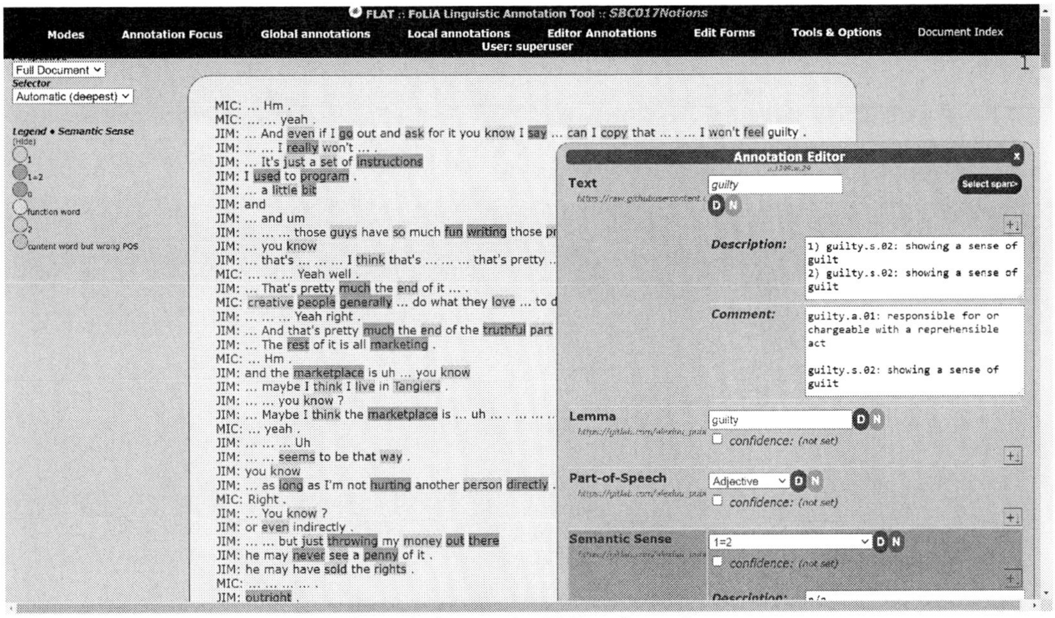

Figure 4: **Annotation Editor** for a token.

Author Index

Association for Computational Linguistics
209 N. Eighth Street
Stroudsburg, Pennsylvania 18360

ISBN 978-1-7138-6739-5

CURRAN ASSOCIATES INC.
proceedings.com